1916

One Hundred Years
of Irish Independence

ALSO BY TIM PAT COOGAN

The IRA

*The Troubles: Ireland's Ordeal
and the Search for Peace*

Michael Collins: The Man Who Made Ireland

*On the Blanket: The Inside Story of the
IRA Prisoners' "Dirty" Protest*

*Wherever Green Is Worn: The Story of
the Irish Diaspora*

Ireland in the Twentieth Century

*The Famine Plot: England's Role in Ireland's
Greatest Tragedy*

1916

One Hundred Years
of Irish Independence

From the Easter Rising to the Present

Tim Pat Coogan

Thomas Dunne Books
St. Martin's Press
New York

THOMAS DUNNE BOOKS.
An imprint of St. Martin's Press.

1916: ONE HUNDRED YEARS OF IRISH INDEPENDENCE. Copyright ©
2015 by Tim Pat Coogan. All rights reserved. Printed in the United
States of America. For information, address St. Martin's Press,
175 Fifth Avenue, New York, N.Y. 10010.

The image credits on page 318 constitute an extension
of this copyright page.

www.thomasdunnebooks.com
www.stmartins.com

Library of Congress Cataloging-in-Publication Data

Names: Coogan, Tim Pat, 1935– author.
Title: 1916 : One Hundred Years of Irish Independence : From the
    Easter Rising to the Present / Tim Pat Coogan.
Other titles: Nineteen sixteen | One Hundred Years of Irish Independence
Description: New York : Thomas Dunne Books, St. Martin's Press, 2016.
Identifiers: LCCN 2016028518| ISBN 9781250110596 (hardcover) |
    ISBN 9781250110602 (e-book)
Subjects: LCSH: Ireland—History—Easter Rising, 1916—Influence. |
    Ireland—History—1922– | Ireland—Politics and government—
    1922– | BISAC: HISTORY / Europe / Ireland.
Classification: LCC DA963 .C628 2016 | DDC 941.7082—dc23
LC record available at https://lccn.loc.gov/2016028518

Our books may be purchased in bulk for promotional, educational,
or business use. Please contact your local bookseller or the
Macmillan Corporate and Premium Sales Department at
1-800-221-7945, extension 5442, or by e-mail at
MacmillanSpecialMarkets@macmillan.com.

First published in Great Britain by Head of Zeus Ltd

First U.S. Edition: November 2016

10 9 8 7 6 5 4 3 2 1

Contents

Introduction

THE ANNIVERSARY OF THE EVENTS OF EASTER 1916 WILL, understandably, be a time of justifiable national pride and commemoration, but it should also be a time of national self-examination. We are currently passing out of the worst crisis to hit the Irish state since independence and there is a natural tendency on the part of official Ireland to accentuate the positive and play down negative statistics and uncomfortable truths. However, it would be a gross insult to the memory of the leaders of the 1916 rebellion and a betrayal of the idealism of those who took part in or supported the Rising to allow a rose-tinted view of modern Ireland to prevail over the uncomfortable realities of what has happened in this country in the years approaching the centenary.

In post-war Ireland, as the revolutionary generation aged and became increasingly unable to deal with the very real problems of emigration and unemployment, and the strictures of Mother Church grew ever more irksome, it became commonplace for criticisms of the Establishment to be referred to as 'letting down the country'. No such approach can be tolerated nowadays. A grim and unpalatable statistic, which is never alluded to in the jargon-laden commentaries about 'recovery' and improved economic performance, is the fact that the number of people who have committed suicide in the seven or eight years since the financial crisis of 2007–8 is higher than the total of those killed in the thirty years of Northern Ireland's 'Troubles'.

Those responsible for creating the climate of austerity that sapped the will to live of so many decent Irish men and women, mainly the banking community and to a degree the accountancy, legal and political elites, have – at the time of writing – escaped virtually scot-free. Had the miscreants been pursued for reckless trading and/or neglect of their fiduciary responsibilities as directors of banks and financial institutions, those of their number who felt disposed to read this book would have had to do so courtesy of a prison library.

Instead, in the unlikely event of their wishing to turn these pages, they are likely to be doing so either on holiday or in their comfortable homes. Obscenely inflated pension settlements and golden handshakes have accompanied a fortunate few decision-makers into luxurious retirement, while emigration, unemployment, poverty – and even suicide – have been the bitter fate of the many. Homelessness is on the increase. On the one hand building costs are too high and, as a result, not enough homes are being built; on the other, rented accommodation soars in cost so that more and more people – men, women and children – find themselves on the streets. The doctrine of 'women and children first' meant that the helpless were the first to feel the pain of slashed state benefits and the loss of support for either challenged children in the classroom or the aged in care. Apart from the destruction of pensions and the savings of retired taxpayers, whom glib stockbrokers induced to place their money in the shares of their golfing companions' banks, the state added further privations such as the withdrawal of medical cards for many over the age of seventy.

These miseries and many many more have occurred almost in direct proportion to the extent to which successive

governments in the late 1990s and early 2000s colluded with
bankers, developers and lobbyists to depart from any sem-
blance of the idealism that permeated the 1916 leadership.

And how were the guilty men treated?

The response of official Ireland recalls George Bernard
Shaw's caustic definition of a government commission being
like a man going to the lavatory. It sits. For a long time nothing
is heard; then there is a loud report and the matter is dropped.

As will emerge from these pages the setting up of a spate of
tribunals was the chosen response to many of Ireland's ills before
the crash. As this book was being written, a government-spon-
sored banking inquiry is being conducted by parliamentarians
who quiz as many of those with either an involvement in or an
opinion on the crash as can be summoned.

Amidst the expressions of regret, obfuscations and denials
of culpability which have flowed from the inquiry exercise, one
comment stands out: it was made by Ms Eithne Tinney, a lady
who served on the upper slopes of finance. She observed that
she saw no real sense of guilt amongst bankers and said that if
left unchecked it could happen all over again.

Her words have been given added weight by the fact that one
side effect of 'recovery' has been the rapid acceleration in house
prices around Dublin and some cities outside it, prompting
fears that another property bubble could well be in the making.

This is obviously undesirable, but the really dangerous nub of
the situation lies in what Ms Tinney had to say about bankers
being ready, willing and able to repeat the sins of the past. For it
is not merely that the banking crash highlighted the fact that the
winds of testosterone blew through banks' boardrooms in what
were termed the Celtic Tiger years prior to the crash.

There is a twofold and deep-rooted problem here. One is the
fact that Ireland was allowed to become a happy hunting-ground

for the multinationals whose profits, garnered elsewhere, as well as in Ireland, could be rerouted through Dublin back to the US in ways that avoided standard taxation. President Obama has made a strong public attack on Irish taxation policies – not at all the soothing tones the Irish have come to expect from the White House, but certainly tones the Irish can expect to hear in the future, to judge from the hard line taken by the US Treasury towards Ireland when the country was floundering in its attempts to bail out the banks.

As education and the effects of TV and social media spread, the Irish have clawed back from the Church a number of freedoms in the area of personal morality. A marked liberalization has occurred in the legalization of contraception, divorce and same-sex marriage. The abortion taboo is increasingly being questioned. In education, moves are afoot to provide school places for children without forcing their parents to have them hypocritically baptized as Catholics so that they can access state schools which, for historical reasons, are still controlled by the Church.

But there are elements of 'I was hungry and ye founded a study group' about all this. When it comes to feeding the hungry, or assisting the homeless, it is very often the Church which is still relied upon to fill the gaps left by state policy. The legendary Brother Kevin Crowley and his Capuchin confreres at the Capuchin monastery in Dublin keep alive both the spirit of St Francis and the memory of the parable of the loaves and fishes as, somehow, in the midst of privation, an ever-rising tide of free meals and food parcels flows out daily from the monastery to an unfortunately ever-growing army of the needy. On the housing front it is a Jesuit, Father Peter McVerry, who champions the plight of another ever-growing army which calls out daily, but without McVerry would scarcely be heard – the homeless. Thus, in the midst of real and disgraceful examples of Church misbehaviour, is witness given that the beating heart of goodness within the Irish Church is not yet stilled.

The laws of the bedroom may have been changed, but no such overhaul occurred for those of the marketplace. And this in the era of the corrupt banker, account and lawyer, the swashbuckling billionaire vulture capitalist, the multinational corporation. The fact is that, on the anniversary of 1916, the Irish legal system is not fit for purpose. It cannot properly control white-collar crime.

On the one hand, civil servants and politicians have greatly subverted the workings of the Freedom of Information Act, so that redactions and costs deter the average citizen from finding out how those who rule, and profit from him or from her, are behaving. On the other, the law, like the Ritz Hotel, is open to everyone. The laws of defamation in Ireland are powerful (and frequently used) weapons in the hands of the rich and the unscrupulous when they wish to cover their tracks.

Where the law-makers are concerned, parliament is very constrained in what it may investigate, even in matters relating to taxpayers' money. Its principal watchdog committee is the Public Accounts Committee (PAC), but there are legal limitations to its ability to investigate the expenditure of public money or to compel witnesses to attend before it. As matters stand the PAC can be, and sometimes is, given the two fingers in its efforts to find out how public money has been spent. The Committee needs to be given the necessary powers to enable it to function effectively in the now-you-see-it, now-you-don't world of electronic banking and deals.

It was hard not to fall prey to feelings of despair when one observed Ireland's refugee policy in the summer of 2015. The Irish attitude to the plight of those fleeing conflict in the Middle East was a disgrace. The Irish naval service had done noble work in plucking refugees from the waters of the Mediterranean, but the government was proposing to admit only a few hundred refugees – nothing like what Ireland should have been able to absorb. When the *Irish Independent* and the *Irish Examiner* placed the image of a drowned Syrian boy, Aylan Kurdi, on their front pages, there was an immediate outpouring of sympathy. As a consequence the government was forced to triple its targets. It should not have required the newspapers' action to force the government's hand. If we can borrow billions of euro to bail out the whited sepulchres which the Irish banks turned out to be, we can surely raise the comparatively few millions required to help ease both the refugee crisis and the situation of the homeless on our streets.

Northern Ireland appears to offer one of the few significant good examples of progress as the anniversary of 1916 approaches. However, there are disturbing signs that a dark heart still beats there. Violence is far closer to the surface than the political Establishments in Dublin, London or Belfast – or indeed the mainstream media – are prepared to acknowledge. A combination of unemployment, sectarianism and the activities of dissident republicans against the backdrop of the approaching anniversary of the Easter Rising, contains a potential for serious trouble that should be met with a renewed concentration on the problem equal to that which preceded the Good Friday Agreement. Here, in this vital area of Irish life, as in the legal system, to paraphrase Lincoln, the price of peace is indeed eternal vigilance.

Tim Pat Coogan
September 2015

1

The Road to the Rising

CATHLEEN NÍ HOULIHAN WOKE. IT WAS THE END OF EASTER
Week, 1916: the guns had finally fallen silent on the
violent events of April – and Kitty found herself suffering from
a hangover historic in its severity. The acute effects of that
hangover would affect Cathleen very much over the next seven
years. Indeed, they would continue to trouble her to a greater
or lesser degree throughout the course of the century to come.

The mythical figure of Cathleen Ní Houlihan personi-
fied Irish nationhood. She had appeared on stage at the Irish
Literary Theatre in 1902, the eponymous subject of a play
written by the poet W. B. Yeats with some help from his literary patron Augusta Gregory – Lady Gregory. Cathleen was
also emblematic, then, of the Irish Literary Revival then taking
shape: that movement in fin-de-siècle Ireland which witnessed
a revival of interest in the country's ancient Gaelic heritage.
In the hands of Lady Gregory and Yeats, Cathleen was an
explicitly and potently nationalistic figure, seeking a sacrifice
of blood and life necessary to transform her from a poor old
woman into a youthful figure 'with the walk of a queen'. As we
shall see, the events of Easter 1916 would make of Cathleen not
merely a symbol of Ireland but one of fiery action in the cause
of national liberation.

In spite of her great symbolic potency for nationalists, however, Cathleen had not been warned to expect any such Easter awakening. Life had been relatively quiet of late, both within her restless family and in its relationship with her powerful British neighbour. She had grown accustomed to living within the constraints imposed by two forms of colonial strait-jacket, one manufactured by Britain and the other by Mother Church. Her political jacket, indeed, had if anything grown somewhat less constraining in recent years. After all, Cathleen had been led to believe that when the Great War, now raging in far-off Europe, was ended, the jacket would be either removed completely or its straps would be loosened to a point where they would no longer trouble her.

Cathleen's inner garments, meanwhile, were restrictive yet also warming. They had been fashioned by Mother Church to help cope with the sharp winds of oppression and economic deprivation, while at the same time keeping at bay the dangerous draughts of independent thought, godless Republicanism and the influence of the Protestant Churches. Indeed, it had been with the assistance of Mother Church that Cathleen had survived the greatest catastrophe to befall her: the devastating Famine of the 1840s and its recurrences in the 1870s and 80s. The charitable efforts of Roman Catholic clergy and nuns, together with a mindset fashioned in schoolroom and pulpit, had helped Cathleen to learn how to adjust her religious strait-jacket so that she could cope with such vexations as clerical authoritarianism and the life-denying teachings of the Catholic Church on the relationships between men and women.

But the heavy, outward cloak with the 'Made in Britain' label that governed her movements in the fields of law and order – this was another matter. Its weight and chafing may have eased a little by 1916, but they had by no means disappeared completely.

Cathleen, of course, had railed against the wearing of that cloak on numerous occasions during the preceding century and before – with disastrous results. Still, she had not expected that this Eastertide would witness another protest against British power and authority in her land. Now, as she surveyed the shocking aftermath of Easter 1916 in Dublin, Cathleen Ní Houlihan was aware that elements in her world were changing before her eyes, were altering violently and breathlessly. There had indeed been a sacrifice of blood – but could Cathleen walk confidently with the walk of youth, with the walk of a queen? A new world of terrible beauty was in the process of being born – so much was abundantly, unmistakeably clear. What Cathleen could not know – what no Irishman or Irishwoman in those days could know – was how much would change and how much would stay the same in the years to come.

★

The century and more leading up to 1916 in Ireland had certainly witnessed its share of turbulence. The Irish parliament – subordinate though it was to Westminster until its partial reform in 1782 – had at least provided something of a national legislature. In 1798, however, British rule was challenged by an uprising of the United Irishmen, spearheaded by a young Protestant-born intellectual named Theobald Wolfe Tone. The rebellion failed, and, in its aftermath, Tone chose to die by his own hand rather than face the hangman. Now, the ties binding Ireland to Britain were drawn tighter still: in 1800, the Irish parliament voted itself out of existence; and in 1801, the Act of Union copper-fastened the link between Great Britain and Ireland. Irish parliamentarians would henceforth assembly not in Dublin, but at Westminster.

Unrepresentative though the Irish parliament certainly had been – it was dominated by the Anglican and landed 'ascendancy' class and it legislated for a country in which, as in Britain, Roman Catholics were disenfranchised by reason of their faith through the Penal Laws – its mere existence had provided the possibility of a gradual, evolutionary political change. Now, however, new circumstances were set in place – and revolution rather than evolution would from this time be the preferred option for a segment of Irish nationalist and separatist opinion. Tone's writings, in this new context, took on a force and authority of their own: for they were inspired both by separatism and by French republicanism – and they left Irish revolutionaries with the concept that the solution to Irish ills lay not in *reimagining* the link with England, but rather in *severing* it completely.

In spite of this new focus, the hopes of those who favoured separation and force as a means of healing Ireland's ills remained largely aspirational throughout the nineteenth century and for the opening years of the twentieth. The 1798 uprising had been crushed savagely by the authorities, the intention being thoroughly to discourage any other large-scale military rebellions during the coming century. The attempted uprising by the young Dubliner and Protestant Robert Emmet against British rule in 1803 is remembered vividly in Irish history – but the facts speak for themselves: this was a small-scale uprising, it was one doomed to failure and it ran its course against the less-than-heroic backdrop of loud cheers and tobacco spits issuing from the drunken mobs who roistered in Emmet's wake through the streets of the Irish capital.

Emmet is remembered for his gallantry in the face of insurmountable military odds – but also for a gleam of glory, in the form of his impassioned speech from the dock:

Let no man write my epitaph; for as no man who knows my motives dare now vindicate them, let not prejudice or ignorance asperse them. Let them and me rest in obscurity and peace, and my tomb remain uninscribed, and my memory in oblivion, until other times and other men can do justice to my character. When my country takes her place among the nations of the earth, *then and not till then*, let my epitaph be written. I have done.

The speech had both an international and a national impact. In the infant United States, Abraham Lincoln learned it by heart; and Emmet's stirring words helped to sustain many a young Irish patriot during the dark night of the soul that gripped Ireland for several decades after his unsuccessful rebellion and death.

Ireland, however, has always brought forth substantial leaders – and in these years it produced one political figure of international stature. Daniel O'Connell demonstrated remarkable political skill in utilizing his segment of the hundred or so Irish parliamentarians at Westminster – generally speaking, he could normally depend on the support of only a third of these – to secure Catholic Emancipation in 1829. It was not an unalloyed plus. The forty shilling freeholders, as they were known – the poorer and most numerous class of landowners – lost the franchise, but the larger property-owning Catholics were entitled to vote, and to rise in the professions. The main beneficiaries, however, were the clergy: the Roman Catholic hierarchy's influence on the Irish educational system began to rival that of the Protestant ascendancy. But O'Connell's greater dream, repeal of the Act of Union that bound Britain and Ireland, failed: and he died a broken man in 1847. And as he died, the greatest disaster in modern Irish history was ravaging the Irish countryside.

As I have argued in *The Famine Plot*, the British government in these years permitted the failure of the potato crop to create a famine – this, in a country that exported food all through the turmoil of these years. Some British cities continued to receive 80 per cent of their meat from Ireland throughout the Famine period. Butter, eggs and wheat were also consistently exported. Generally speaking, the Irish peasantry, some three million of them, lived in primitive conditions and on small plots of subdivided land, suitable for producing one crop only – the potato. Some of the most powerful British statesmen of the period, such as Lord Palmerston, were also the owners of vast Irish estates: such men argued that the chaotic, uneconomic condition of the Irish land system could only be rectified by a removal of the excess population on the land.

The population of Ireland had been nearing nine million when blight struck the potato. By the time the Famine officially ended in 1852, it had fallen to six, and it would continue to decline steeply in the following decades. In spite of this horror, however, the political life of Ireland, and its political energies, managed to sustain itself. In 1848, for example, with the Famine at its peak, the country had a modest taste of the radical spirit then sweeping Europe in that Year of Revolutions. It was administered by a group of idealistic young intellectuals known as the Young Irelanders, who might be considered as providing the intellectual component of nationalist ideology in these years. Protestants such as Thomas Davis and John Mitchel, through the medium of *The Nation* and *United Irishman* newspapers, promoted the idea of a nation and of a coming-together between Protestants and Catholics. These individuals and such others as landowner William Smith O'Brien and lawyer Charles Gavan Duffy were men of stature and integrity, and their circle had a lasting impact on Irish nationalist and republican thought – even if their attempt at militarism, an abortive attempt at a rising in that year, was a fiasco. For the school wedded to the concept of 'physical force' in Ireland, this abortive rebellion bolstered their theory of a rising erupting in the country with every generation: whatever its chances of success, each such rebellion passed the flame from one generation to the next. And less than twenty years later, the truth underscoring this theory was evident once more, as members of the so-called 'Fenian' nationalist group agitated in Ireland, Britain and North America against Britain's rule of Ireland.

Ireland witnessed further upheavals in the 1870s, sparked on this occasion by the issue of land agitation. As a result of Catholic Emancipation, increasing numbers of Irish children had been able to benefit from education, albeit through use of officially prescribed textbooks teaching them that they were in fact intrinsic members of a larger British state. Nevertheless, the expansion of education in general led inexorably to social and political change – and to the formation in 1879 of the National Land League, established specifically to address the vexed issue of land reform. The League operated against a context of years of tumultuous agitation usually referred to as the Land War. Under the leadership of such figures as Michael Davitt and Charles Stewart Parnell, the League had by the 1880s succeeded in introducing a measure of equity to the system of land tenure in Ireland. Unusually, the League also included in its numbers two significant female figures: Parnell's sisters Fanny and Anna Parnell. When their brother was imprisoned, these two women took over the running of the League – although both were in due course sidelined, and their energies marginalized.

As the League's efforts bore obvious fruit, Irish nationalists began to hope that their larger objectives might at last be
within reach. Certainly Parnell, now the undisputed leader
of the Irish Parliamentary Party and of nationalist Ireland,
wasted no time in pursuing his ultimate political aim: that
of Home Rule, and of an independent parliament restored to
Dublin. Parnell was a highly skilled politician and member of
the House of Commons, and adept at using the patterns of
British electoral ebb and flow in the 1880s to extract concessions from William Gladstone's Liberal Party, and to bring the
tantalizing prospect of Irish Home Rule ever closer.

But there were four provinces in Ireland – and in the fourth,
Ulster, with its large Protestant population, the majority of
people did not share Parnell's vision. They would not willingly wear green clothes which they saw as being designed
by a pope in Rome – and in London, the Conservative Party
saw the opportunity to play on their fears, and did so very
deliberately. Randolph Churchill, writing to his friend Lord
Justice FitzGibbon, said: 'I decided some time ago that if the
GOM [Gladstone] went for Home Rule, the Orange card
would be the one to play. Please God it may turn out to
be the ace of trumps and not the two.' Churchill also gave
the unionists their watchword at a meeting held in Belfast's
Ulster Hall in February 1886: 'Ulster will fight and Ulster
will be right.' In that phrase lies the reason six of Ireland's
north-eastern counties are today part of the United Kingdom.
In vain did Catholic Ireland vote in successive elections for
Home Rule, sometimes by majorities as great as five to one.
In London the Conservatives, and an immovable anti-Home
Rule majority in the House of Lords, were able to make
the Ulster Crisis sufficiently an issue to prevent Home Rule
passing into law.

Ultimately, however, it was not the travails of Westminster politics that caused hopes for Home Rule to crash. Instead, a scandal in the life of Parnell ended his political life – and caused at the same time the ruin of Home Rule. Parnell had for years been in a discreet relationship with Katharine O'Shea, the estranged wife of an Irish Parliamentary Party MP, Captain William O'Shea. In 1889 O'Shea was induced by Parnell's opponents to bring a divorce suit in which Parnell was cited. Divorce court proceedings had moral and political repercussions both in Catholic Ireland and the Nonconformist section of Britain on which Gladstone depended to carry Home Rule. The result was a hugely damaging split as Parnell's leadership was challenged from right and left. Denunciations flowed from Land League leaders like Davitt and from the Irish Catholic bishops. Parnell fought back, but died under the strain in 1891, seemingly taking Home Rule to the grave with him.

The Irish Parliamentary Party splintered, political momentum stalled – but now another, more potent pulse began to beat in the Irish nationalist community. As the land issue calmed and the effects of education began to spread further, a new consciousness was abroad in the land: that of the meaning of Irishness itself, what this could and *should* mean. As the nineteenth century came to its close, the Gaelic League and the Gaelic Athletic Association were born, and the Literary Revival began to flower, carrying with it an interest in Irish language, in Irish singing and dancing, in Gaelic football and in the ancient Irish sport of hurling. And in the midst of these activities could be discerned the yeast-like effect of the Irish Literary Theatre, founded in 1899 and in 1902 renamed the Abbey Theatre. The principal Abbey figures were Yeats and Lady Gregory, together with the playwright John Millington Synge and a host of dramatists, actors, designers and directors whose work in putting forward the value of an Irish identity inevitably had an impact on swelling nationalist and republican themes.

In Westminster, meanwhile, the diligent and honourable John Redmond began, slowly, painfully, to resurrect the riven Irish Parliamentary Party. Redmond was much less charismatic than his predecessor Parnell – but in the opening years of the twentieth century, Westminster parliamentary arithmetic, and a Liberal government once again in power after 1906, suggested that Home Rule might again be attainable. Redmond built his party into a position of numerical and strategic strength in the House of Commons once more. The House of Lords veto, which hitherto had sunk every Home Rule proposal, was abolished by means of the Parliament Act (1911); and in due course, limited proposals for Irish Home Rule seemed on the verge of being passed into law.

These new laws envisaged an Irish government consisting of the monarch and of two legislative houses: a Senate and a House of Commons. The head of the Irish executive would not be the leader of the majority Irish party – but rather a Lord Lieutenant, appointed by the British prime minister, who would also nominate Irish ministers and the members of the Senate. Judicial appointments would also be the Lord Lieutenant's responsibility. The British House of Commons would retain the right to make laws involving foreign relations, the army and navy, international treaties and trade, navigation and merchant shipping. It would also control taxation; and while Irish representation at Westminster was to continue, the ranks of Irish MPs were to be reduced from 100 to 42.

This was hardly revolutionary stuff, but its opponents managed to make it look as though it was. Once more the Orange card was played in Belfast. In 1913, backed by the Conservatives and led by the Dublin-born barrister Edward Carson, Ulster unionists formed the Ulster Volunteer Force

(UVF) militia. The UVF had pledged to resist any attempt by the British army or navy (to say nothing of the democratically elected government of the United Kingdom) to impose Home Rule on Ulster. Two years later, this militia engaged in running guns from Germany; and it drilled openly, with the obvious support of the police and the tacit approval of the vast number of younger sons of Anglo-Irish families who had made their career in the British army and navy. All such activities were, of course, quite illegal and constituted a militarist challenge to parliamentary democracy. As the clouds of conflict gathered over Europe, it is a matter of record that some of the Kaiser's advisers thought the war could be won as Britain was preoccupied with the apparent threat of disorder on the home front.

Tacit support became open defiance in 1914 when British officers stationed at the Curragh military camp west of Dublin declared that, even if ordered to do so, they would not move to impose Home Rule on Ulster. On the face of it, this was threatened mutiny – but in fact the officers were merely taking their cue from the Conservative Party leader, Andrew Bonar Law, who two years previously had raised the spectre of civil war as the consequences of forcing Home Rule on Ulster. Speaking at Blenheim Palace in July 1912, he told his listeners:

> The Home Rule Bill, in spite of us, may go through the House of Commons. There are things stronger than parliamentary majorities. I can imagine no length of resistance to which Ulster will go to which I shall not be ready to support them and in which they will not be supported by the overwhelmingly majority of the British people.

This was an extraordinary repudiation of the democratic process, coming from the lips of the leader of one of the great British parliamentary parties. Understandably, no less a person than Herbert Asquith, the then Liberal prime minister, described the speech as 'a declaration of war against constitutional government'. He described the proceedings at Blenheim as 'a reckless rodomontade... furnishing for the future a complete grammar of anarchy'.

In response to the UVF's actions, a nationalist volunteer force was set up to defend Home Rule, should it be resisted by force of arms. These Irish Volunteers also imported small numbers of guns from Germany (landed at Howth and Kilcoole in the summer of 1914) and they too paraded and drilled openly. In addition, they were joined by a smaller group of militants. This was the Irish Citizens' Army (ICA), founded by James Connolly, who was born in Scotland of Irish parents. Connolly was a socialist interested in alleviating the conditions of the poor by controlling the means of production: subsequently, he gave every indication of intending to use his new militia to stage a workers' revolution.

What Connolly, in spite of his planning, did *not* know – what very few people knew – was that the much larger Irish Volunteers militia was in fact controlled by the Irish Republican Brotherhood (IRB), a small society which was planning to make use of the coming war in Europe to stage a nationalist uprising to take from a preoccupied Britain what it would not otherwise willingly give – political independence. This was the aim of radical Irish nationalists, and this independence was to be achieved by means of an armed uprising against British rule in Ireland, and sustained by use of arms imported covertly from Germany. Yet, the irony is that not even the most tempestuous of the IRB leaders imagined that they could actually defeat their British enemy. They did intend, however, to bring about a protest in arms for which they were prepared to give their lives if necessary – believing that in the aftermath of such a gesture public opinion would swing to their cause. Already, quietly, painstakingly, the stage for Easter 1916 was being set.

Among these leaders was a young schoolteacher, poet, intellectual and barrister named Pádraig Pearse. He was a prime proponent of that theory of 'blood sacrifice' then prevalent in many nationalist circles in Europe. In 1915, at the funeral of the nationalist and IRB member Jeremiah O'Donovan Rossa, Pearse would set in oratorical form his sense of an Irish nation that was now within reach of its destiny – and his sense too that this destiny could not come without violence:

The Defenders of this Realm have worked well in secret and in the open. They think that they have pacified Ireland. They think that they have purchased half of us and intimidated the other half. They think that they have foreseen everything, think that they have provided against everything; but the fools, the fools, the fools! – they have left us our Fenian dead, and while Ireland holds these graves, Ireland unfree shall never be at peace.

Pearse was a fine educator. His school, St Enda's at Rathfarnham in south Dublin, was a progressive and enabling place, reflecting Pearse's belief that the contemporary colonial education system was a mind-numbing 'murder machine' designed to stultify rather than draw out the best in children. And he was able to influence profoundly the thinking and ideology of many nationalist young men and women, using his oratorical skills to powerful effect: 'We are young today as men were young when to be young was to be a hero... and we are about to attempt impossible things, for we know that it is only impossible things that are worth doing.' Another statement by Pearse, meanwhile, also resonated in later years. 'I think,' he said, 'the Orangeman with the rifle a much less ridiculous figure than the Nationalist without a rifle.'

A hitherto unpublished letter from Pearse, to the old Fenian John Devoy in New York, gives a clear analysis of the IRB situation in the run-up to the proposed uprising against British rule. It also contains a clear-eyed analysis of the divisions within the ranks of nationalism and of the perceived weakness of Redmond's position vis-à-vis the British. I consider the document to be so important as to merit being published in full.

Turlough
Rosmuck
Co. Galway

12 August 1914

A Chara Chroidhe,*
I have come back here after a few busy days in Dublin, and send you the following chronicle of events.

First, to remove some misimpressions which I and others may have given you. I think I told you that the number of guns landed at Howth was 2500, and Tom Clarke in his cable to GXX [illegible] says 2000. We have both exaggerated, relying on rumour. The actual number was only 900. The number landed at Kilcoole was only 600. That gives 1500 in all. They were 11 [illegible] Mausers of a rather antiquated pattern, without magazines, and are much inferior to the British service rifles and even to those which Carson's men have. Moreover, the ammunition landed is useless. It consists of explosive bullets, which are against

* Irish, 'Friend of my heart'.

the rules of civilised war, and which, therefore, we are not giving out [illegible] to the men. As to these 1500 rifles, the Provisional Comtee insists on sending as many as possible to Ulster – which means to Devlin's Hibernians – and unheard-of efforts will be made to keep guns out of the hands of men not known to be loyal to Redmond. In fact, the last meeting of the Provisional Comtee. was largely devoted to a squabble as to who is to get the guns. Redmond's men roundly charged us with attempting to steal them, and a Comtee. was appointed to ascertain the whereabouts of all the guns and send as many as possible north. Well, the European crisis finds the Irish Volunteers with 1500 or, allowing for other small quantities landed, 2000 rifles, and no ammunition. It is obvious that before we can intervene, or even pretend to intervene, in the crisis to any purpose we must have arms. Hence the one great urgent duty of the hour, the duty wh. overshadows every other duty, is to get guns and ammunition into the country. It is up to the American Comtee. to act <u>at once</u> and <u>on a large scale</u>. You are as much alive to the need as I am. Every penny you can command must be expended now and the goods sent to us with as little delay as possible. A supreme moment for Ireland may be at hand. We shall go down to our graves beaten and disgraced men if we are not ready for it.

<u>Publicly</u>, the movement has been committed to loyal support of England: not officially, so far, but by implication. I enclose cuttings wh. show the latest phase. They are from the 'Independent' of the 11th inst. To everyone in Ireland that has any brains it seems either madness or treachery on Redmond's part. Query: has he got terms secretly – I mean, has he any pledge from Asquith? His

followers on the Prov. Comtee. passionately resent any suggestion that all is well. The Prov. Comtee. at its last meeting took no action either way, but simply leave it to Redmond to speak and act for the whole movement in this grave crisis, and quelches any attempt even to discuss his action! Last week the Dublin Co. Board of the Volunteers made an attempt to set things straight. They drew up a resolution for adoption by the battalions expressing readiness to co-operate with Ulster for the defence of Ireland but unwillingness to support the Brit. Govt. against foreign nations with wh. Ireland has no quarrel. Three out of five Dublin battalions adopted this unanimously and parade in front of Prov. Comtee's office during a meeting and sent in a spokesman to convey the resolution to the Comtee. The reply of the Prov. Comtee was to order the Dublin Co. Board and all concerned to apologise and promise not to adopt resolutions dealing with policy again, on pain of suspension! In the meantime the Companies everywhere are adopting resolutions <u>approving</u> of Redmond's offer of loyal help. In other words, Volunteer bodies are free to pass resolutions supporting Redmond, but not free to pass resolutions or take any action even indirectly dissociating themselves from his offer of loyal help. Redmond's capture of the government of the volunteers is absolute and complete.

I had hoped that the original members would ask to gather and save the movement from complete capture. That hope has proved vain. All Hibernians and Redmondites I with the honourable exception of Judge, vote with the new members, and steadily vote us down. I personally have ceased to be any use on the Comtee. I can never carry a single point. I am now scarcely allowed to speak. The moments I stand up there are cries of 'Put the Question', etc. After the last meeting I had half determined to resign, but have decided to stick on a little longer in the hope of being useful at a later stage.

I blame MacNeill more than anyone. He has the reputation of being 'tactful', but his 'last' consists in bowing to the will of the Redmondites every time. He never makes a fight except when they assail his personal honour, when he bridles up at one. Perhaps I am wronging him, as I am smarting under the remembrance of what I regard as very unfair treatment of me personally and of all who agree with me at the last meeting. He is in a very delicate position, and he is weak, hopelessly weak: I knew that all along.

Now it is perfectly clear that whatever is to be done for Ireland in this crisis must be done outside the Prov. Comtee. The men are sound, especially in Dublin. We could at any moment rally the best of them to our support by a coup d'état: and rally the whole country if the coup d'état were successful. But a coup d'état while the men are still unarmed is unthinkable.

The Brit. Govt. will arm and train us if we come under the War Office and accept the Commander in Chief in Ireland as our generalissimo. Details plans are already drawn up and have been tentatively submitted. So far, the Prov. Comtee. is unanimous against it. But if Redmond directs them to submit? Then, I think the split will come.

I am sending a letter in similar terms to McGarrity do not use any of this for publication.

Sincerely Yours

P. H. Pearse

'MacNeill' was Eoin MacNeill, the ostensible leader of the Irish Volunteers, a Gaelic scholar and professor at University College Dublin. MacNeill had envisaged the corps as having a purely defensive role, coming into action only if the Conservatives and Ulster unionists combined to frustrate the will of a majority of the people in both islands that Home Rule should be introduced. MacNeill, however, had no idea that he was in fact being used as a figurehead while plans for a revolution went on behind his back. There were other factors at work too. Connolly's very obvious drilling and marching of his tiny militia force was the reason the IRB leaders began to worry that he might bring the authorities down on them as part of a general swoop on agitation, and snuff out whatever prospect the proposed rising might have had. Accordingly Connolly was detained and brought – somewhat forcibly – to a meeting with the IRB leadership: he was informed of their (still far from ripe) plans and agreed to throw in his lot with them. In effect, Connolly's decision had the important political consequence that henceforth the aims of labour would become subsumed in the cause of nationalism.

Thus Ireland resounded to the sound of marching feet in both unionist and nationalist boots, drilling for different purposes, between 1912 and 1914. The onset of war in the late summer of 1914, however, altered the flow of events: as war loomed, the vast majority of the Irish Volunteers left on the advice of John Redmond to rename themselves the National Volunteers and join the British army. Redmond had acted in the belief that generosity and co-operation on the part of the Irish in Britain's hour of need would be reciprocated when the war ended. For Home Rule had now been passed at Westminster, though its implementation was paused until the war with Germany was over. Redmond's expectation, then, was that the British government would reciprocate in decency and generosity and implement Home Rule when the war was over. It cannot be argued that Irish history was rich in examples of incidents which bore out this belief; Redmond, however, was influenced by his personal friendship with such leading Liberals as Augustine Birrell, who was the Irish Chief Secretary and a member of the cabinet.

A small minority of the Volunteers, led by MacNeill, refused the call to join Britain's war effort. This radical rump, which retained the name Irish Volunteers, would be increasingly controlled by the IRB for its own rebellious purposes. As the Great War began to tear Europe apart, the IRB's quiet preparations for an Irish uprising continued, and now a tentative date was mooted: that of Easter 1916. Emissaries were sent to Berlin to secure weapons and other practical assistance from the German government. These preparations were unknown to MacNeill – and when he discovered them, very late in the day, another split in volunteer ranks ensued; and MacNeill himself placed a notice in the *Sunday Independent* calling off all parades and volunteer activities scheduled for that fateful Easter weekend.

Meanwhile, IRB leaders were discovering that the scale of assistance to be expected from Berlin was far less than they had been led to believe. So much less, in fact, that the rebels' representative in Germany, Roger Casement, made his way back to Ireland aboard a German submarine, in an attempt to call off the now hopeless uprising before it ever began. Casement, however, having been put ashore on Banna Strand in Tralee Bay on 21 April 1916, was captured and the small shipment of arms which he had managed to secure was scuttled by its German commander after fruitlessly sailing up and down the Kerry coastline awaiting signals which never materialized.

*

Thus Easter Monday in Dublin, 24 April 1916, dawned strangely and tentatively. It was to be a day of revolution with no prospect of military success – but pregnant with enormous, albeit largely unforeseen, potential. And as events transpired, it would become clear that this potential would be realized not so much through Irish efforts as through British actions and errors.

The plan or, rather, the hope, was to echo Robert Emmet's plan for an uprising in Dublin that would spark uncontrollable rebellion across the country. The 1500-odd rebels, as they fanned out across the city that Monday morning, intended to seize strategic buildings and locations, pin down British forces, bunker down – and hope for the best. At first, some of these plans succeeded: the rebels seized City Hall, well located on high ground south of the river and adjoining the centre of British power at Dublin Castle, which, had the rebels realized it, was theirs for the taking since it had been left virtually unguarded because of the Easter holiday. But the chance was missed, and the General Post Office – which commanded views up and down the wide boulevard of Sackville (now O'Connell) Street – became the principal command centre. They also seized ground inside St Stephen's Green, where they began to dig trenches across the smooth lawns of the park. But lack of manpower meant that they did not seize the easily defensible quadrangles and grounds of Trinity College, or the main railway stations.

The rebels' strategic shortcomings soon became all too evident. By the end of that first day, order was breaking down across Dublin; the rebels encamped in St Stephen's Green became the prey of snipers on the roofs of the surrounding buildings and were forced to take shelter in the Royal College of Surgeons building; British control of the railway network enabled a secure flow of supplies and resources – and inexorably the noose began to close around the rebels, who had few weapons and resources and no artillery. Machine guns played little or no part in their plans; and the main weapon they had to hand was their courage. This enabled them to withstand bombardment and to hold their centres in Dublin for almost a week against a modern army equipped with artillery and resources in manpower which enabled thousands of troops to encircle the rebels.

Certain locations, certain figures, certain episodes are especially remembered. One such is the General Post Office, which became headquarters for the duration of the Rising and the base of, among others, Pearse, Connolly, Michael Collins – who would play a central role in later Irish history – and Thomas Clarke. Clarke had become an icon of the physical force school because of his part in a dynamiting campaign in England organized by the Fenians towards the end of the nineteenth century. He served a lengthy prison sentence in grim conditions under the alias of Wilson and his case aroused such sympathy in Ireland that even John Redmond was forced to campaign on his behalf. On his release he went to America and returned to Ireland in 1907. His little tobacconist's shop in Parnell Square in Dublin and his newspaper, *Irish Freedom*, became focal points for a new generation of would-be Fenians. Chief amongst these was Seán Mac Diarmada, who grew up as part of a family of ten brothers and sisters, raised in a tiny cottage on a remote Leitrim hillside. A bad hip meant that he walked in pain and with the aid of a stick, but he became the IRB's principal organizer, travelling the country, allegedly in his capacity as general manager of *Irish Freedom* and in a real sense literally walking in Clarke's footsteps. Clarke went into the GPO to take part in the fighting, even though he was then fifty-nine years old, and was suffering from a bullet wound in his elbow, sustained during revolver practice a few days before the Rising.

Another location was the rebel post in Boland's Mill which, under the command of the American-born Éamon de Valera, was the last to surrender to the British. The area under his surveillance included Mount Street Bridge, the surroundings of which accounted for half of all the British casualties sustained in the Rising. De Valera himself was out of contact with his men in the Mount Street area for much of the Rising period – but this did not prevent his reputation from being substantially burnished in retrospect. The Mount Street Bridge scenes, indeed, encapsulated all the bravery, all the tragedy and all the folly, not alone of Easter 1916 but of how warfare in general was conducted in the era of what was euphemistically termed the Great War.

Firstly, the bridge was held by command posts containing only a handful of men, reduced in number because the Irish rebel leader commanding the posts, Michael Malone, sent a half a dozen or so of his youthful troops home in order to save their lives. The remaining men were only lightly armed – though Malone himself held in his possession a Mauser automatic pistol, and this had the potential to be a lethal weapon when wielded with skill; interestingly, this pistol was given to Malone by de Valera when he discovered that his men at Mount Street were short of weapons. But they had enough in their possession to inflict losses on the British.

The first to walk into the Mount Street trap was a party of Home Guards, mainly middle-aged men who were marched from Dún Laoghaire, some six miles away, when news of the Rising broke. Their tunics were inscribed Georgius Rex. As a result they had been nicknamed 'gorgeous wrecks'. They had no ammunition for their rifles and were mowed down when they encountered Malone's men. The next party to arrive was a battalion of Sherwood Foresters who had only recently disembarked at Dún Laoghaire, having travelled from a training camp in England. Some of them were so raw and inexperienced that they had to be shown how to fire a rifle on disembarkation. They marched, hot and footsore, from the harbour at Dún Laoghaire, to be cut down in a deadly fusillade from Malone and his men. Amongst the Foresters was a Captain Frederick Dietrichsen, who had earlier sent his Dublin-born wife Beatrice and their children back to Ireland, as a safer location in a Europe gripped by war. Marching towards the sound of gunfire with his men, Captain Dietrichsen was astounded to see his wife and children walking along the footpath. The family had a brief, joyful reunion before he had to run to catch up with his men. Dietrichsen was subsequently killed in the fighting.

The death toll would have been much less had General William Lowe, the British commander in Dublin, not ordered his troops to march along Mount Street to the city centre, clearing out the rebels en route. His staff pleaded with him to allow them to take flanking routes to bypass Mount Street itself, but he insisted that his men march this route, to their deaths. How much of the slaughter which occurred in the trenches during the Great War was caused by similar pig-headed instructions from brass hats to their men? On the rebel side, meanwhile, both Malone and his deputy, James Grace, were eventually killed in the fighting. Malone's Mauser passed into the hands of a British officer – who in his turn many years later returned it to de Valera. In a very real sense, de Valera's power flowed from the barrel of that gun.

Though the rebels had little by way of weaponry, they did have at their disposal the power of symbolism. In particular, the text of the Proclamation of the Irish Republic, read that Easter Monday by Pearse from his position in front of the GPO, has taken on a power and authority of its own:

IRISHMEN AND IRISHWOMEN: In the name of God and of the dead generations from which she receives her old tradition of nationhood, Ireland, through us, summons her children to her flag and strikes for her freedom.

Having organised and trained her manhood through her secret revolutionary organisation, the Irish Republican Brotherhood, and through her open military organisations, the Irish Volunteers and the Irish Citizens' Army, having patiently perfected her discipline, having resolutely waited for the right moment to reveal itself, she now seizes that moment, and supported by her exiled children in America and by gallant allies in Europe, but relying in the first on her own strength, she strikes in full confidence of victory.

We declare the right of the people of Ireland to the ownership of Ireland and to the unfettered control of Irish destinies, to be sovereign and indefeasible. The long usurpation of that right by a foreign people and government has not extinguished the right, nor can it ever be extinguished except by the destruction of the Irish people. In every generation the Irish people have asserted their right to national freedom and sovereignty; six times during the past three hundred years they have asserted it in arms. Standing on that fundamental right and again asserting it in arms in the face of the world, we hereby proclaim the Irish Republic as a Sovereign Independent State, and we pledge our lives and the lives of our comrades in arms to the cause of its freedom, of its welfare, and of its exaltation among the nations.

The Irish Republic is entitled to, and hereby claims, the allegiance of every Irishman and Irishwoman. The Republic guarantees religious and civil liberty, equal rights and equal opportunities to all its citizens, and declares its resolve to pursue the happiness and prosperity of the whole nation and of all its parts, cherishing all of the children of the nation equally, and oblivious of the differences carefully fostered by an alien Government, which have divided a minority from the majority in the past.

Until our arms have brought the opportune moment for the establishment of a permanent National Government, representative of the whole people of Ireland and elected by the suffrages of all her men and women, the Provisional Government, hereby constituted, will administer the civil and military affairs of the Republic in trust for the people.

We place the cause of the Irish Republic under the protection of the Most High God, Whose blessing we invoke upon our arms, and we pray that no one who serves that cause will dishonour it by cowardice, inhumanity, or rapine. In this supreme hour the Irish nation must, by its valour and discipline, and by the readiness of its children to sacrifice themselves for the common good, prove itself worthy of the august destiny to which it is called.

Signed on Behalf of the Provisional Government,

THOMAS J. CLARKE,

SEAN Mac DIARMADA,   THOMAS MacDONAGH,

P. H. PEARSE,   EAMONN CEANNT,

JAMES CONNOLLY.   JOSEPH PLUNKETT.

At the time, however, such symbolism was lost on many. There was a good deal of disquiet in the Irish population itself in the face of what was playing out on the streets of Dublin. The British army was heavily reliant on Irish troops in units such as the Dublin Fusiliers, meaning that split loyalties were a fundamental part of the Irish response to what was taking place on the streets. Moreover Dublin was filled with 'separation women', so called because they received a separation allowance while their husbands were abroad fighting at the front. And quite apart from the separation allowances, the women – and for the moment a sizeable section of public opinion too – were conscious of the fact that their absent husbands were engaged against a mighty foe and could be regarded as having been stabbed in the back at home as they wrestled with the Hun. For the organizers of the Rising, then, the first signs were decidedly inauspicious: the initial response on the part of public opinion was of exasperation and anger, not to mention horror at the destruction of large areas of their city by artillery fire.

Only modest numbers of Volunteers had taken part in the uprising – but they had killed or wounded some 1350 police and soldiers. As for 'collateral damage', as it is now known – civilian casualties inflicted by both British and Irish fire – this added to the Volunteers' immediate unpopularity. Even before the full extent of the damage became known, the *Irish Catholic* commented on 29 April:

> ... the movement which has culminated in deeds of unparalleled bloodshed and destruction of property in the capital of Ireland was as criminal as it was insane. Only idiots or lunatics can ever have supposed it could prove successful. Traitorous and treacherous as it undoubtedly was, it was most traitorous and treacherous to our native land.

Press and pulpit joined in the denunciatory chorus of the separation women. The Catholic bishop of Ross, Dr Denis Kelly, termed the Rising 'a senseless, meaningless debauch of blood'. But the Anglican archbishop of Dublin, Dr John Bernard, wanted more blood. In a letter to the *Times* on 4 May, he urged the government to take 'the sternest measures' against the rebels, saying: 'This is not the time for amnesties and pardons; it is the time for punishment swift and stern.' The *Irish Independent*, *Sunday Independent* and *Irish Catholic* took up the theme of the archbishop's letter on 10 May. Speaking on behalf of bourgeois Ireland, the *Independent* thundered: 'When, however, we come to some of the ringleaders, instigators and tormentors not yet dealt with, we must make an exception. If these men are treated with too great leniency, they will take it as an indication of weakness on the part of the Government.'

All in all, then, Catholic Ireland was not best pleased. Press and pulpit were largely against, as were the large farmers profiting from the shipment of cattle at Great War prices; in addition to which, both Protestants and Catholics had a great number of their husbands, fathers, brothers and uncles serving in the army against which the rebels had risen. As for Protestant-dominated Ulster – which would lose five times as many of her sons that year on the first day of the Somme as had taken part in the Dublin Rising – the unionist population was angry, embittered and strengthened in its perception of Dublin and the south of Ireland as being a treacherous sink of popery and rebellion.

As for the response of the British themselves, Sir John Maxwell, the British general plucked off the shelf of obscurity to crush the rebellion, was not a cruel or a stupid man. He read up on Irish history, and correctly identified an essay by Arthur Griffith as the best way of reconciling the crown with nationalist aspirations. Griffith is known as the founder in 1905 of the small Sinn Féin movement – but this piece on *The Resurrection of Hungary* is significant, for in it he proposed an Irish solution of dual monarchy along the lines of the Austro-Hungarian model, as the means by which Ireland's destiny, and future harmony with Britain, might best be secured. Whether or not Maxwell agreed with Griffith's other ideas, such as that of economic self-sufficiency (Sinn Féin translates as 'We ourselves'), we do not know – but Maxwell was certainly appalled at the slums of Dublin, the frightful condition of which he thought could easily have been improved and rectified. He would also come to the view that the Irish were a warm-hearted and generous people who could have been placated with such a reasonable settlement of their political ambitions.

Unfortunately, Maxwell also began taking steps to ensure that, as so often happens in Anglo-Irish affairs, reason and moderation were to be in very short supply – for now he began executing the leaders of the rebellion. And as he did so, the words of Pearse over the grave of O'Donovan Rossa began taking on a new and terrible contemporary relevance. Pearse himself was executed on 3 May, the first of sixteen executions associated with the Rising. Clarke, too, met his end in this way. He spent the immediate aftermath of the Rising in an enclosed space at the back of the Rotunda Hospital on Parnell Square. The prisoners spent the night in the open, Collins attempting to keep Clarke warm by wrapping his arms around him. A British officer, Captain Lee-Wilson, seeing nurses looking out the window of the hospital, went to see what they were looking at – and had Clarke stripped naked and paraded before them. Clarke was executed on 3 May. A few years later Michael Collins had Lee-Wilson shot in Wexford.

As acts of historical reprisal go, the Irish executions were comparatively mild. But their transformative effect was well described by Yeats when he wrote in his poem 'Sixteen Dead Men':

> O but we talked at large before
> The sixteen men were shot,
> But who can talk of give and take,
> What should be and what not
> While those dead men are loitering there
> To stir the boiling pot?
>
> You say that we should still the land
> Till Germany's overcome;
> But who is there to argue that
> Now Pearse is deaf and dumb?
> And is their logic to outweigh
> MacDonagh's bony thumb?
>
> How could you dream they'd listen
> That have an ear alone
> For those new comrades they have found,
> Lord Edward and Wolfe Tone,
> Or meddle with our give and take
> That converse bone to bone?

The sixteen included the signatories of the proclamation and a number of other prominent figures. And one who was not so prominent: Pearse's younger brother, Willie, was shot principally because of his family connection to Pearse. They were shot in batches, the process lasting until 12 May when Connolly, who was so badly wounded that he was unable to stand, was shot sitting on a chair. Roger Casement, meanwhile, would be hanged in Pentonville gaol in August.

In spite of clerical and press condemnation of the rebels, however, it is clear that anti-British sentiment had never truly left Ireland – and the backlash against the executions was not long in gathering pace. Bishop Edward O'Dwyer of Limerick had previously been critical of nationalist militaristic behaviour – but when General Maxwell wrote to him complaining about the pro-nationalist activities of some of his priests, O'Dwyer replied (on 17 May 1916):

In your letter of 6th inst., you appeal to me to help you in the furtherance of your work as military dictator of Ireland. Even if action of that kind was not outside my province, the events in the past few weeks make it impossible for me to have any part in proceedings which I regard as wantonly cruel and oppressive. You remember the Jameson raid, when a number of buccaneers invaded a friendly state and fought the forces of the lawful government.

If ever men deserved the supreme punishment it was they. But officially or unofficially the influence of the British Government was used to save them and it succeeded. You took care that no pleas for mercy should interpose on behalf of the poor young fellows who surrendered to you in Dublin. The first information which we got of their fate was the announcement that they had been shot in cold blood.

Personally I regard your action with horror, and I believe that it has outraged the conscience of your country. Then, the deporting of hundreds and even thousands of poor fellows without a trial of any kind seems to me an abuse of power, as fatuous as it is arbitrary, and altogether your regime has been one of the worst and blackest chapters in the history of misgovernment of this country. I have the honour to be, sir, your obedient servant.

Edward O'Dwyer, bishop of Limerick.

The bishop sent the letter to the papers and it was cut out, bedecked with tricolour ribbons and hung in windows up and down the country. That letter had a profound effect in post-Rising Ireland. And while the high-toned proclamation which the rebels had issued on seizing the GPO had initially made little impact, the seasons soon changed, and with them public opinion – and before long, the executions at Kilmainham and Pentonville had made the proclamation a revolutionary text.

This effect of dramatic and rapid recalibration of the public mood may be gauged by the attitude on the streets of Dublin to the prisoners captured in 1916. As they were marched off to Dublin's docks to be taken to prisons scattered throughout Britain, they were booed and jeered. When they returned only a few short months later, having been released by a British government increasingly worried by the effect their incarceration was having on the prospects of American support, on which rested Britain's hopes for a successful war effort, they were met by cheering crowds and carried shoulder-high through the streets. This change of climate would have extraordinary and radical effects in the years to come.

2

Towards Independence

I N THE MONTHS AFTER THE EASTER RISING, IRISH PUBLIC attention shifted to the prisoners in British jails. The term 'Sinn Féin prisoners' was now generally in use, principally because the British authorities and media habitually referred to the Rising as having been a Sinn Féin rebellion. In fact this movement, founded in 1905 to work towards a self-governing Irish state, had nothing to do with the Rising, and in its immediate aftermath remained relatively small. Its founder Arthur Griffith, however, was well known as a result of his writings – and Griffith had been picked up in a widespread and indiscriminate post-Rising sweep of nationalist figures. From modest beginnings, Sinn Féin was now on the cusp of being the dominant force in Irish politics.

In a curiously prophetic occurrence, the two most important prisoners, Michael Collins and the better-known Éamon de Valera, remained apart during the post-Rising period. De Valera had been the only volunteer commandant to escape the firing squads. This was partly because of his position on the list of rebels to be executed. The command to cease the executions was given *before* the authorities had reached de Valera's name on the list. Maxwell had been coming under pressure from Prime Minister Asquith over the executions policy because of the negative effect it was having on American opinion. De Valera's name on the list of those to be executed occurred just below James Connolly's. Maxwell ran his pen down the list and asked the Crown Prosecutor, William Evelyn Wylie, who de Valera was. 'Is he someone important?' 'No,' responded Wylie. 'He is a school-teacher who was taken at Boland's Mill.' To which Maxwell's answer was: 'All right, we'll go ahead with Connolly and stop with this fellow.' De Valera was placed instead in Dartmoor prison and was subsequently moved between a number of British prisons, remaining in custody until a general prisoner release in June 1917.

Michael Collins, meanwhile, was amongst the large group of prisoners who were transferred from various British jails to North Wales where Frongoch prison camp, close to the market town of Bala, had been constructed on the site of an old whisky distillery. Today, Frongoch is an idyllic, dreamy spot: the River Tryweryn flows through the district and there is little to mark the bitter struggle conducted there, other than a verdigrised plaque set into a boulder on a main road a few hundred metres away, which notes the fact that there was once a prison camp there. At one time, however, the abrasiveness of the relationship between prisoners and prison authorities was such that one prison doctor drowned himself in the Tryweryn. The unfortunate doctor broke under the strain of the moral dilemma posed between his professional calling on the one hand and, on the other, the fact of having to obey the camp commandant's instruction not to minister to prisoners who were refusing to give their real names to the camp authorities. The prisoners feared that this would identify them and lead to their being conscripted.

Two significant events occurred at Frongoch. The first was that the interned men enthusiastically took up that tradition of

Irish prisoners that regards jail as another battlefield on which to continue the struggle that had landed them there in the first place. The prisoners' battles with the prison authorities and the incessant complaints about the regime to which they were subjected – complaints which they managed to transmit to friends and relations outside – made Frongoch an ever-growing and potent source of propaganda.

The second major event within Frongoch was the reorganization of the IRB by Collins himself. Anticipating the eventual release of most or all of the men, Collins took note of the name and address of every likely recruit within the camp – and so, when the prisoners were indeed released and returned to Ireland, Collins could count on the support and local knowledge of IRB agents placed in every corner of the country. And in addition, these agents were radicalized, as political prisoners tend to be, by proximity to other revolutionaries and through exposure to books and conversations they would normally never have encountered on the outside.

By Christmas 1916, the Rising prisoners were being released. The strain, the logistical issues and the political problems facing the British government had mounted inexorably. In particular, the authorities now hoped that this gesture would assuage angry Irish-American opinion which was proving a serious obstacle to the prospect of the United States joining the war in support of Britain and its allies. The now released Collins was put in charge of the National Aid Association (NAA). This was a prisoners' relief fund, largely financed by money from America channelled through John Devoy and other ex-Fenian leaders – and Collins was appointed to the position by Kathleen Clarke, the widow of Thomas Clarke. His position sealed by the Clarke imprimatur, Collins now joined de Valera as a dominant figure in Irish affairs. He was able to use his post to further increase the potent intelligence network he had begun building in Frongoch. The NAA, indeed, provided the perfect vehicle for his unique combination of two conflicting talents – the philanthropic and the conspiratorial.

The Frongoch prisoners returned to an Ireland so remarkably changed, in their eyes, as to be almost bewildering. They had departed as criminals and, a little more than six months later, they had returned as heroes. Their popularity began translating itself into electoral success: a series of fortuitous by-elections occurred in the course of 1917 – and a series of figures associated with 1916 and with Sinn Féin were returned. The first of these electoral victors was George Plunkett, whose son Joseph had been one of the executed leaders of the Rising, and who stood successfully in the Roscommon constituency. Plunkett essentially stood as a sympathy-vote candidate, but the next by-election victory was more significant. The candidate in this case was Joseph McGuinness, who stood in the Longford South constituency as a declared Sinn Féin candidate, while still a prisoner in Lewes jail in southern England. His election poster showed a man in convict uniform under the slogan 'Put him in to get him out!' The British tried to counter the force of the Sinn Féin tide threatening to sweep through Ireland by setting up a political convention on 25 July to which all shades of political opinion were invited. Sinn Féin, however, boycotted the convention, which ended in failure.

Apart from being a demonstration that, in post-1916 Ireland, the sands were running out for the Irish Parliamentary Party, this electoral scene provided the first of many disagreements between Collins and de Valera. Collins gauged sentiment on the ground in Ireland, favouring the gamble of attempting to capitalize on post-Rising sentiment and possibly risking defeat at the polls. Meanwhile, de Valera, in his English jail cell, argued that an electoral loss might damage Sinn Féin's growing popularity. In June 1917, however, de Valera too was released from prison, and now he dropped his reservations about elections and stood himself for a by-election in Co. Clare, where he defeated a popular Irish Parliamentary Party candidate.

John Redmond's star was clearly dimming. He had not accepted a post in the British cabinet on the outbreak of war because he feared that this might damage his standing with his Catholic and nationalist followers; however, the Ulster unionist leader Edward Carson, who had led the unionist revolt, *did* accept the offer of a cabinet seat. Post-Rising Ireland did not and would not understand Redmond's self-sacrificial motives, instead assessing the Carson elevation as a demonstration of who was 'in' and who was 'out' in official British eyes.

Sinn Féin too, of course, was 'out' – but in a rather different and certainly more beneficial way. It was outside the parliamentary arena; and though a considerable state of ebullition was building up in the country, particularly amongst the youth, it was difficult at this point to forecast with any certainty where all the excitement was leading. This was particularly the case as time went on: as excitement began to abate, indeed, Sinn Féin was defeated in a series of by-elections in the course of 1918.

At this juncture, however, something occurred which was second in importance only to the Rising itself in underpinning Sinn Féin's popularity – the British attempt to extend conscription to Ireland. The Great War had halted emigration and the country was full of young men whom important right-wing figures in Britain, such as Field Marshal Sir Henry Wilson, thought would make excellent conscripts and cannon fodder. Wilson and others like him now began thundering about slackers and shirkers of duty who skulked in safety while brave men died in defence of the empire. By this stage in the European conflict, however, early enthusiasm among the Irish public for warfare had faded. Tales of mustard gas, and the ever-lengthening casualty lists amongst the men who had answered Redmond's call, had had their effect. Indeed, one of the reasons why the prisoners in Frongoch had banded together in stratagems such as refusing to give their correct names and addresses was that they feared conscription – and as the news from the front worsened, the same fear hung over every Irish home with a son, husband or a brother of military age.

The British moved to introduce conscription on 16 April 1918. John Redmond had died in March, and now his successor as leader, John Dillon, in protest led the Irish Parliamentary Party from Westminster, thereby ending a tradition of Irish participation in British constitutional politics which had lasted for over a century. Sinn Féin, meanwhile, was presented with a priceless weapon. A delegation led by de Valera descended on a meeting of the Roman Catholic hierarchy at Maynooth and urged the Irish bishops into issuing a statement condemning conscription: 'We consider that conscription forced in this way upon Ireland is an oppressive and inhuman law which the Irish people have a right to resist by every means that are consonant with the law of God.'

This statement was read out at every Mass in the country the following Sunday. Sinn Féin, meanwhile, organized a nationwide campaign of protests in every corner of the land, which ultimately forced the British to withdraw the threat of conscription. And while all of this was taking place, behind closed doors at Westminster another idea was forming: David Lloyd George, the Liberal prime minister, was taking steps to introduce formally to the political stew the notion of Irish partition.

The idea of partition, of course, had already been floated in public. The Home Rule Bill – which had been postponed, because of the onset of war and the opposition of the Conservatives and Ulster unionists – had been intended to apply only to twenty-six counties of Ireland. As a sop to the unionists, the six north-eastern counties of Ireland – Antrim, Down, Armagh, Derry, Fermanagh and Tyrone, some though not all of which had Protestant majorities – were excluded from the terms of the Bill, for a period which was carefully not specified. Lloyd George had written in May 1916 to both Carson and Redmond setting out this proposal. Redmond – with the same blind trust in British good intentions which he had continually shown – declared publicly (on 25 June) that there was no question that the Home Rule proposals meant that partition would be permanent. If there had been any question of this, he said, he would not have supported the proposals.

What the hapless Redmond had not known, however, was that a month earlier (on 24 May), Lloyd George had assured Carson in writing that the direct opposite was in fact the case:

My dear Carson,
I enclose Greer's draft propositions.
    We must make it clear that at the end of the provisional period Ulster does not, *whether she wills it or not*, merge in the rest of Ireland.
    Ever sincerely,
    D. Lloyd George

P.S. will you show it to Craig?

Now, in the aftermath of the conscription crisis and with political turbulence increasingly widespread, the country's political temperature was rising – and this would have been the case even if Lloyd George's discreet letter to Carson had been public knowledge. There was widespread military drilling (Collins' IRB organization being responsible for a good deal of it), while arrests multiplied under the stern terms of the Defence of the Realm Act.

And now a new idea began to circulate: that of the so-called 'German plot'. This was a fiction concocted by the British based on the idea of a Sinn Féin–German conspiracy, and it allowed the authorities to conduct another sweep of Irish nationalist leaders similar to the one that had followed the 1916 Rising. This new dragnet resulted in most leaders of nationalist political thought, amongst them Griffith and de Valera, being rounded up yet again.

Michael Collins had been aware of this brewing plot and had warned de Valera to alter his movements in order to evade capture – but the latter had disregarded the warning. The widespread arrests now had the effect of leaving Collins and his close friend Harry Boland in *de facto* control of the nationalist movement. As president of the IRB, Collins was also secretly regarded as being the real president of Sinn Féin, a fact which de Valera in particular was to find singularly objectionable. But Collins and Boland made use of the crackdown to select candidates of a 'forward' nature to stand in the Sinn Féin interest in the forthcoming general election of December 1918 – 'forward' meaning those who would be more inclined towards war than peace.

In the election, Sinn Féin decimated the Irish Parliamentary Party, winning 73 out of 105 seats, to its rival's total of six. Unionists, principally in the north-east, won twenty-six. Labour did not contest the election so as not to split the vote; and subsequently it was said that James Connolly had marched the Labour Party into the GPO and it had never managed to march out again. Irish politics was now in a state of high excitement. If leading Irish nationalists were not already in jail (thirty-six of the Sinn Féin candidates elected to the first Dáil (parliament) were in prison at the time), then they were engaged in activities calculated to get them there by way of clashes with the Royal Irish Constabulary (RIC). The country rang to the echo of seditious speeches and bands playing martial music and rebel songs as they marched at the head of columns of fiery idealists who would join the ever swelling ranks of nationalist volunteers. These individuals, however, as yet only carried on their shoulders what were known as 'Tipperary rifles': not real guns, but rather hurling sticks which proved themselves formidable implements of political persuasion in a variety of exchanges with RIC batons. The tradition of regarding jail as another battlefield had re-asserted itself – and hunger strikes became a potent weapon in the prisoners' fight for political status.

Lloyd George's political antenna and his daily intelligence reports told him that open hostilities were now inevitable. But he resisted the temptation to strike first, wanting the Sinn Féiners to be seen as the aggressors. By this time General Maxwell had been withdrawn from Ireland, having being made a scapegoat for the post-Rising swing to the rebels. He was transferred to a nondescript post in the north of England, and his place in Ireland was taken by one of the many senior military figures who had joined the Curragh Mutiny against enforcing Home Rule on Ulster. This was Field Marshal Lord (John) French, who received the title of Lord Lieutenant of Ireland. French was warned by Lloyd George to put the onus of shooting first on the Sinn Féiners. He would not have long to wait.

The first Dáil held in Ireland after Sinn Féin's general election triumph was convened at Dublin's Mansion House on 19 January 1919. The intention was to disdain the Westminster parliament to which each deputy had been elected, and to demonstrate in practical and symbolic terms that the country had set out instead on a new path. The veteran activist Cathal Brugha presided: he took the roll call of deputies, not all of whom were present – and the reply in Irish made on behalf of many of these was '*as láthair, faoi ghlas ag Gallaibh*' ('absent, imprisoned by foreigners'; for indeed, many of these newly elected members of parliament were imprisoned in British jails). Brugha then read out the title deeds to the Democratic Programme of the first Dáil.

Inspired by the 1916 Proclamation, it read as follows:

We declare in the words of the Irish Republican Proclamation the right of the people of Ireland to the ownership of Ireland, and to the unfettered control of Irish destinies to be indefeasible, and in the language of our first President, Pádraig MacPhiarais, we declare that the Nation's sovereignty extends not only to all men and women of the Nation, but to all its material possessions, the Nation's soil and all its resources, all the wealth and all the wealth-producing processes within the Nation, and with him we reaffirm that all right to private property must be subordinated to the public right and welfare.

We declare that we desire our country to be ruled in accordance with the principles of Liberty, Equality, and Justice for all, which alone can secure permanence of Government in the willing adhesion of the people.

We affirm the duty of every man and woman to give allegiance and service to the Commonwealth, and declare it is the duty of the Nation to assure that every citizen shall have opportunity to spend his or her strength and faculties in the service of the people. In return for willing service, we, in the name of the Republic, declare the right of every citizen to an adequate share of the produce of the Nation's labour.

It shall be the first duty of the Government of the Republic to make provision for the physical, mental and spiritual well-being of the children, to secure that no child shall suffer hunger or cold from lack of food, clothing, or shelter, but that all shall be provided with the means and facilities requisite for their proper education and training as Citizens of a Free and Gaelic Ireland.

The Irish Republic fully realises the necessity of abolishing the present odious, degrading and foreign Poor Law System, substituting therefor a sympathetic native scheme for the care of the Nation's aged and infirm, who shall not be regarded as a burden, but rather entitled to the Nation's gratitude and consideration. Likewise it shall be the duty of the Republic to take such measures as will safeguard the health of the people and ensure the physical as well as the moral well-being of the Nation.

It shall be our duty to promote the development of the Nation's resources, to increase the productivity of its soil, to exploit its mineral deposits, peat bogs, and fisheries, its waterways and harbours, in the interests and for the benefit of the Irish people.

It shall be the duty of the Republic to adopt all measures necessary for the recreation and invigoration of our Industries, and to ensure their being developed on the most beneficial and progressive co-operative and industrial lines. With the adoption of an extensive Irish Consular Service, trade with foreign Nations shall be revived on terms of mutual advantage and goodwill, and while undertaking the organisation of the Nation's trade, import and export, it shall be the duty of the Republic to prevent the shipment from Ireland of food and other necessaries until the wants of the Irish people are fully satisfied and the future provided for.

It shall also devolve upon the National Government to seek co-operation of the Governments of other countries in determining a standard of Social and Industrial Legislation with a view to a general and lasting improvement in the conditions under which the working classes live and labour.

The absence of labour as a political force in the new parliament may be gauged from the fact that Collins had had the following two paragraphs excised from the programme on the grounds of being too socialistic:

The Republic will aim at the elimination of the class in society which lives upon the wealth produced by the workers of the nation but gives no useful service in return, and in the process of accomplishment will bring freedom to all who have hitherto been caught in the toils of economic servitude.

It shall be the purpose of government to encourage the organization of the people into trade unions and co-operative societies with a view to the control and administration of the industries by the workers engaged in the industries.

Many a Sinn Féiner coming from a conservative small-farm background had similar reservations about the remaining socialistic-tinged content of the document. Yet, broadly speaking, the Democratic Programme represented the spirit of post-1916 nationalist Ireland. It was idealistic, separatist and looked to a new dawn based on republican principles. Arthur Griffith had always had his reservations about said principles: he had argued that Ireland should be governed by the 'King, Lords and Commons' of Ireland, as a separate state headed by the monarch of both Ireland and Britain, his idea being that this device might attract the unionists. The reality, however, may be gauged by the fact that, although invited, unionists who had won seats in the 1918 election ignored the summons to the Mansion House that winter day. And Michael Collins did not attend either, for he was engaged in another major act of illegality. He was in Britain with Harry Boland, rescuing Éamon de Valera from incarceration in Lincoln jail.

After the sitting of the first Dáil, the use of the term 'Irish Republican Army' (IRA) came into general use, as a means of describing that group of armed individuals sworn to defend a state that had not as yet come into being. And even as the Dáil was meeting, two of these individuals fired first. Volunteers Dan Breen and Sean Treacy deliberately shot two RIC men at Soloheadbeg, Co. Tipperary, who were accompanying a cartload of gelignite. Both policemen were killed. This act, moreover, crystallized the tensions between the 'force' versus constitutionalism advocates. The latter position was summed up for me once by my uncle, Monsignor Tim Toal, himself the son of a Tipperary mother. He shook his head and said: 'If Dan Breen and Sean Treacy wanted that dynamite, all they had to do was ask those two men to hand it over. Their rifles were slung over their backs and they could have done nothing even if they wanted to.'

The shooting, however, was mythologized by the 'force' school in terms summed up in a popular ballad which can still be heard in parts of such republican areas as Tipperary and Kerry:

Give me the flag of Ireland boys
And bravely lead me on.
Through rebel Cork and Kerry
And through Clare and Garryowen.

To Solohead and Tipperary Town
And good old Sliabh na mBan
For the flag for which Tom Barry fought
Is good enough for me.

Tell them up in Tipperary that
Their land will soon be free
For the flag of Breen and Treacy boys
Is good enough for me.

Collins was one of those who exulted at the news. The British put a price of ten thousand pounds on Breen's head, for they too appreciated the significance of what had happened. War was coming, but Collins was determined that it would be a new kind of war. There was a degree of context in Collins' planning: he had learned from history, and he had learned from those who had witnessed this history at close quarters. John MacBride – who was executed along with the other leaders of the 1916 Rising – had been on a morning stroll that fateful Easter Monday morning, when he came upon the rebels around St Stephen's Green and promptly joined in. MacBride was a former leader of the Irish Brigade who had fought the British during the Boer War, and with this experience in mind he warned the Volunteers after the surrender that in the next round of fighting they must learn from experience; that they must not find themselves surrounded in buildings or city parks; that they must learn to turn the terrain to their advantage.

Collins, after his experiences in the GPO, fully agreed with him. He too had studied the successful tactics of Boer leader Christiaan de Wet and other guerrilla fighters during the South African Wars – and he also was determined that in the next round there would be no more seizing of buildings in which insurgents could easily be blasted into submission by superior numbers and modern artillery. Collins had learned that his tactic must be to emulate de Wet's tactics. He therefore decided that this time the Irish would fight out of uniform. In putting these ideas into practice, it may be said that Michael Collins pioneered modern urban guerrilla warfare.

More policemen fell as Collins proved the truth of his dictum that the British might replace a detective – but the new man could not step into the shoes of the dead one and his knowledge. The political detectives, or 'G Men' as they were known, had in effect been the eyes and ears of the RIC and of the army. Without them the authorities would be largely consigned to fighting blind, not knowing who in Sinn Féin was or was not significant, and who was or was not in the IRA. Collins now created a special squad to eliminate the G Men, as well as government informers and other political targets. Irish gallows humour promptly christened the hit men the 'twelve apostles'.

There was little humour in the British response to the insurgency designed by Collins; instead, it became increasingly bloody and more counterproductive. Martial law was introduced in Ireland, as was another, terrifying tactic: undercover army-sponsored death squads. Inevitably their operations could not be controlled – and inevitably, the wrong people were arrested, shot or hanged. British reprisals were also aimed at damaging local economic life: throughout the country, for example, creameries – vital centres of the dairy trade in Ireland – were burned as a reprisal for IRA activities.

Yet it was soon evident that the British authorities were inexorably losing control of the situation: not only on the ground, and not only in terms of Irish hearts and minds – but also in the court of *global* public opinion. In particular, American public opinion became increasingly sympathetic to Ireland, even as that country showed every sign of slipping from the British grasp. There were other factors for the authorities to consider, in particular the example that the disorder in Ireland was giving to other potentially restive colonies of the British Empire. Therefore, in order to give the appearance of combatting not a movement for national independence, but a *criminal* movement and a *terrorist* movement, Britain developed the concept of a 'police war'.

This entailed the drafting in of new forces, with new titles. The first body, recruitment for which began in January 1920, consisted of former soldiers – and it was established in such haste that no uniforms were provided for its members, who instead wore an outfit comprising a black tunic and khaki trousers; they soon became known as the Black and Tans. The second, founded in the summer of that year, were known as Auxiliary Cadets: former British officers whose role soon came to consist of visiting reprisals on Irish citizens as payment for IRA activities in their area.

Neither of these corps was subjected to the restraints of normal military discipline. The Black and Tans, being the more visible of the two, are still recalled vividly as hate figures in Irish folk memory. Their mission statement as issued by Dublin Castle was to make Ireland 'an appropriate hell for rebels'. This was heady stuff for men hardened and already brutalized by their experiences in the Great War, and who furthermore were allowed access to alcohol in great quantities – indeed, in many cases simply taking their supplies at the point of a gun.

The Black and Tans soon racked up a record of shootings, killings and indiscriminate violence against civilians across the country. Among the significant acts of destruction attributed to the Black and Tans and the Auxiliaries was the burning of large sections of Cork city in December 1920; the 'Tans' were also responsible for the burning, in September 1920, of the north Co. Dublin coastal town of Balbriggan, along with many other acts of violent incendiarism.

The best remembered day of horror is Bloody Sunday. On that day – 20 November 1920 – Michael Collins' assassination teams killed fifteen suspected British intelligence officers in a series of operations across Dublin. That afternoon, members of the British security forces fired on a crowd at Dublin's Croke Park – the principal Gaelic Athletic Association stadium in the country – killing fourteen; one of the dead was Michael Hogan, a member of the Tipperary team, after whom one of the stands in Croke Park is named today. The official version of what occurred is that the authorities believed that there were armed IRA men in the crowd and that the ground was cordoned off to allow a search for weapons to take place – but that some unknown men fired on the troops, who returned fire with lethal effect.

Bloody Sunday concluded with the capture, torture and death of one of Collins' principal aides, Dick McKee, together with volunteer Peadar Clancy and a student of Irish, Conor Clune – whose death would prove to have far-reaching consequences. Clune was a nephew of Bishop Joseph Clune of Perth, Western Australia, who gave David Lloyd George a first-hand account of the Tans' activities and who achieved worldwide publicity for the Sinn Féin cause when he told a press conference that the men he had met in Ireland were not criminals but 'the cream of their race'.

The best-known Irish leader of the period missed most of these events, for de Valera was in America. While incarcerated at Lincoln, he had decided that he could win rather more political gains propagandizing in America than by staying in Ireland – and had to be persuaded by Cathal Brugha to return to Ireland after his escape, lest a departure for America be regarded as cowardice. In June 1919, however, de Valera achieved his American goal, with Collins smuggling him out of the country with the help of Irish seamen. De Valera's eighteen-month spell in the United States was undoubtedly a political and propaganda success – and yet the price of that success was considerable, and was not fully understood at the time.

Many aspects of de Valera's story, indeed, were never aired in Ireland throughout his career, and so it may be helpful at this point if some attempt is made to unravel the complexities and contradictions of this extraordinary man, who bears out in spades Napoleon's dictum that the most important quality in a general is that he be *lucky*. De Valera was indeed supremely lucky at various key junctures in his life. He was lucky in his early life: a priest from his area chanced to meet a Holy Ghost Father on a train journey from Limerick and mentioned the case of a bright student who had won a scholarship but who didn't have all the money required to further his education. The Holy Ghost Father offered to take the impecunious lad into Blackrock College – and de Valera wrote to his mother in America, telling her in effect to either send him the balance of the school fees, or his fare to join her. She sent him the fees.

De Valera as a result benefited from both a first-class education and a lifelong association with Blackrock, where he went on to teach mathematics. In the throes of the 1916 Rising he was lucky again, this time on two scores. The first was that – even though the post under his command at Boland's Mill was, as we have seen, so far from Mount Street Bridge that he could not even follow, much less direct, Malone's raid on the British forces approaching the bridge – de Valera was nevertheless able to take credit for the fact that approximately half of the total British casualties sustained in the Rising happened on his watch. It became a triumph for de Valera: the fact that his command post actually witnessed comparatively little action was little remembered. Nor were certain other episodes recalled: such as the fact that he suffered a near-nervous breakdown in the course of his command. His anxious men brought him to a nearby railway siding where he was directed to a carriage and told to go to sleep. He awoke disoriented and thought that he had died and gone to heaven, until he realized that the angels and cherubs flying about over his head were the decorations on a carriage specifically designed for royal visits! This part of the de Valera legend of 1916 did not emerge for several decades afterwards.

He then escaped execution in the aftermath of the Rising – another stroke of luck. And, as we will see, his luck would continue to hold. He was also lucky in a more personal sense. Given the social mores of Irish society at the time, he was profoundly lucky that his foes did not find out that he had, most likely, been born illegitimate; instead, most people in Ireland accepted his version of his origins, which was that his mother, Catherine Coll, an emigrant from Bruree in Co. Limerick, had married one Vivion de Valera, a musician in New Jersey. In fact, it would appear that de Valera was born in a foundling home in New York, and was brought back to Ireland as an infant by Catherine's younger brother Patrick because she, working in service, could not support him in the US. He was then reared in the rather loveless surroundings of his uncle's labourer's cottage, and was forced to combine the normal farm chores with continuing his studies to scholarship level.

His attitude to his home environment may be gauged by the fact that he preferred to spend Christmas in Blackrock rather than return to Bruree. The contrast between de Valera and Collins – between the former's uncertain background and Collins' upbringing as the youngest and most doted-upon of a family of eight on a reasonably sized holding for the time (ninety acres) – simply could not have been more stark. And de Valera's austere, strangely un-Irish persona – which both set him apart and at the same time bore him up on the Irish political landscape – was in binary opposition to that of the hurling-playing, outgoing, rambunctious Collins, one of whose favourite pastimes was to wrestle opponents for a 'bit of ear': that is, biting his victim's ear after successfully pinioning him in a wrestling hold.

De Valera eschewed such roughhouse tactics, controlling through being tall, remote and speechifying in a curiously unmelodic and harsh accent that commanded attention. Conservative and exuding *hauteur*, de Valera said of himself: 'Every instinct of mine would indicate that I was meant to be a dyed-in-the-wool Tory, or even a Bishop, rather than the leader of a Revolution.'[1] The only part of that description with which one could quarrel, indeed, is that he viewed himself as a mere bishop – and not a cardinal! For he exuded the loftiness and authority of a cardinal, together with a cardinal's expectation that his pronouncements were to be accepted with the force of dogma – even to the point of risking the anger of otherwise supportive organizations or followers. During his period in America, in a bid to bring the Irish-American leadership under his control, de Valera split the powerful Friends of Irish Freedom (FOIF) movement and set up his own rival organization. A leading Irish-American businessman of the day – one John P. Grace, of Grace Shipping Line fame – described de

Valera's performance at a crucial ten-hour meeting during the row over the break-up of the FOIF:

> I confess before heaven that de Valera was that day revealed to me as either labouring under some psychopathic condition or that the evil spirit himself had taken hold of the Irish movement... Judge Cohalan, humbling himself under insults repeated constantly during those ten hours... Did everything humanly possible or imaginable to bridge the chasm. De Valera had not only been the aggressor, but repeatedly the aggressor, and perhaps encouraged to go a little further as each aggression was overlooked... De Valera's attitude was one of infallibility; he was right, everybody else was wrong, and he couldn't be wrong... Bishops and priests, Protestants and Catholics, aged men born in Ireland and young men born here worked for those ten hours to bring President de Valera to the point of amenability... I beg to repeat that not having seen him before, as for those ten hours he unfolded himself, I thought the man was crazy.[2]

This facet of de Valera's character, however, remained largely unknown in Ireland – until he had returned from America and set off on a path that led ultimately to civil war. In Ireland his supporters, who at this point still included Michael Collins, sided with de Valera against the existing Irish-American leadership of John Devoy and Judge Daniel Cohalan. Collins refused to be swayed to Devoy's side even after the latter printed a lead story with a photo of Collins in his *Gaelic American* newspaper under the heading 'Ireland's Fighting Chief', thus making an unstated but obvious contrast with Ireland's orating chief who operated from the luxurious safety of New York's Waldorf Hotel.

De Valera attracted both huge attention and vast funding –
some of which, as we shall see, he would later use in dubious
fashion – when in the United States. But at an official level,
his feuding with the Irish-American bosses meant that neither
the Democratic nor the Republican Party, faced as they were
with two contending Irish-American lobby groups, emphasized
Irish-oriented policies in their presidential programmes at the
selection conventions held in America during his stay in the
country. None of this, however, percolated back to Ireland in
such a way as to affect his standing.

De Valera's American trip had one damaging consequence
for Ireland. The sheer length of his visit meant that de Valera
himself was removed from the realities of the Irish struggle and
unable to conduct a proper impression of the ability of Collins'
secret army to continue waging war. Rapturous receptions
from Irish-American crowds both boosted de Valera's ego and
gave him an unrealistic assessment of how the war in Ireland
should be tailored to the requirements of public relations in
America. Judging that the down-and-dirty nature of guerrilla
warfare had a damaging effect on such public relations, he
made the extraordinary suggestion that ambushes should be
abandoned in favour of fighting one substantial battle every
month or so, consisting of 500 men on either side. This, de
Valera considered, would have a better effect.

And to be sure, it would – that is, for the British who would
have destroyed the IRA in a matter of days, had the guerril-
las attempted open warfare against a major European army
that had just emerged victorious from the Great War. When
de Valera did get his way in staging a major engagement – a
daylight raid on Dublin's Custom House – the attack on the
famous building did attract worldwide publicity but it also
resulted in the capture of much of the Dublin Brigade of the

IRA. And this his fundamental tension over strategy under-scored an emerging rift with Collins – who throughout this critical spell remained in Ireland and emerged as the rival star in the firmament of Irish leadership.

*

By the end of 1920 it was obvious to Lloyd George that despite fierce right-wing opposition, the situation in Ireland demanded that the rebels be dealt with by means of negotiation. Peace feelers began to flow from London – and in America, de Valera realized that the endgame was approaching. In December 1920 he was smuggled back to Ireland, his path once more smoothed by Collins, and now de Valera set about establishing his author-ity over both Sinn Féin and the IRA.

One of his first substantive actions was an attempt to get Collins to leave the country and go to America in his stead. Apart from being dismaying for Collins personally, this would have stopped the war effort in its tracks: not only did Collins have drive and flair, he also possessed a unique and unrivalled *personal* knowledge of the vast web of contacts and intelligence sources which made the underground campaign possible in the first place. Collins accordingly and successfully resisted the attempt to remove him from the scene. In July 1921, however, just as peace efforts finally bore fruit in the form of a truce, Collins was singularly defeated and humiliated by de Valera. The Irish were invited by Lloyd George to send a delegation to London to discuss the way forward. De Valera headed this delegation – and he took with him to London Arthur Griffith, Cathal Brugha and Austin Stack.

In de Valera's absence, these last two men had become pro-gressively estranged from Collins. Brugha was nominally the minister for defence in the illegal Dáil – but although a man of legendary courage he possessed none of Collins' ability, and was generally regarded as hating the younger man for sidelining him. Stack also intensely disliked Collins: the latter had publicly highlighted his lack of ability on at least one occasion by telling him before witnesses that his department (Home Affairs) was 'a bloody disgrace'.

By taking two men of lesser ability with him while leaving Collins at home, despite the latter's pleas to the contrary, de Valera was clearly demonstrating his authority. His stated reason, of course, was a little different: if Collins went to London, he claimed, this would give the British the opportunity to take photographs of him, and this would be a security risk. The fact, however, that had he succeeded in persuading Collins to go to America, photographs could have been taken of him *there* did not appear to trouble de Valera.

In London there occurred a set of meetings which have been curiously underplayed by Irish historians and certainly glossed over by a majority of de Valera's many biographers. For a number of days de Valera met with Lloyd George alone, leaving the rest of his delegation to pass the time as they wished. These men were probably the two shrewdest politicians in Europe at the time, and at the end of their meetings de Valera was in no doubt as to what Britain was offering. Lloyd George's solution would confer Dominion status on Ireland, equivalent to that prevailing in New Zealand, Newfoundland, South Africa, Australia and Canada. It involved the swearing of an oath of allegiance to the British monarch and the presence of a Governor-General in Dublin. The most significant element in this deal was that Ireland would be subjected to partition.

By this time, indeed, partition was essentially in existence. The king had already inaugurated a separate parliament in

Belfast, on 22 June 1921. George V's speech on the day held out the hand of friendship to the southern Irish – and this speech provided the basis in the first place for calling the truce and holding the peace talks. However, de Valera pretended at first to be so outraged by the British departure from the concept of an all-Ireland Republic, as imagined in the 1916 Proclamation, that he refused even to agree to take the proposals back to Dublin with him when Lloyd George handed them to him. Later that day, however, and without reference to his earlier disdain, he sent a messenger around to Downing Street to bring the proposals back to him at his hotel.

Therefore it is clear that after his London visit to Lloyd George, de Valera was fully briefed on what the British were offering. He was certainly aware that partition was a fact, and he was aware that this new offer contained a far greater measure of independence than the original, pre-war Home Rule proposals – yet de Valera had no intention of engaging in any more negotiation with Lloyd George at this point. Back in Dublin, he began laying the groundwork for the future he envisaged. As tensions mounted once more, both in Ireland and between Ireland and Britain, as the summer of 1921 passed into autumn, and as written communiqués went back and forth between the two sides, de Valera decided that he would not go back to London to face Lloyd George again on the July proposals.

Rather, he would send Michael Collins into the field on his behalf. What flowed from this decision was to have momentous and tragic implications for Ireland.

3

The Treaty Saga

THE DOCUMENT TO BE NEGOTIATED IN LONDON WAS OF the utmost importance in determining the destiny of Ireland – perhaps the most important since the twelfth century when an English pope, Adrian IV, had issued a papal bull, *Laudabiliter*, bestowing upon the Normans the right to colonize Ireland. Now, eight centuries on, the objective was to produce a document *decolonizing* Ireland – or most of it, at any rate. One might have thought at this juncture that de Valera would be anxious not merely to be present at the signing of such a document, but also to play a significant role in its composition.

De Valera, however, shirked both these responsibilities – and one could advance a number of theories as to why this was the case. Perhaps it was as a result of a long sojourn in the United States, in the course of which he had allowed himself to be described as the president of the Republic – a republic which he now knew, following his recent tête-à-tête in London with Lloyd George, was not achievable. Perhaps he realized that his public pronouncements on Irish independence could not readily be set aside, that the terms of Lloyd George's proposal would simply not be acceptable to many of his followers, and that he therefore needed an exit strategy as a means of securing his political credibility.

In any case, de Valera's return to Dublin, after his meetings with Lloyd George, was followed by a bout of sparring by letter which went on for over two months, in the course of which he unsuccessfully attempted to force the British prime minister to commit to holding peace talks on the basis of the self-proclaimed Irish Republic. The final agreement to hold talks was on the basis of two highly significant letters exchanged between Lloyd George and de Valera. Lloyd George's letter opened by stating that:

> His Majesty's Government... cannot enter a conference upon the basis of this correspondence. The position taken up by his Majesty's Government is fundamental to the existence of the British Empire and they cannot alter it. My colleagues and I remain, however, keenly anxious to make in co-operation with your delegates another determined effort to explore every possibility of settlement by personal discussion. We, therefore, send you herewith a fresh invitation to a conference in London on 11th October, where we can meet your delegates as spokesmen of the people whom you represent with a view to ascertaining how the association of the people of Ireland with the communities of nations known as the British Empire may best be reconciled with Irish national aspirations.

De Valera's response, which was actually drafted by Arthur Griffith, contained the following: 'Our respective positions have been stated and are understood, and we agree that conference, not correspondence, is the most practical and hopeful way to an understanding. We accept the invitation and our Delegates will meet you in London on the date mentioned "to explore every possibility of settlement by personal discussion".'

The realpolitik of accepting talks on the basis of Lloyd George's letter, however, stemmed from de Valera's acknowledgement that a republic along the lines of the 1916 Proclamation had now effectively been rolled up and taken off the table. And clearly also this furling of the flag of liberty would indeed be unacceptable to a significant number of die-hard republicans: de Valera understood after his London visit that when an agreement was signed, such a deed would call for 'scapegoats'.[*] The mystery, however, is why Collins allowed himself to become the principal scapegoat. After all, he was fully aware that de Valera, to whom he referred as 'the long hoor', had tried to get rid of him by sending him to America – and he had bluntly stated that he would not be got rid of so easily. And he had been humiliated by being forced to remain in Ireland, rather than accompanying de Valera to London after the truce had come into force in the summer of 1921. And yet, in October of that year, he agreed to go to London to negotiate a treaty which he acknowledged, after he had signed it, also meant signing his own death warrant.

On one level, perhaps, Collins was overawed by de Valera, who generated an incredible psychological force field when he had a mind to do so. Collins' was one of the most brilliant minds ever to come out of Ireland – but quite apart from the remarkable loyalty to his chief which he was known to possess, he may also have been in awe of the older man's educational attainments. De Valera had, after all, been a professor of mathematics at Blackrock College; by 1922, he was Chancellor of the National University to boot. Collins, in contrast, had

---

[*] Mrs Tom Clarke confronted de Valera with his remark – 'We must have scapegoats' – in the Dáil on 17 December 1921. He at first attempted to deny that he had made the remark, but after some prevarication admitted that he *had* made it.

left school in his mid-teens, having completed his entrance exams for the Post Office in Clonakilty in Co. Cork. He then moved from the Post Office to a job with the Morgan Guaranty Company: here he acquired a financial training that stood him in good stead, managing a successful national loan during the Anglo-Irish War – this in spite of the fact that the British regarded such a transaction as illegal. And all of the money was safely accounted for as he effectively fought off British intelligence, the Black and Tans, the British Army and a number of unacknowledged murder gangs, all the while travelling around Dublin on his pushbike with a price on his head. Collins, when his life is viewed in this light, had little to feel inferior about!

But, leaving speculation as to a possible inferiority complex to one side, what is certain is the fact that Michael Collins now knew better than anyone in Ireland how little real military strength his side actually possessed. The Irish War of Independence was in reality a war between two secret services: it was a war which in effect the Irish had won – but it was also a war which could not be won twice. The IRA's greatest weapon, secrecy, was gone. Collins had already warned his colleagues, as the truce neared, that it meant that their secret army would resemble rabbits coming out of their holes, when hostilities ceased. As, militarily speaking, taking on the British once more was not an option, Collins' motivation in going to London may have been that contained in the dictum 'hold what you have and get what you want'. He would later openly accept that the Treaty did not confer full independence – but that it could be used as a stepping stone: as he put it, 'freedom to achieve freedom'.

However, even while Collins was negotiating in London, de Valera again demonstrated his fundamentally different approach to the issue of what sort of military engagement with the British might take place – should it again become necessary. He went about the country, often in the company of Collins' adversary Cathal Brugha, inspecting units of the Volunteers who were being re-organized into a regular army. Clearly such an army, bereft as it was of either tanks or heavy artillery, could never have hoped to compete with the British in open warfare – regardless of how bravely its members fought. But de Valera also had in mind another re-organizational scheme.

He had already persuaded Collins to cause the IRB to alter its constitution so as to recognize the president of the Dáil (in effect de Valera himself) rather than of the IRB as the real president of Ireland. Then, late in 1921, de Valera also made a serious attempt to have the Volunteers brought under his control. For Collins, however, this was a bridge too far – and he used his IRB influence to abort the proposal. Not yet knowing of Collins' plans, de Valera convened a meeting of the GHQ staff in Dublin – significantly *after* Collins and Griffith had finished briefing him on the state of negotiations thus far, and had set off again by train and boat to London to carry on their exhausting discussions with the British. De Valera's purpose at the GHQ staff meeting was to inform its members that the army was now being re-organized and that they would have to take an oath of loyalty to the Dáil. Quite apart from Collins' opposition to this change, those present had already taken the volunteer oath and demonstrated their fidelity to it, by fighting bravely against the British while de Valera was out of the country.

Against this context, the 'New Army' proposals, coming at a time of great tension in Ireland, were regarded at best as ill-advised and at worst as insulting – and were rejected. But, when de Valera realized that he was being stymied, he indulged in one of those egotistical outbursts that had so appalled observers in the United States. He pushed his table away and, jumping to his feet 'half shouting, half screaming', thundered: 'Ireland will give me a New Army'. With the likelihood of hostilities breaking out again should the Treaty negotiations fail, however, even de Valera realized eventually that the time was not opportune for his proposal, and so he dropped it.

It was against a backdrop of such manoeuvring that Collins and Griffith in London faced perhaps the greatest negotiating team Britain has ever deployed. Its members included Winston Churchill, who ranked fourth in cabinet seniority to Lloyd George; the Conservative leader Austen Chamberlain; and the Lord Chancellor, Lord Birkenhead (F. E. Smith). Lloyd George had included Chamberlain because he reckoned, shrewdly and correctly, that any deal he concluded would be so detested by Tory die-hards that he would need moderate Conservatives on his side to get it through the House of Commons. His team also included several other lesser political luminaries, some of the best civil servants in Europe and an immensely efficient secretarial back-up.

The Irish delegation consisted of Collins himself, with Griffith, Eamon Duggan, Robert Barton and George Gavan Duffy; its secretary was Erskine Childers, Barton's cousin, who in the summer of 1914 had brought ashore at Howth the guns smuggled from Germany on his yacht, *Asgard*. Ostensibly Griffith was the leader of the delegation but because of the state of his health, the real task of leadership inevitably fell to Collins. De Valera later admitted that he had deliberately built dissension into the delegation, balancing Griffith and Collins with the others, because he claimed he thought that they could be trusted to hold out for the republican ideal. And the Irish delegation was already weakened by the fact of de Valera's absence; his talent lay in negotiation and this talent was sorely needed. Collins and Griffith, however, made the best of it. They managed to centralize authority in their own hands by setting up a system of subcommittees on which they – and mainly Collins – were the principal negotiators. The Irish delegation lacked depth, therefore, but it could at least rely on a sense of focus.

Throughout the weeks of negotiation, de Valera did not speak with either Collins or Griffith, nor did he acknowledge the signs of alarm which members of the delegation – and others, feeding on rumours – brought to him concerning the trajectory of the negotiations and their likely outcome. Childers too kept de Valera informed of what was happening. In the week before the Treaty was signed, there was an acrimonious meeting of Dáil members in Dublin at which the likely final shape of the Treaty document was made known. Yet even now, no clear-cut directive came from de Valera as to what course should be taken; and, as he had done ever since the question of negotiation had arisen, he refused all entreaties that he should go to London himself.

This left de Valera in a position of being able to simulate shock and horror in the days after the Treaty was signed and its contents published on 6 December 1921. He put this strategy in motion in the small hours of the morning of the Treaty's signing. The epoch-making news of the signing came in a telephone call from London to the home of the businessman Stephen O'Mara in Limerick, where de Valera was staying at the time. The call was from Gearóid O'Sullivan, a member of the Irish army's GHQ staff, to inform Richard Mulcahy, another house guest and O'Sullivan's Chief of Staff, that the Treaty had just been signed. De Valera refused to come to the phone when invited to do so by Mulcahy. He commented, 'I didn't think the British would give in so easily.' He subsequently professed ignorance of the Treaty's signing until he saw a newspaper in Dublin later that evening, prior to presiding at a Dante commemoration event in the Mansion House – this, although the news was breaking on the streets before his train had even left Limerick. The holding of a function to honour the creator of the *Inferno* might be taken as heavily symbolic, in the light of what was to follow.

Before the commencement of the Dante commemoration, Eamon Duggan – who had been dispatched from London for the purpose – handed de Valera the text of the agreement, telling him that by agreement it was about to be published. De Valera flew into a rage, exclaiming 'What! Published, whether I've seen it or not – whether I approve it or not?' He later described the signing without consultation as an act of treachery 'unparalleled in history'. His apparent rage at being presented with a fait accompli drove him to issue a statement after the Treaty's contents were published in which he said:

> In view of the nature of the proposed treaty with Great Britain, President de Valera has sent an urgent summons to the members of the Cabinet in London to report at once, so that a full Cabinet decision may be taken. The hour of meeting is fixed for twelve o'clock noon tomorrow; a meeting of the Dáil will be summoned later.

This was the first public intimation of divisions within the cabinet and marked the beginning of what would become known as the Great Split. Privately, de Valera put a motion before the cabinet members still in Dublin that the London delegation be dismissed. As Barton, Griffith and Collins were still en route to Dublin, he confidently expected that he would have a majority consisting of himself, Brugha, Stack and W. T. Cosgrave, who normally deferred to him. To his astonishment, however, Cosgrave objected, refusing to support the dismissal, at least until after the delegates had been heard. Subsequently Cosgrave supported Barton, Collins and Griffith in voting that the Treaty issue should not be decided by the cabinet alone, but by the Dáil as a whole.

After this decision – one which Childers correctly foresaw would mean defeat for de Valera's position – Childers asked de Valera where he could now expect to find support. The latter replied in a phrase that was to govern his actions for several years thereafter. He told Childers that he would attract 'extremist support', and played on the fears and uncertainties generated by his previous statement to the press by issuing an even more inflammatory and disruptive document:

You have seen in the public Press the text of the proposed Treaty with Great Britain.

The terms of this agreement are in violent conflict with the wishes of the majority of this nation as expressed freely in successive elections during the last three years,

I feel it my duty to inform you immediately that I cannot recommend the acceptance of this Treaty, either to Dáil Éireann or the country. In this attitude I am supported by the Ministers of Home Affairs and Defence.

A public session of Dáil Éireann is being summoned for Wednesday next at 11 o'clock. I ask the people to maintain during the interval the same discipline as heretofore. The members of the Cabinet, though divided in opinions, are prepared to carry on the public services as usual.

The Army as such is, of course, not affected by the political situation and continues under the same orders and control. The great test of our people has come. Let us face it worthily without bitterness and above all, without recriminations. There is a definite constitutional way of resolving our

differences – let us not depart from it, and let the conduct of
the Cabinet in this matter be an example to the whole nation.

This ominous announcement was the first indication to the
public at large that there were major divisions within Sinn Féin.
The more politically-minded began to realize that Irish history
was about to enter a new and perilous phase.

De Valera was certainly not the only one in the ranks of Sinn
Féin to oppose the Treaty. For many an ardent young volunteer,
the retreat from the ideal of the Republic was intolerable. For
experienced IRA leaders like Rory O'Connor, Ernie O'Malley,
Liam Lynch and Oscar Traynor, such a retreat was something
to be fought against just as hard as they had fought the British.
All of these men combined, however, did not attract a fraction
of the public support and adulation of de Valera. And his influence helped both to deepen the split between former comrades
and to attract more support to the extreme republican side than
it could ever have hoped to gather otherwise.

De Valera maintained his position of utter rejection
throughout the ensuing Treaty debates, held in the Dáil in
January 1922. He and those who agreed with him concentrated their fire mainly on the clauses relating to the oath of
allegiance sworn to the British monarch, and to the presence of
a Governor-General in the vaunted new Dominion of Ireland.
The elephant in the room, the substantive matter of partition,
was scarcely mentioned – although in his defence of the Treaty,
Collins choose to take on the issue directly, bracketing it with
his 'freedom to achieve freedom' argument. He said:

> In my opinion it gives us freedom, not the ultimate freedom
> that all nations desire and develop towards, but the freedom
> to achieve it. We have stated we would not coerce the

North-East. We have stated it officially. I stated it publicly in Armagh and nobody has found fault with me. What was the use of talking big phrases about not agreeing to the partition of our country. Surely we recognise the North-East corner does exist, and surely our intention was that we should take such steps as would lead to mutual understanding.

Collins was one of the very few figures of the time who either understood that, while for twenty-six counties freedom to achieve freedom meant just that, for many Irish nationalists in the north-eastern six counties the Treaty was a betrayal: the placing of a large, resentful and fearful minority under what they perceived to be a particularly mean-spirited and unjust majority. Precisely how mean-spirited and how unjust time would rapidly tell – although it would be many more decades into the future before the British authorities would at last move to tear down much of what the Treaty allowed the unionist majority to establish in the new entity of Northern Ireland.

In these tense hours, however, de Valera largely dominated the debate. He forgot about his urgings that the conduct of the cabinet should be an example to the nation. His performance was both egotistical and almost dictatorial. He spoke 250 times, his comments covering a total of thirty-nine pages of the official Dáil record as compared to a combined total of twenty pages for *both* Collins and Griffith. He interjected at will, disregarding normal parliamentary procedure, because he claimed that he had the right to follow his own procedures. His main contribution to the debate was one he subsequently withdrew: 'Document Number 2' was a version of the Treaty which recognized partition but dispensed with the oath and the Governor-General. This document, however, served to cloud the issue: it confused the rank-and-file republicans; and it held no attraction for Collins and Griffith who, after their experiences in London, had a fairly clear idea of the reception awaiting any Irish delegation demanding the replacement of the Treaty with de Valera's brainchild.

Throughout the Dáil debate, Collins – ironically – suffered from the electoral strategy that he and Boland had earlier pursued in their selection of 'forward' candidates: now, the members of the Dáil were rather more republican than was sentiment outside it. Nevertheless when the vote on the Treaty was ultimately taken, on 7 January 1922, it was carried by sixty-four votes to fifty-seven.[*] De Valera responded to the outcome of the debate by leading his followers out of the Dáil, thus leaving Ireland with a ship of state – the new Free State, now headed by Collins – from which the captain and half of her crew jumped overboard before she even began her voyage. That voyage was destined to be long, bloody and tumultuous – for now de Valera did indeed seek the 'extremist support' of which he had earlier spoken.

*

After the Treaty was accepted by the Dáil, the British began evacuating their barracks across Ireland and commenced the handover of Dublin Castle, the seat of British administration in Ireland for centuries. This action had enormous political

---

[*] The story of the debate deserves very considerable space, it being the longest protracted conversation concerning the country's future to take place in an Irish assembly either before or since 1921. However, the tense and bitter exchanges have been captured in a single volume, *Dáil Eireann, Suíonna Príobháideacha an Dara Dáil (Private Sessions) 1921–1922* and can be read at leisure. To dwell on this debate now would detract us from gaining a clear picture of the aftermath to 1916 as it played out in subsequent decades.

and psychological implications. Irish people could see that the Treaty was indeed bringing tangible progress towards independence: the British were visibly leaving the field and handing over to the Irish.

Unfortunately, nothing in the Anglo-Irish relationship is ever that straightforward. Events now began to make nonsense of de Valera's incendiary statement to the public in December – before the cabinet had even met to discuss the Treaty – in which he claimed that the army would not be affected by his activities and would continue under the same control as before. And so, as the split in the Dáil over the Treaty began to be replicated throughout the country, the British withdrawal meant that the vacated barracks began, dangerously, falling into the hands of both pro- and anti-Treatyites.

The IRA was now, of course, the properly constituted army of the Free State: but many of its members could not swear an oath of allegiance to such an entity – and so they broke away to form, essentially, a fifth column rejecting the new government, a guerrilla army in the new Ireland. This sizeable proportion of IRA members who did not agree with the Treaty may or may not have acted as they did without de Valera's incitements. But his words and actions certainly helped to inflame the situation. Though the reality of his control over the army has always provided subject for debate, de Valera's opponents say flatly that he caused the Civil War. He and his apologists, in contrast, have always maintained that he acted as a peacemaker and that his actions had no bearing on the military campaign.

In one letter, de Valera himself wrote that he had been 'condemned to view the tragedy here for the last year as through a glass darkly, powerless to intervene directly'. This, however, is simply not true. The seizure in April 1922 of Dublin's Four Courts building – the heart of legal life in the country and the home of the national archives – by a group of IRA volunteers was clearly a climactic moment. The occupation of the building was both strategically and symbolically significant, and it called for a cool response. De Valera's response, however, was far from cool: he issued what he called an Easter Proclamation couched in incendiary terms:

> Young men and young women of Ireland, hold steadily on. Those who with cries of woe and lamentation would now involve you in a disastrous route you will soon see rally behind you and vie with you for first place in the vanguard. Beyond all telling is the destiny God has in mind for Ireland, the fair, the peerless one. You are the artificers of that destiny. Yours is the faith that moves mountains, the faith that confounds misgivings. Yours is the faith and love that begot the enterprise of 1916.
>
> Young men and young women of Ireland, the goal is at last in sight – steady, altogether forward. Ireland is yours for the taking. Take it.

This cannot be described as the language of someone helpless to influence events looking 'through a glass darkly'. De Valera showed himself capable of exercising influence even over the most dedicated leaders at various times during the conflict. A notable example of this came when an IRA leader, Liam Deasy, who was awaiting execution by the Free State authorities, realized that the military position was hopeless and issued an appeal to his former comrades asking them to lay down their arms. De Valera drafted a letter of rejection – but had Liam Lynch, the principal republican leader left standing at that time, sign it. And so, the truth of this vexed matter perhaps lies somewhere in the middle. De Valera may not have actually caused the war, but he certainly helped to make a bad situation worse – and used his great prestige to further extremism for his own ends.

Events moved bewilderingly fast as civil war engulfed Ireland in that flaming year of 1922 – much too fast, indeed, for most of Irish society, which had just come to terms with the bloody and materially expensive destruction of 1916. And, although the people of Ireland could not yet know it, another horrendous human and material bill was now in the offing. The infant Irish state would find itself picking up the tab for RIC pensions and for the cost of reprisals which the British had inflicted on the country in the course of the War of Independence. These reprisals had caused economic hardship across swathes of Ireland – and now all such acts of war would have to be paid for.

But this was all still to come – for now, and in addition to all these bills, the Irish state was about to inflict a whole range of new and expensive wounds on itself. Civil war deaths amounted to approximately 1500: losses on the anti-Treaty side probably numbered roughly the same as those of the Free State forces. Given the conditions of the time, the republican death toll has not been accurately computed, and may in fact have been higher than on the Free State side. Nor was this the end of the catalogue of bitterness and destruction. In the south-eastern area of the country, notably around Waterford, serious agrarian warfare broke out after labourers' wages were reduced. Meadows were spiked, cattle driven off and farmers retaliated by attacking labourers and burning their homes.

But the government always had the upper hand: aside from the fact that the pro-Treaty forces had the bulk of the citizenry behind them, the Free State authorities commanded considerably more men in the field than the IRA. In the whole country, IRA strength did not exceed 8000 at that time, and against them the Free State authorities had built up a force of at least 38,000 combat troops. The possession of barracks, armoured cars and artillery emphasized the overwhelming Free State strength. Amongst the additional forces brought to bear on the anti-Treaty forces, meanwhile, was a pastoral from the Catholic hierarchy denying the sacraments to the 'Irregulars', as the anti-Treaty forces were called. The rebels certainly did not lack courage – but they did lack anything remotely approaching the power raised against them.

In London, the British authorities watched as disorder in Ireland spiralled upwards. Churchill in particular was outraged, and pressure was piled on Collins to put an end to the flagrant breaches of the Treaty. Collins, however, hesitated to attack his old comrades: partly out of loyalty and old friendship and partly because he hoped that the new Constitution called for by the Treaty, and which was now in the process of being written, would be republican enough to satisfy the anti-Treatyites. He hoped to buy peace at least until his new Constitution emerged and the general election called for by the Treaty, pencilled in for June 1922, could be held.

To further this aim, he concluded an electoral pact with de Valera – an agreement which in itself was flagrantly anti-democratic. The idea was that the electorate be given a slate of Sinn Féin candidates – both pro- and anti-Treaty – for whom they would be called upon to vote. Apart from the fact that this notion excised from the political process other interest groups, such as the Labour movement and the farmers, it also envisioned cabinet posts for de Valera and prominent anti-Treaty figures like Erskine Childers.

Collins' cabinet colleagues were appalled at this action, and Griffith and Collins, in the brief period of life left to them, were never again as friendly as they had been prior to the pact. Collins was caught, not merely between a rock and a hard place, but between several rocks and a multiplicity of hard places. On the political front, de Valera kept up his litany of 'extremist support'-seeking speeches. These may be taken as having commenced at Dungarvan, Co. Waterford on 16 March 1922:

> The Treaty... barred the way to independence with the blood of fellow Irishmen. It was only by civil war after this that they could get their independence. If you don't fight today, you will have to fight tomorrow; and I say, when you are in a good fighting position, then fight on.

The next day, in Tipperary, de Valera continued:

> If the Treaty was accepted the fight for freedom would still go on; and the Irish people, instead of fighting foreign soldiers would have to fight the Irish soldiers of an Irish government set up by Irishmen. If the Treaty were not rejected, perhaps it was over the bodies of the young men he saw around him that day that the fight for Irish freedom may be fought.

Subsequently, he told an audience in Thurles:

> If they accepted the Treaty, and if the volunteers of the future tried to complete the work of the Volunteers of the last four years had been attempting, they... would have to wade through Irish blood, through the blood of the soldiers of the Irish government, and through, perhaps, the blood of some of the members of the government in order to get Irish freedom.

And at Killarney he thundered:

> If our Volunteers continue *and I hope they will continue until the goal is reached*... then these men, in order to achieve freedom, will have, I said yesterday, to march over the dead bodies of their own brothers.

All such rhetoric and bluster helped to further the inexorable march towards tragedy.

The general election of 16 June 1922 was a great success for pro-Treaty forces. In the crucial Dáil vote on acceptance or rejection of the Treaty the winning majority had been only seven votes. But in the election, the Collins-Griffith faction won fifty-eight seats, Labour seventeen, the Farmers Party seven and independents six, with four unionists returned from Trinity College Dublin. The de Valera faction, meanwhile, won only thirty-six seats. The Irish had voted overwhelmingly for the Treaty and peace – but they were not to get the latter. The British government now reacted swiftly to what it saw as the growing instability of the new state on its doorstep. The authorities were particularly outraged by the assassination in London on 22 June of Sir Henry Wilson, who had been advising the new Northern Ireland government on counter-insurgency methods directed against the IRA and the Catholic population generally.

In this fraught context, the order was given to General Neville Macready, the officer commanding the remaining British forces in the Free State, to take the Four Courts. The objective was to stamp out the rebel garrison still stationed inside the building, which in British eyes had come to symbolize a state operating freely and dangerously within a state. Churchill delivered a speech to this effect on the floor of the House of Commons:

The presence in Dublin of a band of men styling themselves the Headquarters of the Republican Executive is a gross breach and defiance of the Treaty. The time has come when it is not unfair, premature or impatient for us to make to the strengthened Irish government and new Irish parliament a request in express terms that this sort of thing must come to an end. If it does not come to an end, if through weakness, want of courage, or some other less credible reason it is not brought to an end and a speedy end, then it is my duty to say, on behalf of his Majesty's Government, that we shall regard the Treaty as having been formally violated, and we shall take no steps to carry out or legalize its further stages, and that we shall resume full liberty of action in any direction that may seem right and proper, or to any extent that may be necessary to safeguard the interests and rights entrusted to our care.

Macready wisely temporized, understanding that a direct British intervention would inflame matters further; and instead, Collins' administration was lent the forces with which to undertake the job itself. An ultimatum was delivered to the garrison in the Four Courts ordering them either to surrender or face being shelled out – and on 28 June, the shelling commenced from an 18-pounder borrowed from the British. The rebels fled or were killed; the building went up in flames, destroying a millennium of national records, and, once more, fighting and fire swept through the centre of Dublin. Ireland's brief but vicious civil war now began in earnest.

In terms of either meeting the requirements of the fledgling Irish Free State, or dealing with the partition issue and the situation in Northern Ireland, the Irish Civil War can justly be described as one of the most useless wars ever fought. It was

marked by hideous atrocities and by bitter fraternal and inter-
necine strife across the country. Revolution devoured her own
children. The anti-Treaty forces carried out sustained attacks
on the economy of the new state. Railways became a particular
target: lines were dynamited, engines were driven into stations
at full speed, bridges and viaducts destroyed. One of the most
notable bridge destructions, directly sanctioned by de Valera,
was that of the Blackwater railway bridge at Mallow, Co. Cork,
which succeeded in severing one of the principal links between
Dublin and the South.

An especially destructive legacy of the Civil War – and
of the War of Independence before it – was the attacks on
the so-called 'Big Houses': that is, the homes of Ascendancy
families and supporters of the Union scattered throughout the
Free State. Apart from forming an important part of Ireland's
architectural heritage, these homes contained valuable librar-
ies, furniture and artworks of all kinds. Another item not
often acknowledged on this bill was the fact that many Irish
Protestants either emigrated from the country altogether or
moved to the perceived Protestant bastion in the North. The
result was to strip the country of a valuable resource, and help
to mould the fledgling democracy, not so much into a Free
State as a Catholic state, cementing the power of the Catholic
Church and adding to the fears of Ulster Protestants.

This voracious appetite for death and destruction reached
its apotheosis early in the conflict with the assassination of
Michael Collins himself, at Béal na Bláth in Co. Cork on 22
August. And with his death, a great potential for good was
lost. He would be remembered in many quarters, to be sure,
for his guerrilla activities, the ability he showed in master-
minding a national loan and in holding his own with Britain's
leading statesmen during the Treaty negotiations. But before he

died, Collins also showed indications of possessing a talent for nation-building: he set down in a memorandum, for example, his ideas for emulating the Swiss use of hydroelectric power and its citizen army; and taking lessons from efficiencies in Danish agriculture; and, in the cultural sphere, on the influence and power of the cinema.

After his death, command of the army devolved upon Richard Mulcahy. He was prevailed upon to hold a peace meeting with de Valera on 6 September – his persuader, an Irish-American cleric, Monsignor John Ryan, told Mulcahy that de Valera was now a changed man. Prior to the meeting, which took place at the home of a prominent Dublin doctor, Dr Robert Farnan, the monsignor blessed Mulcahy and de Valera with holy water. Unfortunately, the type of water chosen was evidently lacking in efficacy. Mulcahy later gave the following account of the meeting:

> I took the initiative in saying that the position in Ireland was that [there] are two things to my mind that were important: 1) That somebody should be allowed to work the Treaty and 2) that if there was to be an army it should be subject to parliament. Given these two things I didn't care who ruled the country as long as they were representative of elected Irish men and women, and I came to a full stop. The 'changed man' still standing in front of me said: 'Some men are led by faith and some are led by reason, but as long as there are men of faith like Rory O'Connor taking the stand that he is taking, I am a humble soldier following after them.'

Following this meeting the Irish cabinet concluded that de Valera intended to continue supporting policies and practices which, if persisted in, would inevitably destroy the new state. It resolved, therefore, to introduce a fearsome piece of emergency powers legislation which gave the government the power to execute persons found committing acts of war. The definition of such acts was drawn widely, and included everything from the destruction of property to being found in possession of a weapon.

The legislation was used to execute, amongst others, Erskine Childers, who was captured in the Wicklow home of his cousin Robert Barton, the Treaty signatory, with a revolver given to him by Collins. Following the shooting dead of Sean Hales, a deputy who had voted for the legislation and a friend of Collins who had been particularly active in Cork during the War of Independence, Rory O'Connor was one of four prominent captured republicans taken out of their cells and placed before a firing squad. O'Connor had been best man at the wedding of Kevin O'Higgins, now justice minister in the Irish government – and now, O'Higgins was one of those who voted for his execution.

In taking this uncompromising line, the cabinet was indicating that it was pursuing a goal of the unconditional surrender of the anti-Treaty forces. O'Higgins summed up the cabinet's attitude in a memorable phrase: 'This is not going to be a draw, with a replay in the autumn.' And indeed, the game came to an end on 21 May 1923, with victory for the government. Frank Aiken, the IRA Chief of Staff, was persuaded by de Valera to issue a statement ordering a ceasefire and the dumping of arms. De Valera issued the following statement under his own name:

Soldiers of the Republic, Legion of the Rearguard:

The Republic can no longer successfully be defended by your arms. Further sacrifice of life would now be in vain and a continuance of the struggle in arms unwise in the national interest and prejudicial to the future of our cause. Military victory must be allowed to rest for the moment with those who have destroyed the Republic. Other means must now be sought to safeguard the nation's right... You have saved the nation's honour, preserved the sacred national tradition, and kept open the road of independence. You have demonstrated in a way there is no mistaking that we are not a nation of willing bondslaves... The sufferings you must now face unarmed you will bear in a manner worthy of men who were ready to give their lives for their cause. The thought that you still have to suffer for your devotion will lighten your present sorrow, and what you endure will keep you in communion with your dead comrades, who gave their lives and all those lives promised, for Ireland. May God guard every one of you and give to our country in all times of need sons who will love her as dearly and devotedly as you.

Thus, weary and sick, did Ireland emerge from the aftermath of 1916. To the statistics of death and destruction already cited, one has to add the terrible bitterness engendered by the Civil War in divided families and communities.

And yet good and efficient nation-building work was accomplished even in these torrid times. The Free State leadership strove to make independence work, by means of setting up an unarmed police force in the middle of a civil war, establishing an incorrupt civil service and an army under civilian control – and desperately trying to find the money to pay for the cost of all that had happened between 1916 and 1923. But this same leadership was enraged by the ongoing actions of its opponents. O'Higgins accurately summed how the cabinet viewed itself in this ferocious period in Irish history. He said:

We were simply eight young men, standing amid the ruins of one administration, with the foundations of another not yet laid, and with wild men screaming through the key-hole.

Subsequent history has borne out the truth of his assessment – though naturally, this is not how O'Higgins' opponents saw the position. As so often happens in Ireland, the best encapsulation of anti-Treaty feelings was to be found in a song:

> So take it down from the mast, Irish traitors,
> It's the flag we Republicans claim.
> It can never belong to Free Staters,
> For you've brought on it nothing but shame.

And thus, with the national flag attracting loyalty from some and execration from others, the Irish state and Irish society began the task of exercising a measure of freedom in twenty-six of Ireland's counties.

4

The Culture of the Time

FROM ITS VERY BEGINNINGS, THE NEW IRISH FREE STATE HAD problems crowding upon it from every point on the compass. But, although the absence of finance and the presence of lawlessness were mighty obstacles to Ireland's progress, the new country did have some assets. It of course could boast a healthy agricultural sector, but it also possessed strengths not always recognized – namely the character of its people and the calibre of some of its public representatives and senior officials.

I once remarked wonderingly to a Maynooth University professor about the number of senior civil servants and writers who hailed from Listowel in Co. Kerry. Why, I asked, was this the case? He replied, 'Simple! High mountains and good teachers, boy!' And Listowel was not the only pocket of learning – nor even was Co. Kerry itself. The famous seminary at Maynooth was formerly in the habit of maintaining records of the counties which yielded the best students – and in these lists, counties Derry and Mayo scored highest. Setting aside the graduates of such elite schools as Clongowes and Blackrock, it is the case that natural ability, teamed with the work of dedicated teachers at primary, secondary and third level, produced people well able to run a new state. This being the situation, it is an unhappy fact that the Irish Christian Brothers have virtually vanished from the Irish educational scene in a cloud of infamy, the reasons for which I will examine later – but they and the diocesan colleges (such as St Kieran's in Kilkenny), founded primarily to educate priests, made a vital contribution to Ireland's ability to stand on its own two feet.

A particular godsend to the new state occurred when, taking heart from the overwhelming pro-Treaty general election result in August 1923, it launched a quest to raise a national loan of £10 million – which was oversubscribed. This was doubly comforting for the new Irish government, not alone because of the still chaotic state of Ireland, but because the Irish banks, mean-spirited and ungenerous to the point of irresponsibility, had previously refused support for a loan sought by the government. Now the cash was in place, and the state could calculate and plan on the basis of these new, albeit modest, cash reserves.

Irish strength lay in the willingness of a majority of the population to make the great experiment of independence work, to accept, for example, long hours and low pay for the greater good. Society was borne up too by a sort of tent-pole philosophy fashioned from a combination of patriotism, religion and a general willingness to postpone gratification until either the next world or somewhere fairly far down the line in this one. The improvement of slums, the deficits, the repair of destruction and other tangible social advances had to be carried out on a shoestring.

Of course it also has to be acknowledged that some factors bore the country down as much as various traits raised it up. There was the burden of the Great Depression later in the decade – and there were also some ham-fisted and miserly responses to the need for retrenchment. One such was cutting a shilling off the blind pension, which led one later academic, Joseph Lee, to describe the people of the period as being subjected to 'the lash of the liberators'. In some cases sheer insensitivity, born out of a privileged upbringing, led government ministers to make revealing statements that fall gratingly on today's ears, but that were common enough in decision-making circles in those years.

One such public representative was Patrick McGilligan, the minister for industry and commerce (today, of course, a ministry synonymous with the creation of employment), who told the Dáil that it was not the task of government to provide work for anybody. As he said this in the course of a debate arising from the fact that a small boy had been found lying dead of starvation on the streets of Dublin, his remarks did not win him many friends even in those times. But the voices challenging such harsh views, including those of the Irish Labour Party, were drowned out by the still-reverberating din of civil war bitterness. As for the Labour Party itself, the words of the taunt seemed now apt: James Connolly had indeed marched the Irish Labour movement into the GPO in 1916 but, bereft of his leadership and adrift ideologically in a predominantly rural and Catholic society, no one had emerged to lead the movement back out again.

Another sector of society not seen to march after 1916 lay at the opposite end of the political spectrum: the former Protestant Ascendancy. The long-ago extinction of the Irish parliament and the shift of political power to Westminster after the Act of Union in 1800 had been a contributing factor in the drift of the former ruling class, the landlords, into a curiously ineffectual space in Irish society. The relationship between the landowner and the peasantry was, in this sense, very different from the situation prevailing in Britain. Whatever one's views on the relationship between aristocrat and peasant, there was at least a functioning relationship between the two classes in the latter society: both certainly regarded themselves as having a working and interacting role to play. In Ireland, however, there was a sense of disconnection between the landowner and the peasant: a gulf lay between the once-powerful Protestant Ascendancy and those over whom they had been ascendant. Terence Dooley has accurately described this:[3]

> Long before the 1870s, the typical Irish Big House had become akin to an artificially created island. By reasons of wealth, social standing, religion, cultural upbringing and political power, landlords and their families had become psychologically distanced from the vast majority of people. By locating their houses amidst hundreds of acres of park-lands and gardens, by building high demesne walls or surrounding their houses with woodland (or doing both), landlords had physically distanced themselves from the local community. A buffer of employees made up of agents, steward, bailiffs and so on maintained this distance.

Keeping distance was not necessarily the leitmotif within the walls of these Big Houses. We are indebted to the writings of Molly Keane for at least one illuminating comment on what sometimes went on in the elegant homes of the hunting, shooting and fishing classes. Keane memorably described the bedrooms during some house parties as 'the saddling enclo-sures'. The occasional exercise of the droit de seigneur was also whispered about as a concomitant of landlord culture. But Dooley is correct: this was a culture which had little input into the lives of the majority population of southern Ireland, the dominant mores of which were rural and Catholic. In this social milieu, it was the bishops who set the tone – both for the mass of the people and for the small but growing middle class bolstered by the spread of Catholic education in post-Famine

Ireland. The influence of Catholicism, indeed, and of the farming community on Irish society ensured that no socialistic lurch to the left occurred in the wake of the Irish revolution. If more conservative revolutionaries existed in Europe, it would have been very difficult to find them. The other Irish colonial power, Mother Church, exerted her influence towards keeping Ireland's gaze fixed on the hereafter, rather than the here and now. In some respects, indeed, it seems a miracle that the Irish had risen in revolt in the first place.

The impact of colonial history and in particular of the Famine had combined with the influence of an authoritarian Church to produce a mentality that might be compared with the condition known to modern psychology as 'learned helplessness'. The term is generally associated with experiments conducted in the 1960s by the New York psychologist Martin Seligman, in which he inflicted electric shocks upon dogs at random intervals, until the dogs reached a helpless state in which they did not try to escape the shocks, even when given the opportunity to do so. It might be argued that a similar learned helplessness prevailed in nineteenth-century Ireland, and that the Famine deepened and embedded this passive condition in the Irish psyche. And other aspects of Famine trauma would linger for generations. Long into the next century, people shrank from early marriage and the prospect of bringing children into a world that might horribly destroy them. Deference to a clergy who had been their main, indeed their only, source of solace during nearly seven years of famine, was ingrained to a degree hardly seen elsewhere in the world. When a French priest was told that the First Vatican Council had passed a decree allotting infallibility to the pontiff on the casting votes of the Irish hierarchy, he replied that he wasn't surprised. He said that not alone did the Irish believe that the pope was infallible, they believed that their parish priests also possessed this quality; and they would beat anyone who argued otherwise.

And this clerical infallibility meant in turn that the Irish hierarchy very speedily began exercising their authority after independence, and with very little opposition began lobbying legislators to ensure that the laws of the new state were brought into conformity with those of the Vatican. Even before independence, the future president of the Executive Council (essentially the prime minister) W. T. Cosgrave made an unsuccessful proposal that, whatever the legislative shape of the new state turned out to be, it should incorporate a sort of theological upper house, which would see to it that no legislation would be brought forward which might offend the Vatican. In his personal life too, Cosgrave was the archetypal devout Irish Catholic. The Rosary was said daily in his house – and callers who arrived during the prayers were expected to join in. And on 11 February 1925, he asked the Dáil to join him in a motion which led to the prohibition of divorce in the new state.

A notable, albeit unsuccessful, refusal to endorse the Catholicization of the legal system came from the poet W. B. Yeats. Yeats' speech to the Senate in June 1925, on the subject of a proposal to ban divorce from Ireland, was one of the best of his life. It was both courageous and far-seeing. He warned of the effect that the introduction of such explicitly Catholic legislation would have on the Protestants of the North, and hence on the prospects for the unity of the country towards which these legislators claimed to be fervently working. But speaking exclusively of the Protestants in southern Ireland, he said:

> This is a matter of very great seriousness. I think it is tragic that within three years of this country gaining its independence we should be discussing a measure which a

minority of this nation considers to be grossly oppressive. I am proud to consider myself a typical man of that minority. We, against whom you have done this thing, are no petty people. We are one of the great stocks of Europe. We are the people of Burke; we are the people of Grattan; we are the people of Swift, the people of Emmet, the people of Parnell. We have created the most of the modern literature of this country. We have created the best of its political intelligence. Yet I do not altogether regret what has happened. I shall be able to find out, if not I, my children will be able to find out whether we have lost our stamina or not. You have defined our position and have given us a popular following. If we have not lost our stamina then your victory will be brief, and your defeat final, and when it comes this nation may be transformed.

The Senate which Yeats was addressing had been conceived of as affording an opportunity for unionist and Protestant opinion in the new state to have its say. The former unionists' belief that this was sincerely meant was greatly weakened by the fact that, during the Civil War, republican elements attacked senators and burned their homes. These actions were abhorred by the more thoughtful of those who claimed to be following in the footsteps of the men of 1916.

For the mass of the population of the Free State, however, the only proper question for the Irish electorate when the bishops said '*jump*' was to enquire '*how high?*' And so, when the bishops demanded censorship as well as prohibiting divorce, contemporary literature vanished from the bookshops and condoms disappeared from the shelves of the chemists. The result was that Protestants (and some better-off Catholics) began sourcing their condoms from Belfast rather than the local chemist.

It is true that illumination began to shine on Ireland's largely peasant population in the 1920s, when the new government built vast hydro-electric works – at the time, the largest such works in the world – to tame the river Shannon at Ardnacrusha above Limerick. The great sluice-gates opened for the first time in 1929, part of a radical process to extend electrification across the country. Rural Ireland now had electricity for the first time, and yet in large measure this remained a land of ghost stories and superstition, where comparatively little of an intellectual light penetrated easily.

The Censorship of Publications Act (introduced in 1929) established criteria for judging works of literature which in effect came down to deciding whether books should be banned or not on the grounds of obscenity. The censors did their work thoroughly. Banned authors over the years included Ernest Hemingway, William Faulkner, Thomas Mann, Jean-Paul Sartre, John Steinbeck, Sinclair Lewis, John Dos Passos, J. D. Salinger, Budd Schulberg, Robert Penn Warren, Ilya Ehrenburg, Truman Capote, Tennessee Williams, F. Scott Fitzgerald, James Baldwin, Alberto Moravia, Norman Mailer, Jack Kerouac, William Saroyan, Samuel Beckett, James Jones, Dylan Thomas, Graham Greene, Joyce Cary, George Orwell and C. P. Snow. Irish writers were attacked with a particularly pathological efficiency. And although, curiously, James Joyce was never banned, practically any other writer of consequence certainly was – be that writer Kate O'Brien in one generation or John McGahern in another.

Irish society was characterized by a narrow Irish variant of Catholicism, by poverty, shabbiness and conformity. All these characteristics were heightened by the continuing effects of the great Wall Street crash which occurred during this period and which hemmed in an already poor people even more narrowly.

But even as late as the 1960s, when a remarkable process of change began spreading through the country, a knowledgeable English visitor to Ireland was able to make the observation: 'Every year when I visit Dublin I find that my friends have the same job, the same suit and an extra child.'

From the outset of the new state, jobs were as scarce as emigration and unemployment were plentiful. In the aftermath of the Civil War, preference in public employment and reconstruction was given to the Free State side and demobilized soldiers were employed before other labourers in, for example, public works schemes. Those who had fought against the Free State were forced to swell the ranks of the emigrants. Political debate was poisoned by civil war bitterness and the defeated were not prepared to concede merit to the achievements of Cosgrave's Cumann na nGaedheal government, the victors in a poisonous civil war. Nor was there any great predisposition on the victorious Free State side to see their opponents' political colouration as being other than wreckers, as Black and Tans with Irish accents. (Some of the Black and Tans were of course Irishmen who had fought in the British army during the Great War.) The defeated republicans, meanwhile, characterized the Free Staters as being subservient to British mores and British fashions: the top hat, for example, became identified with the Cosgrave regime, and de Valera and his followers at one stage took to wearing felt hats, the better to distinguish themselves from their political rivals.

In one area, however, the 'Made in England' description was certainly justified. Balancing the books in the Department of Finance was a particularly fraught exercise: quite apart from the cost of reconstruction, slum clearance and other such infrastructural projects, the Irish administration was all too keenly aware that in the upper echelons of Whitehall, there existed a good deal of hostility towards this new regime of 'Shinners' which a little earlier had been killing British soldiers. Cosgrave, however, succeeded in having a friend of his, C. W. Gregg, seconded from the British Treasury to run the new Irish Department of Finance – and so in many ways, the style of the department continued in the same mode as had existed under Dublin Castle.

And yet it was an efficient department, and it supervised and financed the establishment of a largely corruption-free civil service, an unarmed police force and a loyal and efficient army. W. T. Cosgrave had chosen well and the *Irish Times* would say of him in a profile, dated 29 January 1959:

> He was probably, when it came to handling men, the ablest of them all. The team he picked for the organisation of the new Civil Service would be regarded as the most out-standing single contribution of the president. Without Gregg, Brennan, Coogan [the author's father] Merrick and McElligot the Civil Service could easily have become both corrupt and inefficient.

It is important to note that, despite the Roman Catholicism which permeated the new state, Cosgrave's administration did manage to keep the grosser aspects of sectarianism at bay. In 1930, for example, Mayo County Council objected to the installation by the local appointments commission of Letitia Dunbar-Harrison as county librarian. She had been chosen on the grounds of being the outstanding candidate. The local councillors objected on the stated grounds that she couldn't speak Irish – but the real reason was that she was a Protestant and a graduate of Trinity College Dublin. The government, however, insisted that she be appointed – and when the council remained obdurate in its opposition to her, it dissolved the body and appointed a commissioner to run Mayo affairs. De

Valera, however, with an eye on his party vote in Mayo, played party politics with the issue. He said that the people of Mayo were entitled to have someone they trusted giving out books to their children. The issue generated such feeling that in 1931, Dunbar-Harrison was moved to Dublin and given a job in the library of the Department of Defence.

This was the only really major sectarian controversy in the Free State during the early days of the state: in general terms, Protestants remained secure in their jobs and in their property. It was certainly the case, however, that Protestants had been murdered during the Civil War – most notoriously at Dunmanway, Co. Cork in April 1922, when thirteen Protestant men and boys were killed – and that sectarian fears had been aroused during the years of turmoil. Sean Moylan, who later became one of de Valera's ministers, made the following statement during the Treaty debates, which could hardly have been described as music to Protestant ears:

> If there is a war of extermination waged on us, that war will also exterminate British interest in Ireland; because if they wage a war of extermination on us, I may not see it finished, but by God, no Loyalist in north Cork will see its finish and it's about time someone told Lloyd George that.[4]

After the British departed, many Protestants went with them. The census of 1911 showed that there were just over three hundred thousand Protestants in what became the Free State – but the aftershock of war and civil war and the increasingly Catholic ethos of the state caused a sharp decline in this figure. By 1926, the Protestant population had fallen by one hundred thousand and it would continue to drop for decades afterwards. And indeed, the circumstance which Yeats had forecast did indeed come to pass: the declining Protestant population of the Free State helped to harden the attitudes of Protestant leaders in Northern Ireland.

Yet the Free State was, notwithstanding its economic fragility and barely healed social wounds, achieving a degree of equilibrium in these years – and for de Valera, this meant having to bide his time, and await his political moment. Political tensions, however, remained at high levels. The existence of the Irish border, for example, remained an incontrovertible fact, in spite of the expenditure of republican energies. One of the Treaty's provisions came into force in 1925, with the establishment of a Boundary Commission to determine the final shape of the border. Collins had thought that the Commission might have recommended the transfer to the Free State of nationalist-majority territory in counties Fermanagh and Armagh. In fact, the Commission's recommendations were relatively insubstantial: it was proposed that small parcels of land on either side of the border be transferred – but the prospect of land transfers from south to north was the cause of great anger in the Free State. In the event, a North–South conflict was averted by the conclusion of a financial settlement which left the border as it was but which shifted onto the Free State the responsibility for some of the bills described earlier, notably pensions for the RIC and war reparations.

As early as the spring of 1924, meanwhile, the new government, having ostensibly crushed its republican adversaries, had to put down a revolt by some of its principal supporters in what was known as the army mutiny crisis. This saw some of Michael Collins' staunchest supporters, notably Liam Tobin and Tom Cullen, unsuccessfully attempt to move the army to what they would have described as a more 'forward' republican attitude to the North. There was a consistency here:

such individuals had fought, from 1916 to 1923, for the ideal of a thirty-two-county Ireland. They knew that Collins had intended further movement on securing for Ireland the six north-eastern counties that flew the Union Jack but banned the tricolour. However, they also knew that the new government had not the slightest intention of following in Collins' footsteps. In addition, as the sound of the Civil War died away and the dull grinding hum of books being balanced succeeded the noises of revolution, they saw that the Free State government was severely cutting the army from its civil war manpower levels. Generalships and colonelcies were no longer as plentiful as they had been in Collins' day, demobilization pay was not generous – and in general, demobilization itself was gathering pace. Had the government been less parsimonious, indeed, the mutiny might not have occurred.

The mutiny took several forms, including the theft of weapons from army stores, the absconding of men from their barracks – and, most dramatically, an ultimatum delivered to Cosgrave's government demanding an end to demobilization. In the event, however, the mutiny ended without a shot being fired. This was in part due to the immediate hard line taken by Kevin O'Higgins, the minister for justice, who demanded – and received – the resignation of the army council. Tobin and the others, meanwhile, having made their protest, ended their mutiny. Although no lives were lost, then, some political careers ended: deputies resigned from the Dáil in sympathy with the mutineers; in the by-elections that followed, they subsequently lost their seats.

O'Higgins himself would eventually fall victim to his anti-Treaty enemies. Three IRA gunmen, acting on their own initiative, murdered him on Sunday 10 July 1927 near his home in Blackrock, as he walked to Mass, in revenge for O'Higgins' signing of orders for the execution of anti-Treaty prisoners during the Civil War. The murderers were never apprehended. They had driven immediately to Kilkenny where one of them was taking part in a football match – and thus circumvented the cordons subsequently thrown around the city, because they appeared to be innocent football supporters driving towards Dublin rather than assassins escaping from it. As for the murder of O'Higgins himself, this was to have the most profound consequences for de Valera and his political fortunes.

By now, de Valera had founded a new political party, Fianna Fáil, which translates as 'Warriors of Destiny'. Such a title – and indeed the anthem sung at party gatherings – sums up this movement's powerful appeal to a particular notion of patriotism and past idealism. The party's name also encapsulated the claim that Fianna Fáil embodied the true legacy of republicanism, an aspect absolutely central to the cult of de Valera. The anthem contains the following:

Up the Republic, they raise their battle cry
Pearse and McDermott will pray for you on high
Eager and ready, for love of you they die
Proud march the Soldiers of the Rearguard

CHORUS

Legion of the rearguard, answering Ireland's call
Hark, their march and tramp is heard from Cork to
    Donegal
Wolfe Tone and Emmet guide you, though your task
    be hard
De Valera leads you, Soldiers of the Legion of the
    Rearguard.

Before launching Fianna Fáil at Dublin's La Scala Theatre in May 1926, de Valera had remained at the head of the old Sinn Féin party – but before very long had realized that the party no longer suited his political ambitions. There remained indeed a sizeable pro-Republican vote in the country – but de Valera realized that there was an even more sizeable one stubbornly in favour of peace. As had been the case when they had first cast their votes for Sinn Féin in 1918, the electors liked Sinn Féin's idealism and ideology, but appreciated even more the preservation of peace and the putting of bread on the table.

And so – quietly, discreetly and without announcing his intention – de Valera gathered such key followers as Frank Aiken, Sean Lemass, Thomas Derrig and Gerald Boland – and began the task of organizing a new party. This new party did not merely steal Sinn Féin's clothes while it was bathing, it actually dried up its river of support. For this support to continue flowing de Valera's way, however, he had to continue his faithful reliance on 'extremist support' and on giving the impression of being more nationalist than the IRA. It would be true to say that in the early days of its formation, Fianna Fáil cumainn (branches) by day become IRA flying columns by night – even if one could never be quite certain of the direction of their flight. The Civil War might have been over, in other words, but there were enough attacks on the police (some of them fatal), as well as arms raids on police stations and abrasive encounters between the IRA and the forces of law and order, to keep the southern political pot well stirred.

The general election of June 1927 saw Fianna Fáil make something of a breakthrough: the party gained forty-four seats to the government's forty-seven: but when Fianna Fáil went to the Dáil to take their seats, hoping to do so without taking the hated oath, Cosgrave had the doors of the chamber locked against them – and de Valera had to withdraw, fuming but impotent. After O'Higgins' death in July, moreover, Cosgrave introduced a bill which stipulated that any deputies that did not take the oath would forfeit their seats. It was time to fish or cut bait. De Valera decided to fish.

His re-entry to the Dáil was made easier by Cosgrave who directed that formalities be kept to a minimum. All de Valera and his followers were required to do was sign a book containing the oath. This was a moment of high tension. Some Fianna Fáil deputies carried revolvers – the drama of the situation was such that they expected to be met with gunfire. As it was, however, de Valera deftly converted the signing ceremony to farce. He signed the book – but speaking in Irish, told the clerk that he was not taking any oath and subsequently argued that he *hadn't* taken an oath because his hand hadn't touched the page. The taking of the oath thus became an empty formula.

Empty it may have been on that occasion – but earlier, during the Civil War, de Valera's refusal to make any compromise on the oath had helped to fill many a grave. And furthermore, following his eventual entry to the Dáil – and as though to complete a political journey in lightning-quick time – de Valera and his supporters very nearly filled the *government's* benches, not those of the opposition. The Labour Party leader, Thomas Johnston, put down a no-confidence in Cumann na nGaedheal – and, with the help of Independents and Labour, de Valera came within one vote of winning. Cosgrave was so certain that he would lose, in fact, that on the night before the vote he gave a farewell party for his staff.

In the event, however, those two indispensable adjuncts of Irish politics – journalism and drink – helped to swing the balance against de Valera on this occasion. The editor of the *Irish Times*, Bertie Smyllie, and a Cumann na nGaedheal supporter, Bryan Cooper, took a fellow Sligo man, Alderman Jinks, for not one, but several drinks prior to the vote of confidence, which Jinks had intended to support. It was no contest, as anyone knowing Smyllie, or indeed any self-respecting Irish editor, could have foretold. Jinks passed out, did not turn up to vote, the 'no-confidence' vote resulted in a tie and now the Ceann Comhairle (chairman) of the Dáil did as he was required to, and cast his vote in favour of the status quo. Cosgrave subsequently declared a general election for September: again, Fianna Fáil did well but Cosgrave did slightly better and was able to continue in power for another five years – during which austerity and exhaustion took their toll on his administration.

De Valera had swallowed an oath – and he was soon to taste the fruits of power.

5

The Age of Dev

A s we have seen, de Valera's political pragmatism had dictated that he would have to ditch Sinn Féin in order to attain power – and having taken this step, he now moved through the political landscape of the Free State with several potent political weapons to hand. One was the tail of the British lion, to be wagged and tweaked as dictated by circumstances; another was his own (unwritten) version of the 1916 Proclamation, which brought the impulses and dogma of Church and state together into one potent ideological machine. As would soon become clear, the efficiency of such a method of politics ensured that ongoing practical issues – rising unemployment, the open wound of emigration, the continuing fact of partition – could be lived with, though never actually addressed or causing any political dangers to de Valera himself. He was able, in other words, to sound militant about the six separated counties without actually doing anything about them.

As the 1920s neared their end, then, de Valera began his rise to power in Ireland. His status, oratory and policies now caught the attention of the people, and voters in increasing numbers drifted away from the incumbent Cumann na nGaedheal government. This administration was embattled and exhausted: it had been pursuing the paradoxical path of attempting to beat toleration and democracy into the ranks of its opponents – while at the same time attempting to follow a route of fiscal rectitude in the teeth of a crippling world recession. This last led the government to embrace startlingly un-Irish policies, such as taxing publicans' profits and, as noted earlier, cutting a shilling off the blind person's pension. A demagogue such as de Valera was very capable of making political hay out of such ill-judged governmental cost-cutting, and of enlisting the support of Irish workers exhausted by years of austerity. And in addition to this, he had the priceless support of two other powerful forces.

One was the IRA and the second was the *Irish Press* newspaper. The first remained composed of volunteers who were idealistic, energetic – and going nowhere, especially insofar as the border was concerned. Nor did that border's continuing existence trouble these young volunteers: they continued enthusiastically to chant 'On to the Republic' at meetings or drill session. No one stopped to enquire as to what this phantasmagorical Republic consisted of or where it lay. The occasional shooting at (or of) a policeman, or informer, the occasional exercise of 'balaclava banking' on a bank or post office – such events were wonderfully invigorating and, when married to tight military discipline in an era of mass unemployment, provided an extremely valuable political adjunct for someone adroit enough and unscrupulous enough to make use of it. On both counts de Valera and his henchmen were ready, willing and able.

De Valera evolved a philosophy that entwined the notion of physical force with democratic methods. In the manner that the party encouraged the Irish people to continue to drink from the pure republican spring that was the blood of the 1916 martyrs, Fianna Fáil might be described as walking backwards towards the future. In March 1928, for example, Seán Lemass – who later became the most able minister and subsequently prime minister in modern Irish history – described Fianna Fáil as follows:

Fianna Fáil is a *slightly* constitutional party. We are open to the definition of a constitutional party but before anything we are a Republican party. We have adopted the method of political agitation to achieve our end because we believe, in the present circumstances, that method is best in the interests of the nation and of the Republican movement, and for no other reason. Five years ago the methods we adopted were not the methods we have adopted now. Five years ago we were on the defensive *and perhaps in time we may recoup our strength sufficiently to go on the offensive.* Our object is to establish a Republican government in Ireland. If that can be done by the present methods we have, we will be very pleased, but if not, *we would not confine ourselves to them.*

The Fianna Fáil attitude towards the government and the Dáil was one of relentless hostility. Any tendency towards civic responsibility on the part of republicans and citizenry alike had to be ruthlessly put down – as *Nationality*, the Fianna Fáil newspaper of the time, observed in February 1929, while the issue of joining the parliamentary process was still being discussed:

We entered a faked parliament which we believed in our hearts to be illegitimate and we still believe it, and we faced a junta there which we did not regard as the rightful government of the country. We did not respect, nor do we now, such a government or such a parliament. Our presence in the Dáil of usurpers is sheer expedience, nothing else.

And as if this somewhat less than ringing endorsement of parliamentary democracy were not sufficient, de Valera himself a couple of weeks later went on to make a definitive statement regarding the position of the IRA in society. In the process, this statement gave that organization a legitimacy which led many a young man to join its ranks. In 1929, de Valera made the following statement, which might be seen as the definitive expression of his and Fianna Fáil's view of the legitimacy of the Free State government:

> I still hold that our right to be regarded as the legitimate Government of this country is faulty, that this house itself is faulty. You have secured a *de facto* position. Very well. There must be somebody in charge to keep order in the community, and by virtue of your *de facto* position you are the only people who are in a position to do it. But as to whether you have come to that position legitimately or not, I say you have not come by that position legitimately. You brought off a *coup d'etat* in the summer of 1922...
>
> If you are not getting the support from all sections of the community that is necessary for any executive if it is going to dispense with a large police force, it is because there is a moral handicap in your case. We are all morally handicapped because of the circumstances in which the whole thing came about. The setting up of the state put a moral handicap on every one of us here. We came in here because we thought that a practical rule could be evolved in which order could be maintained and we said that it was necessary to have some assembly in which the representatives

of the people by a majority vote should be able to decide national policy. As we were not able to get a majority to meet outside this house we had to come here if there was to be a majority of all of the people's representatives in any one assembly. As a practical rule, and not because there is anything sacred in it, I am prepared to accept majority rule as settling matters of national policy and therefore in deciding who it is that shall be in charge of order.

I for one, when the flag of the Republic was run up against an executive that was to bring off a *coup d'etat*, stood by the flag of the Republic, and I will do it again. As long as there was a hope of maintaining the Republic either by force against those who were bringing of that *coup d'etat* or afterwards as long as there was an opportunity of getting the people of this country to vote again for the Republic.

My proposition that the representatives of the people should come in here and unify control so that we would have one government and one army was defeated and for that reason I resigned. *Those who continued on in the organisation which we have left can claim exactly the same continuity that we claimed up to 1925.* They can do it...

You have achieved a certain *de facto* position, and the proper thing for you to do with those who do not agree that this state was established legitimately, and who believe as a matter of fact there was a definite betrayal of everything that was aimed at from 1916 to 1922, is to give these people the opportunity to get the Irish people as a whole again behind them. They have the right to do it. You have no right to debar them from going to the Irish people and asking them to support the re-establishment or if they so wish to put it, to support the continuance of the Republic.

> The executive have been trying to use force and have
> been using it all the time. If they are going to meet force by
> force, then they cannot expect the cooperation of citizens
> who wish that there should not be force.[5]

A comparison may be made here with the British Conservative leader, Andrew Bonar Law, who noted that there 'was nothing sacred about parliamentary majorities'. This was a statement remarkable in itself – but it should also be pointed out that de Valera's speech was delivered at a time when IRA intimidation and violence had made it difficult, if not impossible, to secure a conviction against IRA members in open court; and when normal judicial process had been, as a result, drastically changed. A military tribunal had been established: presided over by military personnel, it now took over the processing of all such vexed cases.

Such utterances helped to bring a very sizeable slice of republican opinion to de Valera's side. But the heaviest cannon to be wheeled out in the propaganda war was certainly the *Irish Press* newspaper. De Valera founded this organ by means of breathtaking financial sleight of hand. He had managed to collect several million dollars for the cause of Irish independence during his triumphant tours of America, while back at home Michael Collins was fighting the Black and Tans. For reasons which have never been satisfactorily explained, however, de Valera did not send all of this money back to Ireland to help the hard-pressed volunteers in the War of Independence. Instead millions were left to lie in a New York bank until the matter was adjudicated on in the New York federal court late in the 1920s. Then, as both the Cumann na nGaedheal government and de Valera were laying claim to the money, the judge decided that the proper thing to do was to return it to the bondholders, mostly poor hard-working Irish emigrants who had subscribed their hard-earned money that Ireland might be free. De Valera's legal advisors, however, had anticipated the judge's verdict – and so the bondholders received a communication from de Valera asking them to transfer the bonds to his name so that he could found a genuinely national Irish newspaper to combat the pernicious influences of the British. This task, he averred, was particularly urgent because, as an accompanying letter from a Jesuit pointed out, the existing press was committing enormities such as encouraging Irish youth to join blatantly British organizations like Baden-Powell's Boy Scout movement.

Through this method and another national loan raised with the help of the Fianna Fáil organization to support the newspaper, the *Irish Press* was born. Partisan though it was, none of its detractors could ever accuse its journalism of being anything other than brilliant. After all, an Irish journalist with a cause is a formidable creature indeed. Led by Frank Gallagher, one of de Valera's most devoted followers for a couple of years until his health gave out under the strain of long hours and short wages, the *Irish Press* in the 1930s became a power in the land. Its staff, like Gallagher himself, saw working for the newspaper as a continuation of 'the cause': that is, the fight for a thirty-two-county Republic based on the principles of the 1916 Proclamation. Such staffers worked more hours for less money than other national newspapers of the period.

All these forces came together at the general election of 1932, the year after the *Irish Press* was founded, and helped to place de Valera in power. Ironically, there was no need for Cosgrave to have gone to the polls when he did: an election was not in fact due, and the economy was now in recovery from the effects of the 1929 crash. However, a Eucharistic Congress was scheduled to be held in Dublin in that year – and the devout Cosgrave could not bear the thought of a host of bishops and cardinals of the world being shaken by the uproar which accompanied Irish elections of the period. And indeed, this uproar was a reality – and a dangerous one at that. The loss of an eye, a tooth, the acquisition of a broken jaw or worse: these frequently accompanied the casting of a vote. In my days as a young journalist, Edward Lawlor was a respected figure who, in his younger days, had covered the politics of the 1930s. He described for me an occasion in which he entered the office of the Cumann na nGaedheal director of elections, J. J. Walsh, to find his desk piled high with knuckledusters which were being handed out to election workers. And at the time, no one saw anything unusual in this.

Cosgrave, then, called an election for 16 February 1932 – which he lost; and momentously, de Valera now formed a government with the aid of Labour. Cosgrave's handover of power, to people who, less than ten years earlier, would have cheerfully killed him, marked a critical moment in the evolution of Irish democracy. In many ways, indeed, it was probably the finest achievement of Ireland's first independent government, taking place as it did against the wishes of sections of the police and army who viewed the prospect of de Valera in power with everything from alarm to outright hatred. But in the event, the transfer of power was achieved more or less seamlessly and without gunfire. The Eucharistic Congress too passed off peacefully. Ireland oozed piety: it was a moment in which the oft-heard term 'Holy Ireland' appeared to have real validity. An altar was erected on O'Connell Bridge in central Dublin for the celebration of High Mass; and the papal Count John McCormack gave a memorable performance of *Panis Angelicus*. The country was bedecked in papal colours – and not a drunken shout, fight or unseemly incident marred the course of the Congress. There was one possible exception – and this took place in the village of Knocknagoshel.

Knocknagoshel, situated in north Co. Kerry, decided that it too should move forward with the nation in the celebration of the Eucharistic Congress: and so it was arranged that a Mass would be held in the flag-bedecked parish church, to be preceded by a solemn procession of nuns, clergy and local dignitaries. Knocknagoshel could not boast a cardinal, a bishop or even a monsignor, but it did have a canon who led the pious procession through Knocknagoshel's prayerful streets. As the procession drew near the church, however, some wits unfurled a banner stretching between the rooftops across the street which proclaimed: 'Arise Knocknagoshel, and take your place amidst the nations of the Earth.'

De Valera was now in power – and he had, with the *Irish Press* and the IRA, yet another ally. This was that indispensable aid to Irish electoral success: the political shopping basket. In political terms, the Cumann na nGaedheal doctrine of non-intervention in employment creation was no match for de Valera's production of a basket from which he provided an attractive array of dole subsidies. He also had an eye for political theatre that few parties anywhere could ever equal. One of his unmatchable ploys, for example, was to enter towns at eventide wearing a long black cloak and mounted on a white horse, preceded and followed by columns of marching men shouldering pitchforks to which blazing sods of turf were affixed. This ritual gave rise to the immortal, but, one is assured, not apocryphal anecdote: that of the man who, seeing this spectacle, enquired: 'who is the long bollocks on the horse?' To which the answer was: 'That's not a horse. It's a mare.'

But there was no joking about the manner in which the *Irish Press* was sold and distributed throughout Ireland. I remember an elderly circulation manager of the newspaper describing to a group of what were then young (and irreverent) journalists how the paper got to a remote part of Kerry. First it arrived to a distribution point by train from Dublin, where it was taken on by bus; then, on arrival at a certain town a bundle of copies was picked up by a local postman on a bicycle and brought to a nearby village – 'and then,' concluded the circulation manager, 'copies were brought on up the mountain by a farmer with a good Fianna Fáil ass'. Throughout Ireland, it was immediately possible to tell the politics of a country town by entering a newsagent. If the owner sold the *Irish Press* then he and his customers were Fianna Fáil; if they stocked the *Irish Independent*, meanwhile, they were Cumann na nGaedheal (or its successor party after 1933, Fine Gael). If a copy of the *Irish Times* were to be had, meanwhile, this was an indication that there were Protestants living in the vicinity. In the more remote parts of the country – west of the Shannon, and especially in the Gaeltacht or Irish-speaking districts where there was little or no employment, there was usually only the *Irish Press*. This was partly because of that superb distribution network, which was modelled on the old Sinn Féin communication system, but it was also partly because of the doles and subsidies which gave Fianna Fáil near-religious status in these areas blighted with unemployment. Nationally, de Valera added to these attractions by introducing pensions for those who had fought on the republican side in the Civil War, as the Free State side had done with its supporters.

Ironically, another major source of strength for de Valera would turn, not on the distribution of largesse, but the withholding of it. Under the Treaty terms, Ireland was committed to paying to Britain the annuities used to pay off the loans raised to buy from the landlords the land which had originally been owned by the Irish but which had been taken from them by force of conquest. Understandably the annuities were not a popular form of taxation, and there was initial rejoicing throughout Ireland when de Valera announced that these levies were to be withheld from Britain. Enthusiasm dimmed somewhat, however, when the public became aware that the annuities would still be collected but retained by the Irish Exchequer. The British retaliated by slapping an ad valorem ('to the value') tax on imported Irish produce – which inevitably made Irish produce, particularly Irish cattle, prohibitively expensive.

As economic war broke out between the two states, cattle prices slumped disastrously. Farmers sometimes found that it was cheaper to abandon their calves to grazing alongside the ditches than bring them home and have to feed them. The bigger farmers were hardest hit: but de Valera escaped much of the effects of their wrath because many of them were Cumann na nGaedheal supporters in any case. He also introduced schemes whereby the now nearly valueless cattle were bought up, slaughtered and the meat distributed free to the needy.

With British ports virtually closed to Irish manufacturers, Fianna Fáil also benefited from the encouragement of native industry behind tariff walls. This was a marked departure from Cumann na nGaedheal's non-interventionist approach, and it helped to broaden Fianna Fáil's support base by attracting supporters amongst the commercially inclined. De Valera also generated favourable opinions in the ranks of the more republican-minded by announcing his intention to belittle the office of Governor-General of the Irish Free State by making of the incumbent a *Seán na Scuab* (a 'Seán of the brushes') – in other words, a figure of little respect, a straw man. He duly moved to neutralize the symbolism of the office by appointing, in 1932, a Fianna Fáil loyalist, Domhnall Ua Buachalla, who was instructed to make himself publicly invisible and in the process to make the office an irrelevance.

De Valera was greatly helped in his process of republicanizing the Free State by two of his predecessors' achievements. These were, firstly, the election of Ireland to the Council of the League of Nations on 17 September 1930. This step recognized Ireland's independence of movement on the international scene, despite strong British objections. The second was the Statute of Westminster, which was passed by the UK parliament on 11 December 1931, and which in effect gave the Dáil the right to repudiate anything it wished in the Treaty, including the hated oath. The statute's thrust was that laws passed in Britain were not necessarily binding on the Dominions; and conversely that the Dominions could pass laws of their own without reference to Westminster. The statute passed into law just a few months before Cumann na nGaedhael fell from power, and de Valera, who had so opposed the Treaty because of the oath, was now in a position to remove both it and the king from Irish affairs.

These removals would inevitably take some time to achieve: and while de Valera was thus engaged, he was assisted in his stratagems by having the forces of the extreme left and right fall on each other's necks and expend their energies by weakening each other. As far as the right was concerned, de Valera had greatly increased the political temperature of fear and an expectancy of the worst by, as soon as he took office, sacking the Garda Commissioner, General Eoin O'Duffy, and releasing the IRA prisoners jailed under the previous administration.

Moreover, while Cosgrave had demonstrated his fidelity to democracy by peacefully handing over power when the ballot box told him to, rank-and-file Fianna Fáil and IRA supporters showed no such reciprocal indulgence towards Cosgrave, who was heckled and shouted down while attempting to hold public meetings. One IRA leader, Frank Ryan, gave the republican hooligans their slogan 'No free speech for traitors'. Another, Peadar O'Donnell, advised the police that the correct political action to be taken, should a guard interpose himself between Mr Cosgrave and an IRA boot, was for the guard to stay at home.

In this tense political atmosphere, a new political movement was born. This was the Army Comrades Association, led by the embittered now-former army officer Eoin O'Duffy. Initially, the ACA's membership was drawn largely from ex-members and supporters of the Free State army, but as economic warfare broke out between Ireland and Britain, this support base was widened to include the larger farmers. Such was the Irish background to the formation of O'Duffy's new corps – but he rapidly moved on to incorporate contemporary European political developments into his movement. There was much talk, for example, of the corporate state coming to Ireland. Then, as certain conservative elements within the Free State began to embrace European fascist ideology, O'Duffy introduced a blue shirt as the uniform of his followers; they would subsequently be known as 'Blueshirts'. Originally, it was claimed that the shirts were worn as a badge of identity, and especially to avoid embarrassing mistakes in the utilization of knuckledusters against their own members instead of the intended Fianna Fáil and IRA targets.

De Valera, for his part, also went for the Blueshirts. He revived the military tribunal which he had abolished on taking office as a placatory gesture to the IRA – and he banned Blueshirt parades after it was announced in the summer of 1933 that O'Duffy intended to lead his followers in military formation to a wreath-laying ceremony at Leinster House in memory of Griffith and O'Higgins. Had this march taken place it would most likely have resulted in a bloodbath – as, quite apart from the presence of the army and the gardai on the scene, the IRA lay in ambush at several Dublin vantage points waiting to fire on the marchers.

In any case, one very ugly shooting incident did arise out of this politically fervid period. In the context of O'Duffy's activities and the uproar on the land caused by the loss of the British cattle trade, de Valera decided that having shorn the Garda Siochána of its Commissioner, he needed a cadre upon which he could depend. An armed wing of the police, known as the S Branch, was set up, drawn from the ranks of those who had fought against the state in the Civil War. I interviewed one such member of the S Branch who told me that he joined it after being woken from his sleep by an old comrade throwing stones at his window. Then he informed him that 'they're forming a new force in the guards – and you can have a job'.

The most notorious task carried out by the S Branch was the Marsh's Sales Yard shooting in Cork. Farmers who were refusing to pay annuities and sometimes rates, because of de Valera's economic policy, had their cattle seized and put on sale at various sale yards around the country. This aroused fierce opposition from O'Duffy's right-wing supporters, particularly the larger farmers. In an attempt to abort one such sale at Marsh's Yard in 1934, a lorry containing Blueshirts was driven through police cordons. But the yard gates were then closed behind them and the unarmed occupants of the lorry subjected to heavy fire from members of the S Branch. One young man was killed: at subsequent court proceedings, the S Branch was described by the presiding judge as an 'excrescence' on the normal force. How the fatalities were confined to one death is a mystery, as several witnesses testified to the intensity of the firing. The funeral of the victim, twenty-two-year-old Michael Patrick Lynch, was attended by several thousand Blueshirts, with O'Duffy delivering the funeral oration. The incident could have prompted a re-enactment of the Civil War – but fortunately the S Branch sword remained in its scabbard, and the rates campaign petered out.

A series of government edicts was now directed at the Blueshirts, as O'Duffy and his advisors indulged in a variety of name changes to avoid legal bans. And it was against this unprepossessing background of social and political uproar that a new political party emerged: this was the business-oriented Centre Party, led by James Dillon and Frank McDermott, which then merged with Cumann na nGaedheal to found Fine Gael ('the Tribe of the Gaels'), under the leadership of O'Duffy himself.

But O'Duffy, though a brave man and a noted organizer, was no political strategist. Moreover, his affection for the Irish oral tradition of Jameson, Smithwick's and Guinness meant that sometimes John Jameson played a rather larger role in his political speeches than was politic. This factor in O'Duffy's political life was frequently and unkindly pointed out in the pages of the *Irish Press*, which sent reporters to cover his actual performances, rather than merely printing the staid scripts delivered to the newspapers by Fine Gael headquarters. Soon, the more conservative elements of the old Cumann na nGaedhael party began to desert O'Duffy.

The IRA, meanwhile, began to wilt in these years. Having helped to bring de Valera to power, the organization was now becoming surplus to requirements; and the military tribunal, though ostensibly reformed to pursue O'Duffy's men, soon had the IRA once more in its sights. If one examines the statistics for the convictions of activists from both left and right during the period, indeed, one finds that de Valera's particular form of justice was dispensed even-handedly. Strikingly, exactly the same number from either side fetched up behind bars: 434 from each side, a total of 868.[6] This was balanced justice, de Valera style. And both the IRA and the Blueshirts further weakened themselves by some of their number leaving to fight on opposite sides in the Spanish Civil War (though the Blueshirts did very little actual fighting).

Even as his position was being appreciably strengthened, de Valera found a well of additional support – from a most unlikely quarter. The Abdication Crisis of 1936 – which saw the new British monarch, Edward VIII, standing aside from his destiny in order to marry Wallis Simpson, the divorced woman of his dreams – opened a window of opportunity for de Valera. British constitutional upheaval enabled him to proceed swiftly with his particular pet project: a written Constitution for the Irish Free State, and a general recalibration of Ireland's constitutional arrangements, including the abolition of the Senate.

De Valera had been angered by the Senate's interference with his legislative war against the Blueshirts, not least because it delayed one of his most cherished pieces of legislation. This was the Abolition of the Oath Bill, which he had in fact tabled on first taking office. The bill removed the necessity for elected Dáil members having to take the oath of allegiance to the crown. Then, during the Blueshirt crisis, the Senate also blocked his Abolition of Uniforms Bill. And so de Valera trained his sights on the Senate itself – and in retaliation for delaying the Oath legislation, brought in a bill to abolish the Senate. That body duly passed into oblivion in May 1936.

This meant that at the end of the year de Valera was able to derive further constitutional benefit – or at least what he saw as constitutional benefit – from the culmination of the Abdication Crisis itself. When Edward at length stepped aside from the throne in December of that year, the Dáil was recalled from its

Christmas recess and rushed into passing two significant pieces of legislation under guillotine. One, Constitutional Amendment Number 27, removed both the monarch and his representative in Ireland, the Governor-General, from their positions at the heart of Irish constitutional arrangements. The other, the Executive Authority Bill, rendered the King's position vis-à-vis Ireland as one of 'external association' on occasions when Ireland acted with other members of the Commonwealth. Thus the link with Britain was weakened even as the connection with the Commonwealth was maintained: the other Dominions still regarded Ireland as belonging to the Commonwealth, as did Britain itself.

The new Constitution was generally regarded by de Valera's supporters as being one of his greatest achievements. In reality, it was an exercise in sleight of hand in which the existing state emerged with the same shape, size and income, and clad in a few new clothes. Even de Valera himself could not give a clear answer to a question which continued to be asked into the next decade. How should the new state be defined? Speaking in the Dáil nine years later, on 17 July 1945, a month before the Japanese surrender ended the Second World War, de Valera decided that the state of the world demanded that he address this question and he collected a set of quotations from various authorities before making what became known as the 'Dictionary Republic' speech. It contained the following:

> The State is what it is, not what I say or think it is. How a particular State is to be classified politically is a matter not to be settled by the *ipse dixit* of any person but by observation of the State's institutions and an examination of its fundamental laws... look up any standard book of reference and get... any definition of a republic or any description

of what a republic is and judge whether our State does not possess every characteristic mark by which a republic can be distinguished or recognised. We are a democracy with the ultimate sovereign power resting with the people – a representative democracy with the various organs of State functioning under a written Constitution, with the executive authority controlled by Parliament, with an independent judiciary functioning under the Constitution and the law, and with a Head of State directly elected by the people for a definite term of office.

De Valera's Constitution of 1937 introduced a markedly sectarian character to the governance of the Irish state. One of his principal advisers in drawing it up was the president of Blackrock College, the Holy Ghost priest John Charles McQuaid, who subsequently became Archbishop of Dublin with de Valera's support. The Constitution, which drew heavily on Catholic social doctrine, and on a number of encyclicals by Pope Pius XI dealing with youth education and Christian marriage, was frankly theocratic in form. It could be said, indeed, to have replaced the crown's position in Ireland with that of God, recognizing as it did the special position of the Catholic Church, consigning women's role in society to the home and laying claim to Northern Ireland 'pending the re-integration of the national territories'.

Until that happy, and carefully unspecified, day dawned, it claimed jurisdiction only over the Free State area. The Pope was shown the Constitution before it was presented to the Irish electorate, who somewhat unenthusiastically passed it into law, with only 39 per cent of the electorate in favour. A further 30 per cent voted against and 31 per cent abstained. Under the new Constitution, the term *Taoiseach* was introduced to describe the prime minister, the official name of the country in Irish was Éire – and in English, Ireland – and the Seanad Éireann was the new name given to the body replacing the former Senate, which had so recently aroused de Valera's ire.

There was little chance of the new body behaving in like manner. Though its membership was given the appearance of having a vocational character, it became a party assembly pure and simple; and one, moreover, in which the Taoiseach – at this time, of course, de Valera – had the power to nominate eleven out of the sixty senators. As the new body only had powers of delay (and that for only ninety days), the Seanad became in effect merely a rubber-stamping body, and one in which government supporters who had lost their Dáil seats might find a safe haven. One aspect of the new arrangements which deserves praise, however, was the creation of the office of president of Ireland. The first nominee to this symbolically powerful post was a Protestant, Douglas Hyde, who had been a founder of the Gaelic League; later, another Protestant, Erskine Childers, would also fill the office. These facts, although they left northern Protestants monumentally unmoved, were a source of reassurance to the small Protestant minority in the South.

The Constitution was regarded as worthy of emulation by such emerging colonial nations as Burma and India – but in general it proved itself unable to cope with the realities of modern life. Several referenda have amended it over the years, removing the provisions prohibiting divorce, the theocratic nature of its preamble, the claim to Northern Ireland and the reference to the special position of the Catholic Church. At the time of writing, the Catholic birth rate in Northern Ireland and the rise of Sinn Féin north and south of the border make the unity of the country a realistic prospect in the future – but the Constitution itself has become a thing of rags and tatters which would obviously have to be reimagined in the event of a united Ireland.

In the context of contemporary politics, de Valera and his acolytes averred that the country was now a republic in all but name. And he used this argument in discussions with the IRA to convince them that they must now put away their weapons: after all, their desires had been met by a republican constitution and by the removal of British symbols of authority from Irish law. This argument fell on many deaf IRA ears, though it would surely have carried considerably more weight had it not been for the small matter of the existence and persistence of the border. And equally, the abolition of the oath and the king from Irish affairs only served to deepen northern unionist intransigence.

For the moment, however, and in the wake of the new Constitution's introduction, Irish eyes were fixed not on the border but on world affairs. The shadows of the Second World War were falling over Ireland – and now de Valera moved to dispel them by engaging in a quite astonishing feat of negotiation which enabled the southern part of Ireland to be spared much of the horrors of war. He negotiated the return by the British of the so-called 'Treaty ports' – deep-water and strategic harbours in Cork and Donegal which had been retained by Britain under the Treaty settlement; at the same time, he negotiated the end of the land annuities dispute – and ipso facto the gruelling economic war with the United Kingdom.

To the fury of a powerless Winston Churchill, who argued against their return, the British prime minister Chamberlain – who had not long to live and was influenced by the politics of appeasement – agreed to give up the Treaty ports for a cash settlement and a guarantee that the ports could not be used to attack Britain. Their return thus enabled Ireland to remain neutral during the war soon to explode across Europe.

The loss of these ports may not, in fact, have been as griev-ous for the Allied war effort as some British historians have argued – but this new dispensation did allow German subma-rines more freedom of action that they would otherwise have had in the early days of the war. And certainly there is some validity in the bitter lines of the Ulster poet Louis MacNeice who wrote, in the face of a calamitous loss of Allied wartime shipping off the coasts of neutral Ireland: 'While to the West off your own shores the mackerel are fat with the flesh of your kin.' It is also indisputably the case, however, that the Irish made an enormous contribution to the British war effort: by providing the manpower which built essential aerodromes, dams and roads; and in joining the armed services. The Irish also differentiated between the treatment accorded to German and British service personnel. The British airmen who crash-landed in Ireland, for example, were returned across the border with large parcels of food unobtainable in rationed Britain – while German aviators were detained for the duration.

Fundamentally, however, two important points must be made concerning the basic unreality of de Valera and Fianna Fáil's policy throughout the decades before and after the war. One: all the constitutional advances and the republicanizing of Irish forms of government, such as the abolition of the oath and the Governor-Generalship, could have been achieved (and indeed were achieved) within the framework of the Treaty and without civil war. The second point is that nothing copper-fastened the independence conferred by the Treaty as neatly as the ability it conferred on de Valera to remain neutral through-out the several years of the Second World War, despite the pressures of both Churchill and the American government.

And, as the lights began going out all over Europe, so de Valera now moved decisively against his one-time allies in the

IRA. Realpolitik and not semantics governed de Valera's attitude towards his former comrades. He dealt ruthlessly with the prospect of a second authority and a rival armed force and claimant to sovereignty: as war broke out, he used the tools of the internment camp and the hangman to deal with irreconcilable elements in the IRA.

As a day of reckoning, this had been comparatively long in coming. From the moment the Treaty was signed, after all, the IRA had faced two problems. One was the fact that the organization was confronting not merely British, but *Irish* opponents. In order to succeed in its aims, the IRA was duty-bound to overcome the police and army of the Dublin-based government before moving on to take care of the Belfast administration. More importantly, there was a basic flaw in the philosophy of armed republicanism. This saw the British as the principal enemy of a united Ireland. But over the years it became glaringly obvious that, while the six-county area was most emphatically under the crown and remained a part of the United Kingdom, the main bulwark for ensuring that it stayed that way was not merely the British but the unshakeable determination of more than a million Protestants that they should remain linked to the United Kingdom – and the IRA never had the military strength, even under Michael Collins, to alter that fundamental reality. It could be challenged – but never overturned. And similarly, the IRA could never, in spite of periodic and largely symbolic attempts in the field, overturn the Irish state either. The first wave of republicanism after the signing of the Treaty had been much the strongest – and yet it had been defeated with relative ease by the Free State army and the force of public opinion.

The IRA, moreover, was by the onset of the Second World War a shadow of its former self. It was suffering from a loss of substance, and in particular from an absence of commanding leadership, particularly when Seán MacBride left the organization in 1937. MacBride had provided intellectual heft and charisma at the top of the organization: he was a son of Maud Gonne MacBride, the woman Yeats had loved passionately and fruitlessly over the course of many years, and John MacBride, a player in the 1916 Rising and one of those whom the British had executed in its aftermath. Seán MacBride was himself now a veteran of conflict too: as a young man, he had come though the upheavals of the War of Independence and Civil War, before becoming Chief of Staff of the IRA in 1936. His departure from the organization – 'The Army', as its members referred to the IRA – in the following year was therefore keenly felt. It continued as a shrunken force to drill and attract new members – but as the world changed, the organization sloughed off the support that it had previously enjoyed. Its disintegrating relationship with de Valera and Fianna Fáil, now enjoying the fruits and trappings of power, marked the apotheosis of this change. And in the meantime, the continued existence of the Irish border underscored the organization's ultimate failure.

And yet it continued to operate – and Britain continued to feel the effects. In the summer of 1939, for example, five civilians were killed in Coventry when an IRA bomb exploded in the city. Coming as they did on the eve of the outbreak of the Second World War, the bombings also caused an exodus of Irish citizens from Britain. As if this were not enough to disturb a government attempting to maintain neutrality in the teeth of the onset of the greatest war the world had ever seen, the IRA in Ireland carried out a number of operations which no government could condone, in either peace or wartime. For example, armed IRA men carried out an attack on Britain's wartime envoy to Ireland, Sir John Maffey, wounding several guards;

and the organization subsequently made off with most of the Irish Army's ammunition.

The Phoenix Park raid, as it was known, carried out at Christmas 1939, resulted in the IRA clearing out the contents of the Irish army's lightly guarded arsenal. Most of this ammunition was subsequently recovered, however, as the IRA had not given sufficient thought to the question of where to hide the trove of stolen munitions. Nor had the IRA given thought to the fact that the Phoenix Park raid consolidated de Valera's base in public opinion and allowed him to crush his former allies. He had at his disposal a battery of wartime emergency legislation which allowed him to introduce internment, military courts, strict censorship and in extreme cases the death penalty – and he made use of each.

Internment was a particularly debilitating process for the IRA. Some 1500 internees were housed in parole huts under army guard, reinforced by barbed-wire fences at the old British military base at the Curragh in Co. Kildare. Here the truth of the statement that in politics, the worst attrition comes from one's own side, was amply borne out. Proximity, boredom and futility formed a corrosive cocktail in which many an old friendship dissolved. Splits and enmities multiplied; and after the war when the internees were released, alcohol completed the work of the Curragh, and destroyed many an idealistic and promising career. Some top-level IRA prisoners, meanwhile, were held in Portlaoise prison where conditions were particularly harsh.

As for public opinion in the face of de Valera's actions: a population which provided some 150,000 recruits to join the Irish security services and another fifty thousand for the British army – to say nothing of the huge numbers of Irish men and women helping in the British civilian war effort – may have regretted, but still supported, de Valera's repressive measures.

Some hundreds of thousands of either first- or second-generation Irish emigrants supported the war effort. As for de Valera himself, he was in no doubt that his harsh policies towards the IRA were correct. On one of their car journeys, he made a remark to his eldest son Vivion which he subsequently repeated on other occasions: 'You know, if it weren't for the executions, the Civil War would still be going on.'

As for public opinion on Irish neutrality itself, it is the case that the Irish people, no matter what side they favoured in the Civil War era, were completely behind Irish neutrality. The policy was a most successful unifier. Given this specific context, it is true to say of the period from the war's outbreak until 1948 (when he was defeated in a general election) that de Valera enjoyed unfettered power – albeit backed by popular support – and headed a dictatorial government the stringencies of which were ameliorated by that peculiar gift for finding Irish solutions to Irish problems. When the concentration camps were opened at war's end, there were widespread feelings of regret in Ireland at not having done more to defeat Nazism. During the war itself, however, only one politician, James Dillon, dissented from the policy of neutrality and resigned his party membership – and his stance earned admiration but not support. And, just as the ending of the economic war and the handover of the ports facilitated neutrality, so the fact of the Second World War itself had helped to *bolster* neutrality: for the policy of self-sufficiency enforced on Ireland by the interference with the normal flow of both exports and imports also led to self-sufficiency in wheat-growing and other cereals.

As for the Irish relationship with the British government during the war: Churchill was quite aware of the facts on the ground – of an essential Irish co-operation with the Allied war effort, and of Irish courtesies extended to Allied soldiers and other personnel. Whatever history will record against de Valera's name for his mistakes over the Treaty and his responsibilities in helping to foment the Civil War, his diplomatic skill in maintaining neutrality in a time of peril has to be regarded as a major diplomatic feat.

And, given the powers he had and the uninterrupted sojourn in power which the war years afforded him, it is not in the least surprising that for all its inevitable alarms and excursions, the Emergency was looked back upon by de Valera with affection. Indeed, as his son Vivion later recalled, his father enjoyed this period most of all because for him, it represented 'the encapsulated personality of the people'.

But every war must come to its end – and when the Emergency in Ireland ran its course, de Valera was faced with new domestic challenges not readily overcome.

6

The Generation Game

THE YEARS OF THE EMERGENCY MARKED THE ZENITH OF DE Valera's powers – although this would, of course, be apparent only in hindsight. In 1946, indeed, he may have been lulled into thinking his power would continue unabated: the Labour Party in Ireland was riven by internal tensions, thus removing one potential rival from the scene in the short term; and soon he had also neutralized the teachers, whose union, the Irish National Teachers' Organization (INTO), had staged a long, bitter and ultimately unsuccessful strike in a quest for more pay.

In the aftermath of the war, however, it was soon apparent that there were new and highly potent changes afoot on the Irish political scene. These came embodied in a new movement: Clann na Poblachta, founded by Seán MacBride. MacBride had, as we have seen, already lived an extraordinary life, and indeed this would continue: later he became a member of the Irish Bar; later still, a leading light in Amnesty International and a recipient of both the Nobel and the Lenin Peace Prizes. Such activities and accolades lay in the future: for now, in the aftermath of war, MacBride's ascent to power had its roots in local politics, and specifically in the attempt by de Valera to crush the power of the IRA.

MacBride had been instrumental in the defence of many of the republicans charged before the special military court – including some who were subsequently executed. Now, with the war over, censorship relaxed and the remains of the executed men returned to their families, Clann na Poblachta arose out of the revived republican sentiment which swept the country in the wake of the funerals and a spreading awareness of what had taken place in the name of state security during the Emergency. This rejuvenated republicanism, coupled with the energetic support of the country's teachers and MacBride's own undoubted charisma – which was itself greatly enhanced by the French accent he had acquired during a sojourn in Paris with his mother – all combined to give Clann na Poblachta a pivotal role in Irish politics in the immediate aftermath of the war.

This culminated in Fianna Fáil's defeat in the general election of 1948: and Clann na Poblachta now became a minor party in a Fine Gael-led 'inter-party' coalition government, headed by John A. Costello. This administration is best remembered, perhaps, for its Republic of Ireland Act, passed in 1948, which took the final constitutional steps towards full Irish independence. The country declared itself a republic, removed the final links which bound it to the British monarch and left the Commonwealth. The bill became law on Easter Monday, 1949, which was the thirty-third anniversary of the beginning of the Rising.

Costello's was always an unstable administration, and it ultimately disintegrated in 1951, as a result of a famous clash between the state and the Catholic Church. This notorious quarrel – for such phenomena were essentially unheard of in post-independence Ireland – had its origins in the so-called Mother and Child scheme of Dr Noël Browne, a Clann na Poblachta TD and independent-minded minister in the coalition government. Browne wished to introduce free health care, otherwise unavailable in Ireland, to expectant and nursing mothers; and it is clear that he regarded such a measure as benign and essentially uncontroversial.

However, the Church, embodied in the powerful form of John Charles McQuaid, Archbishop of Dublin since 1940, deplored the scheme as a plan to introduce socialized medicine to Ireland and to permit the state to meddle in family life. And there were other powerful interests who now marshalled in opposition: in particular, the Irish Medical Association, whose members equally feared any state interference in their private practice. In the face of such a powerful coalition and such pressure, the scheme was abandoned. Browne resigned his ministry, to the pleasure of some even of his own colleagues in the unwieldy coalition, and the government fell shortly afterwards.

The remainder of the decade saw power shift between de Valera's Fianna Fáil and further Fine Gael-led coalitions. This was a drab, shabby, depressed decade. Irish society was beset by chronic emigration, a steadily falling population, unparalleled unemployment and ever-growing pessimism as to the country's future. The pessimism was accurately summed up by a cartoon in the humorous journal *Dublin Opinion* which depicted Cathleen Ní Houlihan enquiring of a fortune teller 'Do I have a future?' The man who answered that question was T. K. Whitaker, an economist, civil servant and Secretary at the Department of Finance, who put it to de Valera that the situation was so bad that people were questioning the economic viability of the state.

De Valera's response was to give Whitaker permission to draw up a blueprint for recovery. With the aid of a group of colleagues, Whitaker took on the challenge, producing in 1958 his *First Programme for Economic Expansion*, which called for a shift away from protectionism and an agriculture-based economy in favour of free trade and an emphasis upon services and industry. The Whitaker plan paved the way for a reduction in tariffs, a gradual end to classic de Valera dogmas such as self-sufficiency – and most significantly, perhaps, a new focus on attaining membership of what was then a relatively small six-nation European Economic Community (EEC). Whitaker's initiative was the greatest single contribution by an individual to Ireland's post-war development; and it would have profound consequences for the future of the state.

On the economic and political front, meanwhile, the climate of innovation was further greatly improved by Seán Lemass's accession to the position of Taoiseach in 1959 – the year that the population of the Republic fell below the psychologically significant three million mark. Even de Valera's most trusted colleagues now recognized that the time had come for a change; and Oscar Traynor, one of de Valera's most loyal colleagues since the days of the Civil War almost forty years earlier, was chosen to tell him so.

In classic de Valera fashion, the announcement of the chief's resignation was made in the course of a potentially embarrassing parliamentary debate sponsored by Noël Browne. He had been given a single share in the *Irish Press* and he used this to exercise his right to examine the books of the company. In the process, he discovered that the newspaper was in fact not only a national institution which supported Fianna Fáil – but an actual de Valera family enterprise. The sound of the explosion of publicity and wrath which this discovery elicited within the Dáil chamber, and in the media, was muffled assiduously by the sensational announcement of de Valera's departure. He was now seventy-seven years old and was subsequently shuffled off to take up the post of president of Ireland – a position which he himself, of course, had created.

Under de Valera, Lemass had already proved himself a man of considerable ability in a variety of posts – both in government and as manager of the *Irish Press*. Now, the swishing of new brooms in Irish political and economic life proved to be of considerable benefit to national society. Economic stagnation began to lessen, and the country to open up tentatively to the modern world. Censorship was relaxed, the provision of secondary education was greatly extended and this mood of optimism and new thinking was symbolized by the arrival on the world scene of two figures who, each in his own distinctive way, had a marked influence on Ireland.

President John F. Kennedy visited Ireland in the early summer of 1963, to a rapturous reception from the Irish public and political class. His speech to the Irish parliament in the course of his visit ranks among his best: emotionally charged, pitch-perfect and replete with Irish references and Irish influences. Quoting George Bernard Shaw, for example, he told the assembled Irish parliamentarians that 'we need men who can dream of things that never were, and ask why not'. Pope John XXIII and his liberalizing Second Vatican Council of 1962–5, meanwhile, had a profound effect on Ireland's religious ethos. New ideas that would have been taboo in previous years now began to be openly discussed: liberalizing concepts to do with reproductive freedom, with divorce and the beginnings of feminist thought, with the power of the laity versus that of the clergy – these ideas and more became part of the national conversation.

The mid-1960s, then, represented an era of transformation – even if people did not at the time recognize the changes that were underway. The South began to shed the republican pieties of earlier days, and to morph into a consumer society – and an unequal one at that. The fiftieth anniversary of the Rising, for example, passed with scant attention paid now to the quaint notion of cherishing all the children of the Republic equally. There were beneficiaries of the anniversary, most notably de Valera, who was returned in the presidential election of that year, even though his vote fell dramatically.

Attention was now focused even more on the possibility of securing EEC membership, and acquiring tickets on the gravy train to Brussels. Ireland's strongly independent policy line at the UN was quietly dropped; subsequently, as Europe would go, so would Ireland follow. Entry to the EEC was delayed just the same: President de Gaulle of France vetoed enlargement of the union as a means of foiling the aspirations of Britain; and both Britain and Ireland had to wait until 1973 for their applications to be approved.

*

From the mid-1960s on, the political process in the Republic was focused at all times on sidestepping the perils presented by the growing disorder north of the border. There was sympathy, to be sure, but also fear of the upheaval spilling over into the Republic. A lack of interest and disengagement grew, as partitionist attitudes inexorably took root: many more people marched throughout the 1970s in the South in protest at taxation levels, for example, than ever protested about what was going on across the border. But in a small country, maintaining a sense of complete apartness was of course an impossibility: and a curious episode known as the Arms Trial demonstrated this vividly.

This saga intimately involved the minister for finance in the Dublin government, Charles Haughey, and it remains one of the more curious political episodes in the Troubles. In the wake of the upsurge of violence in Belfast and Derry in the late 1960s, some powerful figures in the Republic had decided that the situation on the Catholic side called for more assistance from Dublin. Haughey had established a reputation as a hawk in his dealings with the IRA, and there was general astonishment in the Republic when, in April 1970, Haughey and another cabinet minister, Neil Blaney, were dismissed from the cabinet of Taoiseach Jack Lynch amid allegations that they had been guilty of securing money for weaponry to be used in Northern Ireland. Haughey denied the charge, and when the case came to court, amid a welter of allegations of perjury, it eventually collapsed. The case became more than a mere footnote, of course, because of the trajectory of Haughey's later career, which ultimately propelled him into the office of Taoiseach. It is true to say that no one man better exemplified the complexities and confusions of the period than Haughey.

The Haughey family had northern roots. His father Seán was a prominent IRA man in the village of Swatragh in Co. Derry during the Anglo-Irish war of 1919–21; and partition meant that he and many like him were forced to come south. He settled first in Co. Mayo where, after a spell in the Free State's army and then a short-lived period farming in Co. Meath, he developed multiple sclerosis. The Haughey family then moved to the blue-collar Donnycarney area of north Dublin, and here he and his six siblings were reared by his remarkable mother, Sarah. Psychologists would probably decide that Haughey's relatively lean early years were what inclined him towards the wastefulness and taste for opulence that destroyed him in later life. Educated by the Christian Brothers, at St Joseph's school in north Dublin, Haughey took a first-class commerce degree at University College Dublin, where he also studied accountancy and law and was elected auditor of the Commerce and Economics Society. He was a good athlete, winning a Dublin Senior Football Championship medal in 1945, and played water polo with the Clontarf swimming club. After he became a Fianna Fáil TD in 1957, he made it clear to those around him that he was heading in one direction only – the top. In 1951 he married Seán Lemass's daughter Maureen. He kicked off his political career by serving in a number of ministries – notably in justice where he helped to put an end to the IRA's border campaign of 1956–62.

In 1966, the fiftieth anniversary of the Rising, Haughey, now minister for agriculture, had his first shot at being Taoiseach. In that year, his father-in-law Lemass stood down from the post amid turmoil in Ireland's economically significant beef industry. Ireland was not yet in the EEC and thus could not export cattle to Europe, a disability that was compounded by a dock strike in its other main market, Britain. Beef prices were therefore a major *casus belli* with the National Farmers' Association (IFA). The stress caused by the dispute was probably a factor, indeed, in Lemass's decision to stand aside. But neither the abrasive Haughey nor his main rival, George Colley, got the top job, which went instead to the deceptively mild-mannered Jack Lynch. In the course of the row with the IFA, however, Haughey demonstrated a trait he would demonstrate throughout his career.

This was a tendency towards news management: Haughey advised the farmers to hold onto their cattle until prices rose, but the IFA leader, Rickard Deasy, contradicted this and advised the farmers not to hold on because prices would fall further. When RTÉ carried Deasy's statement immediately after that of Haughey, he rang the station and caused the IFA statement to be dropped. Haughey told the Dáil afterwards: 'I think it was a very unwise thing, to say the least of it, for Radio Teilifis Éireann to follow that solemn advice of mine given as minister for agriculture with a contradiction by one organization.' Deasy's response was to lead a farmers' march from Bantry in

Co. Cork to Dublin, a distance of 210 miles. Farmers joined in on the way, with the result that 30,000 farmers arrived in Dublin on 9 October 1966. Haughey, however, refused to meet the IFA leaders. It was a this point that Lemass stood down, and the dispute was resolved under the new Taoiseach, Jack Lynch. However, the joust with the farmers caused damage with rather longer-term implications than the temporary wounding of Haughey's hopes of becoming Taoiseach. Hereafter, the government placed farmers' interests above all others; as a result, when Ireland came to negotiate its accession to the EEC, its rights to exclusive fishing of its coastal waters were virtually given away. The loss to the Irish exchequer was – and is – incalculable.

Haughey nearly had an end put to his own career, through either his own actions or those of others, on at least two occasions: one in September 1968, the other in April 1970. In the former, he was returning from working on an unsuccessful referendum campaign to abolish proportional representation when his state car hit a bridge on the Dublin–Wicklow road. For years afterwards, the bridge was generally known as Charlie's Bridge. Less generally discussed was the rumour that the imperious Haughey, with a drink or two aboard, had hit the bridge after insisting that he take the wheel from his garda driver. What I do know of the aftermath of this incident is that one day shortly after it, Vivion de Valera came into my office to tell me that he had just been talking to his brother Dr Éamon de Valera, who had come from visiting Haughey in his hospital room – and found him 'with brain fluid trickling from his nostril'. I often wondered subsequently whether that crash may have affected Haughey's judgement.

The second incident occurred in April 1970, during his stint as finance minister – and it prevented him from delivering his own Budget speech on 22 April; his speech was read by Jack

Lynch. Three conflicting versions of the causes of the accident circulated, two of which were semi-official. The first was that, in dismounting from a horse that morning, Haughey had fallen after grabbing at a drainpipe which gave way. A second, from his family, said that his head had struck a beam while riding. A third, and definitely unofficial, version which subsequently found its way into print at various junctures was that he had been hit on the head with an iron bar in a pub row. However, one associates Haughey with fine restaurants, not pubs.

If I had to choose from all the rumours, I would choose to believe – while stressing that I cannot substantiate it – that Haughey was hurt in an altercation with detectives as he was discovered attempting to remove his own files from their care in the small hours of Budget morning. The files were said to contain material which had a bearing on something that undoubtedly did happen two weeks later, while the accident-prone Haughey was still in hospital. Lynch went to his bedside to sack him on account of the Arms Trial saga. Lynch told me himself that even at that stage Haughey's state of consciousness was not good, and that he appeared not to fully understand what was happening. So, however sustained, the traumas to Haughey's head may have to be reckoned as having had a bearing on his career. Certainly some force seemed to hold him back where Northern Ireland was concerned. Despite his sulphurous reputation, largely stemming from the Arms Trial, he disappointed those who expected him to take a proactive policy towards the northern statelet. This failure to act is sometimes ascribed to an incident which occurred while he was minister for finance. On a Friday the British, as a courtesy, informed their EEC colleagues that they were planning to devalue the pound on the following Monday. That Friday afternoon there was heavy advance purchase of sterling in certain Swiss centres. These purchases were eventually traced back to Dublin and, it is said, compromised Haughey in his subsequent dealings with the British.

Much of the Arms Trial saga remains in the realms of speculation, what is not speculation is the fact that Haughey and his two colleagues and friends, Brian Lenihan and Donnacha O'Malley, became the epitome of what I termed the 'men in the mohair suits'[7] whom Lemass brought in to Fianna Fáil after succeeding de Valera. Brash, hard-living, hard-drinking, they encouraged their friend John Healy, the leading political journalist of the day, to refer to them in his 'Backbencher' column in the *Irish Times* as forming part (and in their eyes, at least, the most important part) of 'the youngest and best cabinet in Europe'. Whatever the effect of his accidents, Haughey certainly had some of the best brains in the public life of his era. And, although it ultimately destroyed him, he probably benefited rather than suffered from the rogue element in his character. He behaved like one of the legendary Irish bosses of the pre-New Deal era in America: men like James Michael Curley of Boston who took from the American WASP aristocracy to enrich the lives of their constituents and themselves, using the philosophy of 'looking after your own' to justify (and to obscure) the enhancement of their own lives. In the Republic of Ireland, however, there were very few WASPS for Haughey to plunder, so he settled for taking what he could from wealthy businessmen. Years later, even as he warned the country that it was living beyond its means, and prescribed a diet of public austerity, he was accustomed to himself living the high life – so much so that it was later proven that his own lifestyle was sustained by means of overdrafts, soft loans and donations from wealthy businesspeople.

In the aftermath of the arms trial, Haughey would claw his way back into the political reckoning to rejoin another Lynch government. Indeed, Haughey went on to make an extraordinary political re-emergence. His potent grassroots Fianna Fáil support forced Lynch to restore him to the front bench in 1975. Although Lynch won an overwhelming majority in 1977, he still had little room for political manoeuvre and was forced to reinstate Haughey to the cabinet as minister for health. By this stage Lynch had served as Taoiseach on three separate occasions and he could justly be described as one of the most popular politicians of the century. He had also been one of the greatest hurlers ever, winning several All-Ireland medals. But his soft Cork accent and diffident manner off the field concealed the steel which served him well both on the sports field and in the political arena.

Ironically, Lynch was also destined to depart in the midst of a farmers' protest: in December 1979, the farmers were protesting because the minister for finance, Colley, had introduced a 2 per cent levy on farm incomes. Farmers who traditionally paid less tax than PAYE workers mounted the barricades once more, and the government backed down. This in turn caused the trade unions to take to the streets. Some fifty thousand people joined a protest march through Dublin organized by the Irish Transport and General Workers Union; and other marches took place in various towns throughout the country. Lynch was preparing to go anyway, but in thinking to deny Haughey the time to organize a successful campaign against his main rival Colley (whom Lynch supported), he stepped down after being approached by five Fianna Fáil deputies who advised him to do so. Lynch's manoeuvres were in vain: Colley was a hopelessly inadequate adversary against the ruthless Haughey, who duly became Taoiseach in December 1979.

Charles Haughey would serve three times in the office in the course of the next thirteen years, but controversy always pursued him. Take the extraordinary episode in 1982, in which he was involved in a scandal generated by the discovery of a double murderer, Malcolm McArthur, in the home of the Irish Attorney General Patrick Connolly. After the arrest, Connolly phoned Haughey on his private island off the Kerry coast to inform the Taoiseach what had befallen his house guest (and former companion in some of Dublin's highest social circles). Haughey, however, was in holiday mode, and did not appear to realize the import of what Connolly was telling him. And Connolly himself apparently felt free to depart on a pre-arranged holiday in New York, which was to prove one of the shortest vacations on record. He was met on arrival by Irish consular officials and returned home immediately. Haughey subsequently described these happenings as 'grotesque, unbelievable, bizarre and unprecedented', a description that was shortened into the acronym GUBU by one of his arch-critics, Conor Cruise O'Brien; GUBU subsequently became a synonym for skulduggery in Irish politics. To say the least of it, Haughey's subsequent career provided ample evidence of the latter.

And to be sure, he was a complex individual: meting out austerity and higher taxes with one hand, while showing his concern for senior citizens, for example, by introducing free travel on state transport services for pensioners, free television licences and some reductions in electricity and phone bills. These did not greatly affect either society or the national budget, but they were of undoubted benefit to the elderly and provided some evidence that there was indeed a caring component to Irish society.

Haughey also brought in tax relief for artists. This gesture illustrated one of his strengths. The idea was suggested to him one night at dinner with the writer Constantine Fitzgibbon and his wife, the film star and sculptor Marjorie Steele. He saw the merit of the proposal and within a short time had translated the idea into legislation. Few politicians of any era had his gift of cutting through bureaucracy and political obstruction and translating word into deed. He also was instrumental in the establishment of Aosdána ('People of the Arts'), a writers' and artists' academy that provided a financial allowance to members, after the idea was put to him by his friend, the critic and poet Anthony Cronin.

In the still largely cleric-dominated Ireland of his time, Haughey somehow managed to avoid any public censure for the open secret that, along with a lavish lifestyle which included the ownership of horses, a yacht and his own island off the Kerry coast, he also maintained a mistress, Terry Keane, who was a newspaper columnist and the wife of Judge – and later Chief Justice – Ronan Keane. Despite this thoroughly unorthodox private life, in public Haughey stoutly defended the sanctity of the Irish family and Church teaching on the issues of abortion and divorce. Although, upon his appointment as minister for health in 1977, he managed to push through a liberalizing measure on contraception, the pill was only to be dispensed by pharmacists and prescribed by doctors who certified that it was being used by married couples not for contraception, but for regulation of the menstrual cycle. Haughey famously described this compromise as being 'an Irish solution to an Irish problem'. The divorce prohibition was only removed from the Constitution in 1995; and abortion still remains essentially illegal in Ireland.

But there was always the tendency towards skulduggery, and at length this engendered a sense of growing disgust with Haughey among certain members of Fianna Fáil, an eventual split in the ranks of the party and the emergence, in December 1985, of the Progressive Democrats (PDs), with a mandate to bring to Irish politics what was described as true republicanism. The PDs translated this as meaning ethics in public life and respect for the rule of law – a laudable, but obviously doomed aspiration, given the pork-barrel nature of Irish politics. This largely middle-class and economically right-wing party also stood for social reform, in particular of the divorce and contraception laws, terrain in which the Church was still powerful. The PDs had some initial success, securing fourteen seats in the general election of 1987. Two years later, another general election saw this slide to six. But six was still sufficient to help them form, with Haughey, the first coalition government in the history of Fianna Fáil: in the eyes of many party stalwarts, a notable, but highly unwelcome innovation for the Warriors of Destiny. Haughey, however, survived as Taoiseach, for the moment.

The arrival of the PDs helped to create a political climate in which neither old nationalism nor even the newest form of socialism held much appeal. While the PDs did grow out of Fianna Fáil, they were also one of the few significant Irish political parties to develop outside the War of Independence and Civil War matrix. However, ultimately the party had little lasting impact on southern society; and its northern policy consisted largely of trying to appease the unionists by cracking down on the IRA, which bore no lasting fruit.

As for Haughey, he remained for several more years at the centre of Irish politics – even after the split in Fianna Fáil and the rise of the PDs. But the world was changing around him. This was exemplified best, perhaps, by the election to the presidency of Mary Robinson in the autumn of 1990. She was a feminist lawyer with a long record of espousing liberal causes in Ireland, and she ran as an independent candidate with the support of the Labour Party. At the beginning of the campaign, her cause was considered hopeless: the Fianna Fáil candidate, Brian Lenihan, was a long-time supporter of Haughey, popular in his own right, and was odds-on favourite to sweep the election; after all, no Fianna Fáil candidate had ever lost a presidential election.

In the end, however, past misdemeanours destroyed the Fianna Fáil campaign. Lenihan admitted his role, in 1982, in the improper pressuring of President Patrick Hillery to refuse a dissolution of parliament in that year: such a refusal would almost certainly have resulted in Haughey forming a new Fianna Fáil government, but Hillery regarded the pressure exerted on him as an act of gross misconduct, and agreed to the dissolution, thus ushering in a general election that brought Fine Gael to power. Haughey dismissed Lenihan from his position as Tánaiste (deputy prime minister); and Robinson was elected to the presidency. Although Lenihan won on the first count, his Fianna Fáil supporters could not bring themselves to give their second preferences to the next in line, the Fine Gael candidate, Austin Currie, and their votes went to the third-placed Mary Robinson.

Two years later, Haughey's own career came to an end, and here, the Progressive Democrats were instrumental in bringing about his fall. Another long-buried scandal, this time involving illicit telephone-tapping, caused the PD leadership to withdraw support from Haughey, who had already been politically weakened by discontent within Fianna Fáil itself. Haughey was subsequently disgraced in the course of both the McCracken and Moriarty tribunals into payments to politicians, which found the former Taoiseach guilty of widespread financial corruption and impropriety.

He was diagnosed with prostate cancer in 1996, but was assured that if the prostate was removed he would survive. However, he was also informed that the operation would render him impotent. He refused to undergo the procedure, even though he was warned that in all probability the cancer would thereby spread and kill him. He refused the operation saying: 'No: there's life in the old man yet.' He died in 2006.

7

A World of Troubles

AND WHAT OF THE PLACE OF NORTHERN IRELAND IN THE history of these years – that artificial six-county entity that was born out of fear, out of sectarian values and in bloody violence, and which was run explicitly as a Protestant state for a Protestant people? Its unhappy origins made it in many ways an unprepossessing place, for its problems were intrinsic to it, were an aspect of its essential nature and could not be readily wished away.

Incredibly, however, even the problems of Northern Ireland appeared amenable to solution – for a little while. In the 1960s, with the sap rising and new ideas on the horizon, Seán Lemass decided, in January 1965, to take himself north of the border and shake hands with Northern Ireland's prime minister Captain Terence O'Neill, a well-meaning old Etonian and scion of an aristocratic unionist family. O'Neill then came south to pay a reciprocal visit to Lemass, and it seemed that, after decades of frigid relations and mutual hostility, things might – perhaps – get better.

Optimism, however, is a dangerous trait where Northern Ireland is concerned. Not long before O'Neill came to Dublin to meet Lemass, there had been mini-riots and a degree of public disorder accompanying a visit paid to Ireland by

Princess Margaret. The car in which she had been travelling was a little damaged; it was repaired – but then, in an unfortunate but appropriate piece of symbolism, this same vehicle was chosen to drive O'Neill to his meeting with Lemass. In the South, however, this aspect of the visit passed unnoticed, and people focused instead on how olive branches might possibly be extended to the North.

In those early days, much had to be overlooked in the cause of bridge-building. Northern Catholics were systematically discriminated against – in, for example, the areas of housing and employment – and the government in the Republic, though fond of much in the way of wearying sloganizing, was less keen on the prospect of taking concrete steps to address such issues. Instead, people began paying heed to unionist suggestions that small, stealthy gestures might improve relationships between the two parts of Ireland. I was asked to play my part in such moves: though the northern entity consisted of only six of Ulster's nine counties, the unionists resented the term 'Six Counties' and wanted their entity referred to as 'Ulster'. During my spell in the editor's chair at the *Irish Press* in the 1960s, I ensured that the paper reflected this and other superficial changes enthusiastically – though in the end, of course, unavailingly. The unionists had been offered the entire province of nine counties at the time of partition, but opted for six only because they could be sure of controlling them. Control, not co-operation, remained the unionists' leitmotif.

The handshakes also proved to be to no avail: for in Northern Ireland, events took a different path, one that would lead instead to bloodshed. One figure in particular ensured that this was the case. As one demagogue – de Valera – slipped into retirement in the Republic, so another, the fiery Co. Antrim preacher Ian Richard Kyle Paisley, made his dramatic first appearances on the political stage in the North. Demagoguery and oratory these two men had in common, but in other ways and in their individual worldviews, they were utterly unalike. De Valera was a pious Catholic of the first stripe, Paisley was a fundamentalist Protestant. And while demagoguery is not something confined to Ireland or to de Valera's time – though it certainly is a trait in Irish and Irish-American politics – Paisley was one of the most successful demagogues to arise in Ireland in the course of the twentieth century, or indeed at any time before that.

In October 1965, when it still seemed possible that Lemass and O'Neill between them might manage to heal the North–South divide, in my naïveté, I put it to Captain O'Neill that surely the activities of Paisley, this strange anti-cleric from the dark ages, could not derail the widely popular process of reconciliation which he and Lemass had initiated. O'Neill looked worried and replied: 'The trouble is: he does all this with the Book in his hand. The Book is very important up here.' And to be sure, Paisley went on to demonstrate just how powerful the Bible was in the hands of an unscrupulous man bent on power. I saw him one evening flummox a BBC interviewer who put it to him that bigotry was being fermented in Ulster. Paisley thundered:

I am a bigot, I glory in the title. During the inquisition the Catholics offered the Protestants the choice of a quick death by strangulation or a slow burning at the stake, they chose the stake and went to their deaths exclaiming that they were right by God. That's how they got the name bigot.[8]

This ringing Reformation-flavoured rhetoric was extremely difficult to counter. He was merely one, albeit the most successful, of a long line of fiercely anti-Catholic northern Protestant clerics. Paisley also hinted at ethnic cleansing in his speeches. He was once captured on television telling a meeting, to thunderous applause, that: 'The last word will be with me and with you and when the time comes I say "Clear the rebels out of here."' That is precisely what the mobs whom Paisley incited thought they were doing when they set about burning out Catholics and attacking them in their homes across the North in the years to come.

As far back as the 1950s, Paisley was stoking the flames of northern politics by means that would soon become his trademark. In 1956, for example, he hit the headlines in extraordinary fashion, when he was involved in the spiriting away to Scotland of a fifteen-year-old Belfast Catholic, Maura Lyons, who left her home because she was having doubts about her faith. The case aroused huge publicity throughout Ireland: Paisley openly challenged the authorities to send him to jail for refusing to divulge her whereabouts, claiming he was doing so to protect Protestant liberties. The case of Maura Lyons, though sensational at the time, in hindsight established the particularly theatrical tone of Paisley's entire career. Meanwhile, during his incessant anti-Catholic tirades – always carefully aimed at 'Rome' rather than individual Catholics – he deployed a variety of props to underpin his rhetoric. He would bring on stage, for example, a woman he claimed to be a former Catholic nun, who would proceed to describe the life of unimaginable vice she had witnessed during her spell within the convent walls.

The same element of demagoguery appeared in 1964, as the general election of that year approached. If one happened to look closely at the window of one of the tiny red-bricked 'kitchen houses' in Cromac Square off the Falls Road at this time, one would have seen a small tricolour displayed by Liam

McMillan, who was standing in the election as a republican candidate. Under the Flags and Emblems Act, the showing of the tricolour was illegal at the time. McMillan would garner only a few hundred votes; Paisley, however, threatened to march up the Falls at the head of a mob of extreme loyalists to tear down McMillan's flag. The Royal Ulster Constabulary (RUC) itself eventually removed the source of the outcry, after first smashing in the door of McMillan's home with sledge-hammers. But riot and uproar continued in Paisley's wake for the duration of the election campaign – a period which saw the first car burnings in Northern Ireland.

Nor was Paisley the only bigot in the Ulster extremist firmament. There was also, for example, William Craig, who as minister for home affairs in the Stormont government banned civil rights marches, and declared like Paisley that the Civil Rights Association was but a front for the IRA. He was subsequently fired by Terence O'Neill, and went on to found his own extreme loyalist movement, named Vanguard. He advocated the keeping of dossiers on the state's enemies with a view to 'liquidating them should the need arise'.[9]

In a very real sense, Paisley and other extremists represented the forces of reaction against those of enlightenment which were beginning to make their presence felt in northern society. The Catholics were coming out of their crouch position, assisted by the post-war Education Acts which, for the first time in Northern Ireland's history gave them the intellectual tools with which to challenge the discriminatory regime enforced by their unionist masters. Playing the normal political game by normal rules had, after all, proved ineffectual: for years in the early days of the state's foundation, the Catholics had boycotted the new parliament, and even after swallowing their distrust and entering it, they found they were discriminated against by an election system that enshrined sectarian constituencies and locked Catholics out of any municipal or national share of power.

And discrimination it certainly was. Even after one has made all possible allowances for the psychological 'encirclement' effect of the Protestants of Ulster by the presence of an overwhelming Catholic majority on the island, one is still left with the undeniable fact of a mean-spirited and ungenerous political culture. In order to hold back the feared tide of Catholicism, the unionist Establishment resorted to two tactics in particular: discrimination and gerrymandering. By introducing a property vote into local government elections, extra votes were given to those who actually owned the property – who were mostly Protestants. By means of a gerrymander, they corralled the Catholics into large constituency wards wherein the larger Catholic numbers in any given area were essentially nullified. For example, in Derry, a largely Catholic city, this gerrymandering effect resulted in a built-in Protestant majority in local and national elections. And in the face of this dispiriting status quo, migration or unemployment became the familiar choices for Catholics. State employment in every sphere, from local veterinarian to county-council road sweeper, was almost exclusively Protestant in nature; and the great engineering and shipbuilding companies of Belfast were also the preserve of the local majority.

In an effort to blunt the increasingly potent educational weapon, the Stormont government unwittingly called forth the first civil rights protests in the North. In 1965, thousands of protesters made their way in a cavalcade of some 2000 cars from Derry to Stormont to protest at the decision to site Northern Ireland's new second university not in Derry, where there were existing third-level facilities at Magee College, but on a greenfield campus outside the overwhelmingly Protestant market town of Coleraine; furthermore, it was suggested that Magee itself be closed completely.

The motorized cavalcade of itself achieved little – the University of Ulster was indeed sited at Coleraine – but it did mark the beginning of a new era of Catholic activism. Young working-class university graduates such as John Hume and Eamonn McCann began appearing on television and radio, out-debating and out-witting their unionist opponents. New ideas permeated northern society: the fresh thinking established by the Second Vatican Council (Vatican II), along with civil rights ideology imported from the American South, all found their mark. Street demonstrations became common, their participants marching now to the strains of 'We shall overcome'. But strain grew in northern society too, as liberalism and increasing nationalist activism clashed with a defensive and increasingly fearful Protestantism, stoked by Paisley's incendiary rhetoric.

Amid this welter of sectarian feeling, a new paramilitary body came into existence. This was a new incarnation of the Ulster Volunteer Force (UVF), which more than fifty years previously had spearheaded the revolt against Home Rule. Some members of the UVF took part in the 1966 killing of the first Catholics to die in what became known as the 'Troubles' – and, ironically, Terence O'Neill had to fly back from the commemorations in France of the sacrifices of the 36th (Ulster) Division at the Somme to officially ban the new organization. Notwithstanding such actions, however, the wave of unrest continued. Paisley developed a tactic of countering the announcement of a civil rights march with a declaration that he would hold a rival protest on the same occasion.

Faced with the prospect of riot and disorder, the RUC inevitably took the line of least resistance by banning the civil rights march. And at the same time, Paisley's actions ensured that social and sectarian tensions spiralled month by month. One of his most infamous slogans was 'CRA [Civil Rights Association] equals IRA', which encouraged loyalists to believe that Catholics in the civil rights movement were either members of – or supported – the IRA.

As the tension and violence increased, it was inevitable that change would come to Northern Ireland. Between the mid-1960s and 1974, indeed, governments and governing arrangements would rise and fall: O'Neill was swept from power in 1969; his successor, James Chichester-Clark, followed him in 1971; the Stormont government itself was suspended in 1972, at which point direct rule from London was imposed by the government of Edward Heath. A short-lived power-sharing Northern Ireland executive, established by the Sunningdale Agreement of 1973 and headed by Brian Faulkner, fell in 1974. And Paisley succeeded in riding the tide: he developed his own sect, the Free Presbyterian Church he had founded in 1951, into a formidable force; and he created his own party, the Democratic Unionist Party (DUP), which would eventually become the dominant unionist party in Northern Ireland.

This was all in the future. For the moment, politicians in the Republic looked on in fear and dismay as the North slid inexorably into chaos. The civil rights marches met with more and more violence and less and less police protection, most notably at Burntollet Bridge in rural Co. Derry in January 1969 when a student civil rights march was attacked by Protestant extremists while the RUC stood by. Protesters were hit with stones transported from a local quarry and with sticks with nails driven through them; some of the marchers were then thrown into the Burntollet river. Many of the attackers, in fact, were actually off-duty police officers. This astonishing assault was documented by numerous press photographers and featured on front pages around the world.

There is a surfeit of violent episodes one could choose to cite – but the events of August 1969 were in every sense the most explosive of the period. In Belfast, Protestant mobs attacked the Catholic Clonard district adjoining the Protestant Shankill Road area, burning out Bombay Street in its entirety. They were led in some cases by the auxiliary 'B Special' police force, whose ostensible purpose was to patrol the border. Stone-throwing Catholic youths kept them from their main targets, the adjoining Clonard monastery and a nearby Catholic school complex. Simultaneously, disturbances broke out in a number of cities and towns across the province, most notably in Derry. Here the long history of gerrymandering worked against the unionists in spectacular fashion. In order to keep the Catholics penned into the South ward and diminish their electoral power, a series of high-rise flats had been built and a relatively large population of underemployed youths was concentrated in the district. These young militants used the height of their apartment blocks to their advantage by raining down stones and petrol bombs on the police and B Specials who attempted to break into the barricaded Bogside, where a 'no-go' area had been declared. And now, with Belfast and Derry alight, it seemed only a matter of time before the entire North went up in smoke. James Callaghan, the responsible minister in the British Labour government of Harold Wilson, now took the momentous decision to send in the troops to keep the peace. It would be a long time before they were withdrawn.

In Protestant areas such as Belfast's Shankill Road, British officers recorded their anger and incomprehension at Protestant mobs who waved Union Jacks at them, shouted 'Ulster is

British' – and then proceeded to throw stones and fire shots at them. The first police officer and the first soldier to die in the 'Troubles' were both killed by Protestants. In the Catholic areas, meanwhile, matters were more complex. The IRA had, after all, become essentially de-militarized over the years, and increasingly devoted its energies to left-wing agitation and protest, to the detriment of what it had traditionally regarded as its ultimate role as defender of the Catholic population. As a result, after the Bombay Street burnings, graffiti reading 'IRA – I ran away' appeared on gable ends off the Falls Road. It was from this context that another IRA developed – the so-called 'Provisional' IRA, sworn to that previous role of defence and to the furtherance of the 1916 Proclamation goal of a thirty-two-county Ireland.

In the first months of the British military presence on the streets, working-class Catholics tended to view the soldiers with something close to relief: they provided a level of protection against Protestant paramilitaries, especially in the sectarian patchwork of small streets and communities in Belfast. (The troops were sent in in August 1969, but the first British soldier to be killed by republicans, Gunner Robert Curtis, did not die until February 1971.) As time went on, however, resentment against the British military presence grew as sectarian fears and resentments asserted themselves, and the security situation continued to deteriorate.

*

On the eve of the Troubles in Northern Ireland, then, Northern Ireland was a profoundly complex and disturbed society. The IRA, though extant, was unsure of its place and position in the world: IRA operatives played their part in the burgeoning civil rights movement, even as other volunteers anticipated a return to full-scale military action against the northern state.

As the Troubles fermented in the late 1960s, nationalist leaders tended to emerge from the left. They were highly educated, by and large, and profoundly influenced by civil rights ideology: and such personalities as McCann, Hume, Bernadette Devlin, Ivan Cooper (a Protestant) and Austin Currie would leave their mark on northern society. In June 1968, Austin Currie staged the first sit-in by 'squatting' in a house at Caledon in Co. Tyrone, thereby causing the London media to examine the issue of discrimination in public housing in Northern Ireland for the first time. Hume would prove himself the leading political thinker to emerge from the ranks of constitutional nationalism: in 1979 he became leader of the constitutional nationalist Social Democratic and Labour Party (SDLP) party, which had grown to become the dominant nationalist party in Northern Ireland; and his career would be crowned in due course by a Nobel Peace Prize awarded for his sustained, courageous efforts both to lead his own people and to find common ground with his unionist opponents over the decades. But the SDLP, dominant though it was, certainly did not speak for all nationalists and republicans.

In the opening years of the Troubles, the voices of those within the republican movement who were still animated by 1916 and the prospect of an all-Ireland Republic attained by force of arms were heard but faintly, if at all, in the outside world. At first, the energies of the IRA were consumed by what amounted to a philosophical debate. Or, rather, by a re-run of an old, old debate: the 'force' versus constitutionalism argument was conducted with much vehemence but without attracting much attention from the outside world. Meanwhile, many members of the Catholic population, faced with Paisley's demagoguery and daily violence, had rather more on their minds than philosophy.

At length, however, two separate events combined to explode the debate into the public arena. The first stemmed from a decision by the IRA's Army Council to drop the movement's traditional policy of abstaining from what they viewed as the illegitimate parliaments of Belfast, Dublin and London. The second was the effect of the frenzied year of 1969, in which rioting and house burning threatened to engulf not merely northern cities but those of the South as well.

In early December 1969, the *Sunday Press* lead story revealed that the IRA was dropping abstentionism. In January 1970, the Provisional IRA – the 'Provos' – was born, its arrival hastened by widespread anger among many IRA members at the direction the organization was now taking; its political wing, Sinn Féin, remained wedded at this time to an abstentionist policy. The Provos were committed to the concept of an armed struggle, although initially they had virtually no arms at all, and resorted instead to the use of nail bombs and suitcases filled with homemade explosives in many of their attacks. But they had one priceless asset, something which had boosted recruitment into the ranks of the Irish physical-force tradition down the centuries. This was a grievance at the flow of history which had created an unjust and fundamentally sectarian Northern Ireland in the first place, and had now brought the British army onto its streets.

The IRA did, of course, take steps to secure arms, and the porous Irish border was, ironically, ideally suited to aid the flow of weaponry from South to North. As this army took to the streets, impelled by widespread violence, Britain came to a decision that was to have long-term and ultimately beneficial effects on physical-force republicans. In a word, Whitehall decided that it could not risk opening a second front and thus being shot in the back by loyalists as the soldiers turned to confront republicanism. In essence, the British government's attitude was that Northern Ireland was, for good or ill, part of the United Kingdom. Loyalism might be dangerous, extremist, and unpredictable and incomprehensible to many members of the British army now patrolling its neighbourhoods, it might bear responsibility for the deaths of actual soldiers and police-men – but just the same, it was not the real enemy. And it was for this reason that internment was introduced in these opening years of the Troubles and that northern nationalists began to encounter the full effects of state security.

The introduction in August 1971 of internment without trial was resented bitterly. It was directed exclusively against Catholics and nationalists. The only Protestant picked up in the mass arrests of 'Operation Demetrius' on 9–10 August was an SDLP representative, Ivan Cooper. And soon this resentment turned to fear and anger as stories emerged of torture methods deployed in Northern Ireland's internment centres: prisoners were hooded, for example, and spread-eagled while forced to stand supported on their fingertips, to the accompaniment of continuous punching and yelling and the use of high-pitched background 'white noise'. Torture and internment had the effect of worsening relationships between Dublin and London: the Dublin authorities were forced to take up the men's cases and what was known as the torture case dragged on through European courts for several years before reaching a verdict which stopped short of finding that torture had occurred. The process which took place, the courts found, was merely cruel and inhuman treatment.

As it happens, the British later turned to a Catholic cousin of mine, Harold Plunkett, one of the North's leading psychiatrists, to attempt to rehabilitate the men: he found many of them so physically and mentally damaged that they died in their early forties. One who survived was Kevin Hannaway, a cousin of Gerry Adams, who told me how he survived more than a week of sleeplessness. Hannaway had memorized the last words of the executed 1916 leaders – and he kept repeating these and saying to himself: 'Look what those men went through; sure, what am I getting? – nothing!' Hannaway's survival, indeed, could be taken as a metaphor for the survival in general of militant republicanism in Ireland in the course of the twentieth century.

Within Catholic society, the inevitable effect of internment was to create a huge rise in IRA recruitment and a surge in the organization's popularity – which never quite died away, regardless of the atrocities the IRA committed during the course of the Troubles. Internment, moreover, failed in its primary stated objective, which was to round up and neutralize the IRA. None of the IRA leaders was ever captured. A re-run of Irish history commenced as the British resorted to the same tactics they had used in the days of Michael Collins, when in order to avoid the appearance of being engaged in a war of independence they devised a concept of a 'police war', of using special forces and auxiliaries to combat the IRA, and so avoid the appearance of being engaged in a 'regular' war.

In his famous book *Low Intensity Operations*,[10] Brigadier-General Frank Kitson wrote of his experiences in Kenya during the Mau Mau campaign – and of the value of forming 'pseudo gangs' in counter-insurgency situations. The advice of the brigadier, later aide-de-camp general to Queen Elizabeth II, fell on willing ears in Northern Ireland. And many a loyalist murder gang was armed and furnished with information about supposed republican activists over the ensuing decades.

Amid a threatened disintegration of society into full-scale civil war, the Stormont government was, in 1972, at last prorogued. The last straw was the episode known as Bloody Sunday: the killings on 30 January 1972 by the security forces of thirteen civilians on the streets of Derry (a fourteenth subsequently died of his wounds) in the course of a civil rights march through the streets of the city. The episode, captured by journalists present on the day, caused shock and condemnation across the world; in Dublin, the British embassy was burned out by a crowd of demonstrators. The British government belatedly set about introducing reforms in an attempt to address Catholic and nationalist grievances: the B Specials were disbanded; the property vote abolished; and a general attempt made to remedy the evils of discrimination and gerrymandering. This was perhaps the greatest vote of no-confidence in a supposedly democratic state ever passed in Western Europe. The ruling unionist elite was judged to be unfit to run a parliament, a police force, a militia (the B Specials), a voting system and a local government system.

The proroguing of Stormont was both a tremendous shock to the unionist psyche and a corresponding boost to the nationalist one. As far as many observers were concerned, the IRA had brought down Stormont. It had survived the attrition of internment and condemnation from press and from pulpit; and its renewed campaign of bombings and shootings received a different reception in many Catholic homes from that articulated in public by the leaders of their Church. The IRA even maintained its support in the face of the horrific atrocity of Bloody Friday on 21 July 1972, when a score of bombs exploded across Belfast killing nine people and injuring 130; again, the horror of the event was captured on television.

There were increasingly urgent attempts, some public and some private, to design a political structure that would support the weight of peace. In the wake of the fall of Stormont in 1972, a top-secret British initiative was undertaken which would ultimately play a major part in the evolution of the IRA's strength. A delegation of republicans was flown under a promise of safe conduct to London to a secret meeting at Cheyne Walk in Chelsea, the home of Paul Channon, a junior minister. Here they met a delegation of senior British politicians led by William Whitelaw. The IRA delegation was led by Seamus Twomey, the then Chief of Staff of the IRA, and included senior figures such as Seán MacStíofáin and Daithí O'Connell. A young Belfast activist, Gerry Adams, acted as a 'watcher', studying the reactions of the other side, and a Dublin solicitor, Myles Shevlin, kept a record of the event which was subsequently published in the *Irish Press*. The talks were significant in that this the first time that the British had received a republican delegation since Michael Collins and Arthur Griffith had gone to Downing Street at the invitation of Lloyd George fifty years earlier – but it produced no short-term result. The British sought an end to the IRA's campaign of violence, the IRA wanted an end to the British presence in Ireland – and such positions resulted in a gulf too wide to bridge.

There was, however, one significant lasting legacy from these talks. Prior to the holding of the Cheyne Walk talks a group of IRA prisoners embarked on a hunger strike in pursuit of a familiar republican demand – *political status*. In order to set the scene for the talks, Special Category status was conceded. In effect, this consisted of the right to free association with fellow republicans, the right to wear their own clothes and the right to educational courses. The prisoners dealt with the prison authorities only through their officers and, depending on the circumstances of prison or compound, had their own areas to which only IRA prisoners were admitted. At Cheyne

Walk, it was agreed that this status could be maintained. As we will see, an eventual effort to remove this status would provide republicans with a golden political opportunity.

The most significant of the *public* moves towards peace was the agreement signed amid the incongruously well-heeled surroundings of Sunningdale in Berkshire in 1973. Sunningdale consisted of the creation of a power-sharing executive between mainstream unionists, the non-sectarian Alliance Party and the newly established SDLP. Radicals and extremists on both sides were excluded. These new arrangements got off to a very rocky start with the British prime minister Edward Heath removing the heavyweight William Whitelaw from his post as secretary of state for Northern Ireland and returning him to Downing Street to help deal with an ongoing miners' strike. Whitelaw was succeeded by the innocuous Francis Pym – though whether either Whitelaw or Pym could have done much to change the path of history is a moot point. In any case, all attempts to exclude the extremists failed: Paisleyite objection to sharing power with the Catholics came to a head with the loyalist workers' strike of 1974, which destroyed the Sunningdale executive.

The loyalist-dominated trade unions had great influence within the power stations supplying Northern Ireland's electricity supply – and, in May 1974, they caused the lights to go out. They even controlled the roads, because barricades set up by hooded members of the Ulster Defence Association (UDA) were not dismantled by the British army; they closed the port of Larne and they cut the supply of petrol to the pumps. Northern Ireland descended rapidly into chaos. By this time a Labour government under Harold Wilson had returned to power in London. With the passage of time it became known, notably through the work of three *Sunday Times* journalists,[11] that both MI5 and the British army actively worked *with* loyalist extremists and *against* their own government and the new power-sharing executive to bring down Sunningdale. Television footage appeared to show armed and uniformed British soldiers standing by as UDA thugs armed with pickaxe handles and clubs prevented people going about their daily lives.

All this has been chronicled in often wearisome detail elsewhere, but one episode deserves to be highlighted because it demonstrates the ongoing hidden relationship between political unionism and loyalist paramilitarism. By coincidence, this chapter was being written in the approach to the Twelfth of July celebrations of 2014, when again, under pressure from the Protestant UVF, unionist politicians temporarily withdrew from all-party talks at Stormont. In this case the issue was, to outsiders, the seemingly trivial issue of the Orange Order not being allowed to march through the nationalist Ardoyne area at the conclusion of a Twelfth of July parade.

In 1974, however, the issue was more serious: whether or not a democratic power-sharing assembly should be enabled to survive. At that time, one of the more enlightened members of the executive was Roy Bradford, minister for the environment, and a graduate of Trinity College Dublin. Knowing Bradford as I did, I would have thought that of all the unionist members of the cabinet he would have been one of those most likely to support the SDLP's John Hume, who had argued that the authorities must hold out against the strikers even 'if the shit were to flow down Royal Avenue'. Bradford, however, broke ranks with his colleagues and resigned, urging that the strikers be negotiated with. He told me later that he took the decision after a visit from two of his constituents, who had 'explained the difficulties of the situation' to him. One was the leader of the paramilitary UDA, the other of the paramilitary UVF.

Bradford had served with British military intelligence during the Second World War and he was suspected of having links with MI5, which supported the loyalist strike. Such links might have had a bearing on his actions but it is also worth noting that while unionist politicians often make the propaganda case that the Provisional IRA was fostered at birth by Fianna Fáil, the idea of a Chief of Staff of the IRA being able to walk into the Dáil to put pressure on a government minister would be unthinkable in southern political life. Bradford's resignation helped to bring down the executive in late May 1974. It would be some twenty years before power sharing was seriously attempted again.

British underground activity, startlingly varied though it was, did not confine itself to arms smuggling, secret talks and the undermining of viable peace accords. Peace feelers were continually extended from British Establishment figures, including not only army generals but such leaders of British political opinion as Cecil King, the newspaper magnate, and William Whitelaw. But it was not the efforts of such figures that eventually changed what had become a frozen political landscape. Rather, it was another episode in the history of Northern Ireland that, tumultuous, violent and traumatic though it was, began to alter the Six Counties in the most profound way.

8

Towards Peace

Everything goes up your bum. The lads are circling around so that the screws don't see the priest slipping us the cigarette box. We roll up the fags in our hands and cram the tobacco into a biro casing. Then one of your mates comes behind you and you bend down and up it goes. The lads make sure that it's well up so nothing will show when the screws search us after Mass. It's amazing what fits up there – one fellow brought out three pencils that way and another hid a pen, a comb and a lighter. You don't feel it unless the casing is too long, but you do bleed all the time, sometimes pieces of flesh come off. Everyone has piles.[12]

THIS INSIGHT INTO HOW WHAT WAS LITERALLY A BATTLE OF the bowels was carried out by IRA prisoners helps to explain how, at the time of writing, the Sinn Féin political party occupies an important place in the parliamentary life of Ireland, both north and south of the border. The reminiscence above, dating from the prelude to the hunger strikes of 1980–1, contextualizes how this came to be the case.

Hunger striking had an established precedent in Irish politics. It was used as a weapon in the Anglo-Irish War, during the Civil War, in the run-up to and during the 'Emergency' by IRA prisoners – and, as indicated earlier, by the IRA in 1972 in order to lever the British authorities into introducing Special Category status for republican prisoners in the approach to the Cheyne Walk talks. This special status outlived the talks, of course – and by 1976, conditions at the internment site at Long Kesh outside Belfast were creating tension in Northern Ireland, the prison being referred to by unionist spokespersons and some of their Conservative allies as the 'Sandhurst of Terror'. The republicans had their own command structure within the camps, wore their own clothes, associated freely with their comrades, received food parcels and, importantly for the development of the Provisional movement, took part diligently in educational courses. The republicans allowed only their own members to join a compound or 'cage', as they called them, with the result that these political prisoners were able to cultivate their own encapsulated and powerful spheres of influence.

All this was, to some, highly objectionable, and in the mid-1970s unionist complaints bore fruit. At this time, new prison buildings began to take shape on the Long Kesh site: these were the 'H-Blocks' – two rows of cells joined in the middle by an administrative corridor. To the IRA's opponents, these had the merit of providing cellular confinement to reinforce the 'ordinary decent criminal'* image desired by the authorities. At this time, the British were engaged in yet another subterranean ceasefire negotiation with the IRA. This was given an air of authenticity by the fact that the British allowed the prisoners' leader, David Morley, out of Long Kesh to hold consultations with IRA leaders in the South.

---

* The phrase was coined by the then secretary of state for Northern Ireland, Merlyn Rees, in the course of explaining the change in prison policy.

It was around this time also that the British introduced a three-pronged strategy known as Ulsterization, normalization and criminalization. The first part of this strategy was based on an experiment carried out towards the end of the Vietnam War, in which the Americans tried to 'Vietnamize' the conflict by getting the natives into the front line; now, similarly, the British intended to put the RUC and the army auxiliary Ulster Defence Regiment (UDR) into the forefront of the war against the IRA. 'Normalization' involved making Northern Ireland society seem as normal as was possible under the circumstances – not merely by pulling back the army to barracks but by moving to rebuild IRA bomb damage almost as soon as the echoes of the detonation had died away. Finally, 'criminalization' aimed at making the IRA not prisoners of war but ordinary convicted criminals. Special Category, therefore, was now brought to an end.

The so-called Diplock courts, introduced in August 1973, were another aspect of the strategy of criminalization. They were named after the law lord Baron Kenneth Diplock, author of one of the many reports into Northern Ireland conditions at the time. Diplock suggested that these courts be permitted to accept uncorroborated evidence and to operate without juries and under the special emergency legislation of the period. While these developments were taking place, ceasefire talks were still in progress – but by 1976, one of the deadliest years of the Troubles, during which both loyalist and IRA death squads exacted a heavy toll, traces of a ceasefire were hard to find. The authorities for a period appeared to be winning the war, with a conveyor-belt system of special laws and special courts sending an ever-increasing flow of IRA prisoners into the H-Blocks.

The first prisoner convicted under the new dispensation was one Kieran Nugent. He refused to wear the prison garb of an ordinary decent criminal. He told me that when it was offered to him he replied: 'They'll have to nail it to my back first.' Subsequent prisoners followed Nugent's example – and so began the 'blanket protest'. The prisoners who refused to conform to normal prison discipline were confined to their cells, from which all prison furniture was removed. They were left with nothing but their mattresses, a chamber pot and a prison blanket to cover their nakedness.

In the initial stages of the blanket protest, attention focused more on the success of the conveyor-belt system as a counter-insurgency tool than on the prisoners' reaction to being criminalized. But in fact, the sheer efficiency of the conveyor-belt system ultimately led to its undoing. As with internment, the indiscriminate nature of the Diplock courts' sentences – themselves in effect a form of internment – meant that not only did prison numbers shoot up, but more and more families became affected, with an ever-greater effect on public opinion. And as prisoner numbers soared, so did the prisoner resistance. By 1980, another dimension had been added to the struggle. The prisoners now introduced a new weapon – their bowels.

Both sides, prisoners and warders, blamed each other for this development. The prisoners said that during the normal morning prison routine of 'slops out, breakfast in', the warders began kicking over the toilet bowls; when the contents were thrown out of the windows the warders threw them back in again. As a consequence, the prisoners began disposing of their faeces by smearing it on their cell walls. The warders, however, claimed that the prisoners had planned to do this all along. They alleged that slop utensils were not kicked over. However, not disputed was the fact that the struggle was quite horrible. I visited a cell in Long Kesh which contained

two twenty-year-olds serving ten- and twelve-year sentences.
Afterwards I described what I saw:

They were pallid and naked except for a blanket draped
over their shoulder. They stood silently, fear hardening into
defiance, I felt, as we looked at the cell.

It was covered in excrement almost to the ceiling on
all four walls. In one corner there was a pile of rotting
blue moulded food and excrement and the two boys had
evidently been using pieces of their foam rubber mattress
to add to the décor as we entered. There wasn't much of a
smell but the light was dim and the atmosphere profoundly
disturbing and depressing. I felt helpless and angry as I
looked at the appalling and disgraceful conditions, prevented by bureaucracy and by history from talking to two
of my fellow human beings who had brought themselves,
and been brought, to this condition of self-abnegation.[13]

I felt weak as I left the cell, but recovered when I heard the
warder and governor talking about a well-known republican,
Martin Meehan, whom they apparently thought had been considering giving up the protest. Now they suggested that I be
shown his cell. But, far from giving up, it turned out that
Meehan apparently had decided to use the protest to display his
powers of imagination. As we entered the cell, we discovered
that Meehan, naked except for a small white towel around his
loins, had used pieces of his mattress to convert his cell into a
tropical island. The 'ocean' came half way up the cell walls, and
palm trees sprouted from it. The scene was so surprising that
it took a few seconds to register the fact that both the ocean
and the trees were brown in colour. Meehan then proceeded
to inadvertently elicit from me one of the bravest actions of my

life. He transferred his faeces-impregnated piece of mattress to his left hand, smiled and gave me his right hand to shake. I did so. Women prisoners incarcerated in Armagh jail joined the protest too, adding to the horror by spreading their menstrual fluids on the walls. How many of the prisoners on this form of protest did not contract some form of virulent disease, I do not know. They also went on a no-wash, no-shave protest.

Despite all the anguish and the shooting of the warders the H-Block protest remained a curiously muted affair, hardly rippling the surface of political opinion south of the border. I, for example, would have been a member of the very small group of southern journalists who took an active interest in northern affairs – but to be frank, I knew very little about the dirty protest or its origins until a Dublin publisher, Phil McDermott, on his way to my office one January evening to discuss a book proposal, encountered a small procession of bare-footed women draped in prison blankets, holding plac-ards saying something about H-Blocks. In telling me about the encounter, he sparked my interest in the protest.

I was so appalled by what my research into the situation revealed that six months later I had produced a book. *On the Blanket*, written in the summer of 1980, highlighted the dirty protest and the dangers it posed. My chief interlocutor and guide during the research period was Father Alec Reid, the Redemptorist priest who would ultimately broker the Northern Ireland peace process almost twenty years later. He lived in the Clonard monastery, which was one of the first points of attack when loyalists invaded the Falls area in 1969, burning out Bombay Street. From this cockpit he learned to understand the situation in deprived and politicized areas of Northern Ireland better than most, and he foresaw that if the dirty protest esca-lated into a full-blown hunger strike, then the fallout in the

North would be immense and would most likely also affect the Republic. My book did something to alert public opinion to the dangers, though not enough to prevent a hunger strike breaking out towards the end of 1980.

That first hunger strike continued until Christmas 1980, when the prisoners' leader, Brendan Hughes, who was himself on hunger strike, called it off. His pragmatic view at that point was that some proposed concessions, such as 'civilian type clothing' (track suits), together with other ameliorations of the prisoners' conditions, would in effect concede a special status on the prisoners and would help to save the lives of the hunger strikers'. One of these in particular, Sean McKenna, had become delirious: it was feared that he would die – or break; and if the latter, then the strike would collapse. If the former, on the other hand, the sacrifice of his life would have been wasted, should the concessions prove to lead the way to a full restoration of political prisoner status.

The concessions, however, turned out to be largely bogus, and Hughes subsequently felt betrayed and humiliated. In the immediate aftermath of the aborted protest, the IRA prisoners began to reorganize and made preparations for a second hunger strike. This time it was laid down from the word go that the strike would be to the death. It would be led by Bobby Sands, Hughes' successor as the prisoners' leader, and now the prisoners began coldly to plan their own deaths and to secure the maximum publicity for their efforts. Information was sought from other hunger strikers around the world, notably members of the Palestine Liberation Organization, as to how long the human body could survive without food. Strikers, meanwhile, were chosen from each of the six northern counties so as to secure the maximum effect.

Bobby Sands was a character who might have made a mark in a different society, had he not been born in Belfast. He was something of a human dynamo. He could have been taken as one of those swift and indifferent men who make their way in life without undue concern for the welfare of others. But Sands left volumes of writings behind which indicate that at his core was a passion, a striving which was concerned with the betterment of others. His statement on embarking on the hunger strike, which he knew would end with his death, could have been taken as being composed in equal measure of a Padraig Pearse-like self-sacrifice and the prophetic. He said: 'Our revenge will be the laughter of our children.'

Sands' family had been intimidated out of their home in Belfast by loyalists when he was a boy. Growing up, he was frequently attacked and threatened. It was virtually foreordained that, like so many boys of his type in nationalist ghettoes, he would join the IRA. He was arrested at a time when the IRA was using its available resources wastefully. The flow of recruits, which continually increased as a result of internment and other security measures, meant that eight or ten young volunteers – both men and women – were sent out on operations for which one or two would have sufficed. The then twenty-two-year-old Sands, for example, impulsively joined such a party in 1976, setting out to burn a furniture store, because another volunteer had failed to turn up. He was captured after a gun battle. His subsequent imprisonment was the beginning of his rise through the rough classrooms of the republican university from where he graduated to a place of immortality in the Pantheon of Irish physical-force republicans.

Following in the wake of the dirty protest, the impact of the Hughes-led hunger strike on nationalist Ireland, particularly north of the border, can be readily imagined. The second wave of hunger strikes of 1981 added greatly to this arousal of intensity. So the reaction to the protracted months of martyrdom which now ensued released extraordinary levels of political energy throughout Ireland, north and south of the border. One manifestation of this was the bloom of black flags on telegraph poles and other vantage points across the country. I remember the comment of an American banker after we met, following a trip he had made to Killarney's scenic beauties. Shaking his head, he said: 'These Sinn Féin guys must have more support than it says in the papers to get all those black flags we saw onto all those telegraph poles.'

In the course of the second hunger strike, through the spring and summer of 1981, tensions rose steadily and excruciatingly. Ten prisoners would die – but, although their deaths took place behind closed doors and barred windows, they certainly did not die in obscurity. The prisoners had gone on strike at staged intervals, and now, as they died at intervals, the levels of publicity rose higher and higher. The British government under Margaret Thatcher, however, refused to bow to the prisoners' demands. After much soul-searching on the part of the Sinn Féin leadership, Sands had been chosen as a candidate in a Westminster by-election for the Fermanagh and South Tyrone constituency. And he won the poll: on 9 April 1981 he was declared elected as a full-fledged member of the House of Commons. His original selection as a candidate had merited one brief paragraph towards the foot of the front page of the *New York Times*. By the time he died sixty-six days later, on 5 May 1981, the television cameras and the journalists of the world had poured into Northern Ireland. As a convicted criminal, however, Sands was disqualified from taking his Westminster seat – and after his death his election agent, Owen Carron, was elected in his stead. The Sinn Féin bandwagon now began to roll.

In the South, meanwhile, H-Block candidates – including a hunger striker, Kieran Doherty – were nominated in that year's general election which saw the return to power of Fine Gael under Garret Fitzgerald, and won a handful of victories. In Northern Ireland, Thatcher's intransigence was a substantial boost to Sinn Féin – and was seen as such even at the time, dismaying the leaders of other parties north and south of the border. In particular, the threat posed by Sinn Féin to the moderate nationalist SDLP was well understood. In an effort to stem the rise of Sinn Féin, Fitzgerald in 1983 convened at Dublin Castle the New Ireland Forum, a grouping consisting of parties in the Republic plus the SDLP, with a view to drawing up a blueprint for a new agreed Ireland. In the North, the unionists scorned its proceedings much as they had done when the first Dáil was established in 1919. All of the parties to the Forum, however, worked diligently to produce three agreed models on which peace might be based. One was Joint Authority, in which both London and Dublin would, as the term suggested, be responsible for the governance of Northern Ireland. The second was a type of federal solution for the island of Ireland; and the third was an all-Ireland unitary state.

The Forum reported in November 1984. Margaret Thatcher responded by holding a press conference in London at which she went through the Forum's three options saying, in each case, 'that is out'. The performance became known as her 'Out, Out, Out' speech – and it damaged the credibility of both the SDLP and the Dublin government to such an extent that Thatcher was persuaded to return to the table. A summit was held in Dublin Castle a year later, and in the historic Anglo-Irish Agreement, signed by Thatcher and Fitzgerald at Hillsborough Castle on 15 November 1985, a modicum of joint authority was conceded. Dublin won the right to be consulted over matters northern; and an Irish secretariat was set up at Maryfield near Belfast. Ulster unionism was livid, but ultimately powerless to alter the course of events.

Off-stage, meanwhile, powerful hidden currents were flowing. Shortly after the Agreement was signed, Father Alec Reid contacted me and suggested that I persuade Charles Haughey – then Fianna Fáil leader – that there was a possibility of a united Ireland, if he would enter into dialogue with the republicans. I did so, and also passed over a document which contained the decidedly appealing suggestion that the armed struggle could be brought to an end and that the IRA would shelve their demand for a British withdrawal – *if* the upshot was a shared government in Northern Ireland in which London had no part.

Haughey, who became Taoiseach for the third time in March 1987, read the document and agreed to meet Reid. But I could never get him to meet Gerry Adams – even though Cardinal Tomás O'Fiaich, the leader of Ireland's Catholics, had promised the ecclesiastical centre at Maynooth as a venue. O'Fiaich had earlier declared himself in favour of a united Ireland in an interview with me in the *Irish Press*. It was an important declaration, in effect aligning the Church for the first time with a united Ireland approach. Maynooth would have been an ideal venue for a secret meeting. It is a huge, sprawling complex with many entrances and exits. Haughey, however, said it would be impossible to meet Adams without the knowledge of the Irish Special Branch. Even at this remove the reason why the Taoiseach was so wary of his own police force has to remain a matter for speculation. But certainly valuable time was lost. It took a further six years of violence before a path towards that objective began to cut through the thickets of bureaucracy, prejudice and history. Haughey did appoint a senior advisor, Martin Mansergh, to liaise with Reid, and there was a secret meeting with republicans in the Redemptorist monastery in Dundalk involving Haughey's ministerial colleague Brian Lenihan – but that was all.

But already, a certain energy had been tapped. Alec Reid formed the first connections between SDLP leader John Hume and Sinn Féin leader Gerry Adams, and now a tentative dialogue began that would gradually and tentatively evolve into a peace process. As news of this dialogue began to leak out, the idea of a conversation with Sinn Féin sent unionist politicians into paroxysms of rage – in which they were joined by Dublin's *Sunday Independent* newspaper, which so criticized John Hume that his health was affected and he almost had a nervous breakdown. He continued, however, with the painstaking persistence that was his trademark; as did Reid and Adams.

Adams is one of the more interesting and important figures to emerge on the Irish political landscape in the twentieth century. Like many of his predecessors, and indeed contemporaries in the Fenian tradition, Adams was hammered out on the anvil of circumstances. Tall, lithe and bearded, Adams' father's and mother's families were significant players in the history of Belfast republicanism over a period of several decades. Adams initially joined the republican movement in the wake of the violence of 1969 – but he first became known to the British and Irish security Establishment when he formed part of the Cheyne Walk delegation (see page 164) in 1972.

Subsequent to the Cheyne Walk talks, Adams was beaten up by the police and imprisoned in the republican compound at Long Kesh. Adams has always denied being a member of the IRA. Inexplicable as this contradictory position appeared to both friend and foe alike, it certainly both made sense and paid dividends at a crucial high point in his career. This was when he successfully fought and won a battle to gain a visa to the United States in January 1994. His opponents, in the absence of any undeniable proof that Adams was in the IRA, failed to label him as a terrorist. And the visit, an overwhelming publicity triumph, had the outcome of convincing the IRA that there was a political alternative to the armed struggle – and so in effect made the peace process possible.

Adams' own conversion to faith in the political process, meanwhile, was formed in the crucible of the H-Block protest and in the successful electoral campaign on behalf of Bobby Sands. Thereafter, under his leadership and that of the formidable Martin McGuinness, the Derry IRA commander who had also taken part in the Cheyne Walk talks, debate within the republican movement began centring on political activity as opposed to violence as a method of achieving the IRA's goal of a united Ireland. This of course exposed Adams to extraordinary dangers: quite apart from the ever-present threat of loyalist and security-force death squads, he had to contend with the fact that some of the most dangerous men in Europe began to regard him as a traitor who would sell out the republican movement and take the hated path of compromise.

As Sinn Féin electoral successes mounted, Adams proved himself to be a master of political analysis and strategy. Internally, he was supported by McGuinness, who was a political, military and diplomatic powerhouse in his own right, and by other republican figures such as Gerry Kelly. Internally also, the Adams machine steamrolled its opponents. One by one the obstacles to political progress informed by traditional republican dogma were overcome. At the 1981 Sinn Féin ard fheis (annual conference), the party's director of publicity, Danny Morrison, routed opponents of the new departure with the celebrated rhetorical question: 'Who here really believes we can win the war through the ballot box? But will anyone here object if, with a ballot paper in one hand and an Armalite in this hand, we take power in Ireland?' The question also encapsulates the reason for the unease that even essentially sympathetic observers felt in the face of this Sinn Féin single-mindedness. For supporters of the Adams bandwagon, however, the path proved inviting and was duly followed. Moreover, the path to peace was smoothed with the help of a fresh ally, in the form of the new incumbent in the Taoiseach's office in Dublin.

Albert Reynolds hailed from Co. Longford. He had made his fortune running dance halls and producing dog food in vast quantities. While a member of the cabinet, as minister of post and telegraphs, he had once appeared on RTÉ dressed like a rhinestone cowboy and crooning 'Put your sweet lips a little closer to the phone'. He was probably the last person in Irish public life whom anyone might have expected to take an interest in Northern Ireland. However, on his first morning as Taoiseach, in February 1992, Reynolds told his officials that his main priority was going to be Northern Ireland, and if that meant that his time in office was going to be of short duration, well, then, so be it. This was not the line that any civil servant in the Republic might have expected to hear from their political master.

As his stunned officials left the room, Reynolds picked up the phone to call an old dance-hall associate, who just happened to be Ian Paisley's right-hand man in the Paisley fiefdom of Ballymena, Co. Antrim. Later, Reynolds told me in detail how the conversation went. He began by informing his friend that he wanted to do something about this 'northern thing': 'if your man wants to deal, I'll deal, but I don't want to waste his time, or have him waste mine'. Reynolds' old contact, surprised – as one can well imagine – at having got this phone call out of the blue, went off to consult 'his man'.

For a week nothing happened – and then a top-level unlisted phone on Reynolds' desk rang. The man from Ballymena began by saying: 'My man won't deal...' Thinking that was the end of the matter, Reynolds interrupted him, saying: 'That's OK. I don't want to waste his time...' with the intention of shrugging his shoulders and moving onto other matters. But the Ballymena man interrupted Reynolds: 'No, no, hear me out! My man says he won't deal – until he gets the top job!' And so there it was. After all the years of bloodshed and turmoil, to which he had contributed so much, Paisley was admitting that his main objective all along had not been 'Ulster' and its Protestant heritage – but power.

Reynolds himself, in his two years and ten months in office, was a key player at this stage of the peace process: after all, if the Taoiseach does not back an initiative on Northern Ireland, there will be no initiative. In my view, indeed, Reynolds was absolutely instrumental in bringing this deal within reach, and he achieved more in a short space of time then all the Irish prime ministers who had preceded him throughout the Troubles. And he was happy to use other contacts at his disposal to further the process or help him with difficult decisions and tense moments. I remember him sending for me one crucial day on which the IRA were holding a meeting in Donegal to decide whether or not to have a ceasefire. He had cancelled all other business and we sat for hours in his office drinking tea and, as he put it, 'trying to call it'. No other government business was done that afternoon. No phones rang. No officials entered the room – except to bring more tea. There was no mistaking either the sincerity of his commitment or his detailed knowledge of who and what was involved. He struck up a genuine personal and political friendship with Jean Kennedy Smith, sister of President John F. Kennedy, who was appointed US Ambassador to Ireland in 1993. I introduced her to Father Reid and she developed a high regard for his insights, piety, shrewdness and contacts, all of which helped to inform her judgements. With the help of her brother, Senator Edward Kennedy, she used her family's unrivalled influence on the White House to bring President Bill Clinton aboard. This led to a key moment in the peace process, the securing of a visa for Gerry Adams to visit America in 1994. This demonstration to rank-and-file IRA members that politics could work was one of the principal ratchets on which the entire process swung. Reynolds also had the benefit of a longstanding friendship with British prime minister John Major: and so an improvement in London–Dublin relationships began to set in. The high point of this relationship was the Downing Street Declaration of 15 December 1993, which declared that, if a majority of the population of Northern Ireland favoured self-determination, London would not stand in the way.

This was a seismic shift – and an undertaking that formed the basis of a peace deal. The IRA declared a ceasefire in 1994: this broke down in 1996 but was renewed in 1997. This was the same year that Tony Blair succeeded Major as prime minister, bringing with him not merely the enthusiasm of ending eighteen years of Conservative rule, but a certain Irish insight in the form of affectionate memories of boyhood holidays in Donegal. In one short year, Blair helped to transform Anglo-Irish relationships, and achieved an extraordinary rapport with Sinn Féin's Gerry Adams and Martin McGuinness to boot.

On occasional Saturday mornings, Adams would set off from his home in Belfast, apparently on constituency business, and McGuinness would do the same from Derry. But in fact the pair would rendezvous at a military airstrip and be flown to London, then driven to the prime ministerial retreat at Chequers where, sequestered for some hours in the Buckinghamshire countryside, the trio would smooth the path to peace. Blair also worked well with the new Irish Taoiseach, Bertie Ahern, whose record in helping to solve Northern Ireland's problems deserves honourable mention, and which certainly vastly outshone his economic performance after he succeeded John Bruton in June 1997.

A deal was finally sealed in the form of the Good Friday Agreement of 10 April 1998. The people of the Republic were pleased to relinquish their state's claim to Northern Ireland in a referendum in the same year; and thereafter, a public sense of disengagement in the woes of Northern Ireland was a palpable element in public opinion in the South. And in Britain too – even in the face of, or perhaps because of, crisis after crisis in the peace process, some of which threatened to derail peace entirely.

There were other developments too: Sinn Féin, as foretold by many, in electoral terms came to eclipse the SDLP, whose Mark Durkan and Seamus Mallon were the principal drafters of the Good Friday Agreement. The Ulster Unionists also declined, overshadowed by Paisley's DUP, which became the dominant unionist party in the years following the peace accord. The SDLP leader John Hume, and his Ulster Unionist equivalent David Trimble, were awarded the Nobel Peace Prize in 1998 – but thereafter Sinn Féin and the DUP would govern Northern Ireland between them. They would govern with tension, and not at all well, but both parties had achieved their dream of power.

And Paisley himself, fifty-odd years after his first firebrand appearance on the political scene, became first minister of Northern Ireland in 2007, governing with Martin McGuinness as his deputy. The pair developed such a good relationship that they became known as 'The Chuckle Brothers', after the television series. It was an extraordinary state of affairs, and one which surely few in Northern Ireland could have foreseen even five years previously. Paisley had capped an extraordinary career – and was lauded for the end results of his political journey, though by no means everyone could forget the damage and destruction that remain an indelible aspect of his legacy. As for the peace process itself: at the time of writing it remains fragile, but intact; and the fact of partition on the island of Ireland is as underscored today as it was almost a century ago.

POBLACHT NA H EIREANN.
THE PROVISIONAL GOVERNMENT
OF THE
IRISH REPUBLIC
TO THE PEOPLE OF IRELAND.

IRISHMEN AND IRISHWOMEN: In the name of God and of the dead generations from which she receives her old tradition of nationhood, Ireland, through us, summons her children to her flag and strikes for her freedom.

Having organised and trained her manhood through her secret revolutionary organisation, the Irish Republican Brotherhood, and through her open military organisations, the Irish Volunteers and the Irish Citizen Army, having patiently perfected her discipline, having resolutely waited for the right moment to reveal itself, she now seizes that moment, and, supported by her exiled children in America and by gallant allies in Europe, but relying in the first on her own strength, she strikes in full confidence of victory.

We declare the right of the people of Ireland to the ownership of Ireland, and to the unfettered control of Irish destinies, to be sovereign and indefeasible. The long usurpation of that right by a foreign people and government has not extinguished the right, nor can it ever be extinguished except by the destruction of the Irish people. In every generation the Irish people have asserted their right to national freedom and sovereignty; six times during the past three hundred years they have asserted it in arms. Standing on that fundamental right and again asserting it in arms in the face of the world, we hereby proclaim the Irish Republic as a Sovereign Independent State, and we pledge our lives and the lives of our comrades-in-arms to the cause of its freedom, of its welfare, and of its exaltation among the nations.

The Irish Republic is entitled to, and hereby claims, the allegiance of every Irishman and Irishwoman. The Republic guarantees religious and civil liberty, equal rights and equal opportunities to all its citizens, and declares its resolve to pursue the happiness and prosperity of the whole nation and of all its parts, cherishing all the children of the nation equally, and oblivious of the differences carefully fostered by an alien government, which have divided a minority from the majority in the past.

Until our arms have brought the opportune moment for the establishment of a permanent National Government, representative of the whole people of Ireland and elected by the suffrages of all her men and women, the Provisional Government, hereby constituted, will administer the civil and military affairs of the Republic in trust for the people.

We place the cause of the Irish Republic under the protection of the Most High God, Whose blessing we invoke upon our arms, and we pray that no one who serves that cause will dishonour it by cowardice, inhumanity, or rapine. In this supreme hour the Irish nation must, by its valour and discipline and by the readiness of its children to sacrifice themselves for the common good, prove itself worthy of the august destiny to which it is called.

Signed on Behalf of the Provisional Government,

THOMAS J. CLARKE.

SEAN Mac DIARMADA.   THOMAS MacDONAGH.

P. H. PEARSE.   EAMONN CEANNT.

JAMES CONNOLLY.   JOSEPH PLUNKETT.

1. The Proclamation of the Republic. Pádraig Pearse's reading of the Proclamation on the steps of the GPO marked the beginning of the 1916 Rising.

2. Thomas J. Clarke

3. Seán Mac Diamarda

4. Pádraig Pearse

5. James Connolly

6. Thomas MacDonagh

7. Eamonn Ceannt

8. Joseph Plunkett

9. Dublin after the Easter Rising: a view of lower Sackville Street across O'Connell Bridge.

10. Éamon de Valera after his arrest, Dublin 1916.

11. Sinn Féin leaders at a meeting of the first Dáil, April 1919. De Valera, the Dáil president, is seated in the centre of the front row, between Arthur Griffith and Count Plunkett. Michael Collins is second from the left, and William T. Cosgrave second from the right.

12. British security forces guard a Dublin street after a shooting on Gloucester Road, 1920.

13. Members of the Irish delegation sign the Anglo-Irish Treaty, December 1921. Seated, left to right, are Arthur Griffith, E. J. Duggan, Michael Collins and Robert Barton; standing behind them are Erskine Childers, George Gavan Duffy and John Chartres.

14. General Michael Collins, now commander of the Free State army, leaves Portobello Barracks, August 1922. By the month's end he would be dead, assassinated by anti-Treaty IRA men.

15. William T. Cosgrave (centre), President of the Executive Council of the Irish Free State, with his cabinet, October 1922. Left to right: Joseph McGrath, Hugh Kennedy, William Thomas Cosgrave, Ernest Blythe, Kevin O'Higgins and J. J. Walsh.

16. Church and state: de Valera, now President of the Executive Council, receives Edward Joseph Byrne, Archbishop of Dublin, during a garden party at Viceregal Lodge (now Áras an Uachtaráin), Phoenix Park, Dublin, 1933.

17. Alex Spain, master of Dublin's National Maternity Hospital and champion of the surgical procedure known as symphysiotomy.

18. Dublin mothers chatting outside a tenement building, *c.* 1945.

19. After mass: churchgoers in rural Ireland, 1943.

20. Dr Noël Browne, minister of health (1948–51). His ill-fated 'Mother and Child scheme' was bitterly opposed by the Catholic hierarchy, which saw it as interfering with traditional Irish family life.

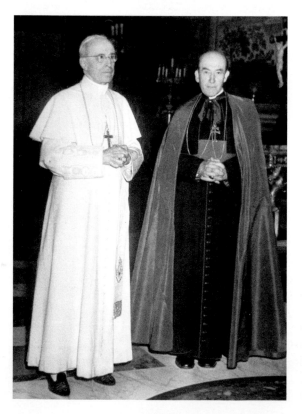

21. The old order: John Charles McQuaid – archbishop of Dublin and Primate of Ireland from 1940 to 1973 – with Pope Pius XII, Castel Gandolfo, 1957.

22. Seán Lemass and Jack Lynch, respectively Taoiseach and finance minister, at 10 Downing Street for talks with the British prime minister Harold Wilson, July 1965. Lynch would succeed Lemass as Taoiseach the following year.

23. Unionist intransigence made flesh: loyalist politician and Protestant evangelical minister Ian Richard Kyle Paisley leads a demonstration in London, 1967.

24. British troops – deployed on the streets of Northern Ireland from August 1969 in the wake of vicious sectarian rioting in Derry and Belfast – arrest a young demonstrator.

25. Derry, 30 January 1972: a British soldier attacks a protestor on 'Bloody Sunday', when British paratroopers shot dead thirteen unarmed civilians during a civil rights march.

26. Charles Haughey and Neil Blaney during the Arms Trial, October 1970.

27. Austin Currie and John Hume, Northern Ireland civil rights leaders and founders of the nationalist SDLP, 1971.

28. Republican martyr: Bobby Sands, leader of the 1981 IRA hunger strike in the Maze Prison (formerly Long Kesh), died on 5 May 1981 after sixty-six days without food.

29. An IRA honour guard fires a volley over the coffin of Bobby Sands, Milltown cemetery, Belfast, 7 May 1981. Gerry Adams looks on. More than 100,000 people lined the route of Sands' funeral cortège.

30. A fire in the early hours of 14 February 1981 at the Stardust nightclub in the north Dublin suburb of Artane killed 48 people and injured 214.

31. Father Alec Reid gives the last rites to Corporal David Howes, who, along with his colleague Corporal Derek Wood, was killed by republicans after the two British soldiers drove their car into the funeral procession of an IRA member; West Belfast, 19 May 1988.

32. Prime Minister John Major with Taoiseach Albert Reynolds, September 1992. Their joint 'Downing Street declaration' of December 1993 would be a key staging-post in the peace process.

33. President Mary Robinson, June 2005.

34. Former Irish premier Bertie Ahern attends a session of the European parliament in Brussels, November 2006.

35. Eamon Casey, the disgraced former bishop of Galway, 1994.

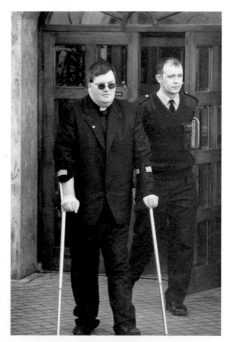

36. Father Seán Fortune leaves court in County Wexford, 1999. He killed himself later that year, while awaiting trial on charges of child molestation.

37. Supporters of same sex-marriage await the result of the referendum in Dublin, May 2015.

38. Taoiseach Brian Cowen and Finance Minister Brian Lenihan at a news conference in Dublin after announcing the EU bailout plan, November 2010.

39. Enda Kenny campaigning for Fine Gael, May 2007.

9

Disillusionment

I N 1966, I PUBLISHED *IRELAND SINCE THE RISING*, A HISTORY of Ireland in the fifty years between 1916 and 1966. The book was suffused with optimism. It was influenced by the promise of what I termed the 'watershed years': the emergence of a new generation of Irish decision-takers with preoccupations and horizons wider than those influenced by the Civil War and clerical domination. They had their eye on the wider world, and had been stimulated by the effects of the Second Vatican Council, the coming of television to Ireland and by far greater state expenditure on and control of what had hitherto been largely the church's fiefdom – education.

Fast-forward twenty years, to 1986, I wrote another book, the stark lack of optimism of which could be summarized by its title, *Disillusioned Decades*. In the present work, as readers will see, I chronicle what can validly be termed the age of scandal and betrayal. What went wrong? Many complex factors can be advanced to explain the problems that befell Ireland during this period. But an accurate and a valid answer may be encapsulated readily enough: a great deal of Ireland's problems may be measured by the extent to which society's leaders departed from the ideals of 1916 and the integrity of those who framed the Proclamation. And this departure can, as we will see, be detected and measured in many aspects of subsequent Irish history: in the ways in which Irish children were used and abused, instead of being cherished equally, as the words of the Proclamation have it; in the attitude of society towards women's rights and freedoms; in our general attitude to the social health and well-being that is necessary in the life of a nation, though all too frequently lacking in Ireland. In other words, what should have been part of the horizon-widening experience of the watershed years, including preparation for and subsequent entry into the EEC, in fact proved to be a factor in a sharp turn away from idealism. This chapter will explore some of the tragic results of this turn. It will look through the prism of, and attempt to explain something of the historical context of, the Irish relationship with what has traditionally been a central pillar of this country's distinctive culture – the Catholic Church.

*

The three monotheistic global religions – Christianity, Islam, Judaism – all use sex as an adjunct to religious power. In the jurisdictions in which they wield power and influence, this concern with matters sexual often manifests itself in an outward appearance of piety, accompanied by inward hypocrisy and cruel and unnatural forms of sexual subjugation. In a specifically Irish context, this can be seen in myriad ways. Take, for example, the fetid Irish Catholic impulse to control Irish female sexuality, which has certainly accounted for some of the nation's bitterest controversies since 1916, and in more general terms for much of the sexual guilt that has permeated Irish society.

Guilt and sex were, for example, conjoined in the infamous custom of 'churching', which was once widespread amongst

Irish women who had had children. Before receiving Holy Communion, women who had recently given birth had to be purified of the stain of sexuality associated with childbirth. Churching was ubiquitous until the 1960s in Ireland; after this point, the influence of Vatican II caused it to fall largely, though not wholly, out of use. Church teaching on contraception and abortion, meanwhile, was – and to a degree, one could argue, still is – responsible for a set of outcomes which were as cruel as they were hypocritical. Catholic teaching forbade the use of artificial forms of contraception, and the general scarcity and unavailability of contraceptives in Ireland until the 1970s was directly responsible for a diverse range of social scandals.

The most obvious and notorious of such scandals, as we will see, is the officially unacknowledged, but nevertheless continuing, passage to Britain of pregnant Irish women in order to terminate unwanted pregnancies. In cases where termination did not occur, meanwhile, poorer women were often faced with being forced into one of the dense network of so-called 'Magdalene laundries': institutions where 'fallen' or otherwise socially rejected women worked, sometimes for years, under the aegis of Ireland's religious orders, the twin objectives being to remove them from the view of society and to use them as a means of turning an economic profit for the orders concerned. Frequently, too, they were simply driven out of the district or country altogether by their families; and in both scenarios, they were forced by socio-religious pressure to give up their babies for adoption. To this day, the Irish landscape contains mass graves: the final resting place of the mothers and babies 'cared for' in such institutions. Many such mass graves are only now being excavated; others remain unexcavated, and their stories untold. We will examine this phenomenon, and that of the Magdalene laundries, in more detail later. Nor were these evils untypical aberrations attributable to the 'few bad apples' syndrome. On the contrary: these were the direct outcome of policies consciously and deliberately followed by both Church and state, which led parents to deliver their children into the hands of unfeeling institutions, rather than helping them to keep and rear their babies.

We have already traced the course of the infamous Mother and Child débâcle of 1949–50. In hindsight it seems almost comical that such an episode could even have taken place, especially given the fact that a subsequent Fianna Fáil government quietly introduced essentially identical measures shortly afterwards. Yet there is nothing at all amusing about the fact that, in a very real sense, this miserable episode was still bringing its malign influence to bear on the lives of hundreds of Irish women years later. I refer, of course, to the symphysiotomy scandal, the impact of which has still not been fully addressed by the Irish state. Symphysiotomy is a medical procedure which involves the widening by means of surgery of a woman's pelvic ligaments: it was introduced at Dublin's National Maternity Hospital by that institution's master, Alex Spain, in 1944, and deployed in Catholic-controlled maternity hospitals in Ireland in the forty years between 1944 and 1984 as a substitute for Caesarean sections. In the Dáil in 2001, the following description was read into the official records:

The operation – and the details are not for the squeamish – involved sawing through the woman's pelvis so that it opened like a hinge. International medical experts repeatedly criticised this practice. They stated that Caesarean section should have been the preferred option for difficult pregnancies. Some Irish doctors persisted with symphysiotomy, because they apparently believed that women who underwent Caesarean section would use contraception to

avoid pregnancy. The use of contraception, of course, con-
flicted with the prevailing Catholic ethos.

To place this comment in the correct context: the medical consensus at the time was that having more than three Caesarean
sections was dangerous. Further pregnancies, therefore, would
have to be prevented by sterilization or contraception, both of
which ran counter to the Catholic ethos. For the most part, Irish
patients were operated on without consent. The consequences of
a symphysiotomy operation include – but are not limited to – difficulties in walking, incontinence and long-term physical pain; to
say nothing of the mental and emotional repercussions that can
flow from the procedure. Defenders of the practice contended that
this barbaric operation was preferable to carrying out Caesarean
sections. However, the real motivation for the practice would
indeed appear to have been religious, and the consequences for
hundreds of patients were shattering. Whether the main church
protagonist in the Mother and Child controversy, Archbishop
John Charles McQuaid, was also the main mover in the introduction of the symphysiotomy operation to Ireland cannot be said
with certainty at this stage. But he assuredly was fully aware of
the practice which was spelled out for him by Spain, who was
a friend of his from his Blackrock College days. At the time of
writing many of the 1500 Irish women who survived the procedure are still struggling to win compensation from the state.

I would like to bring a personal reflection to bear now, on these
subjects of Ireland, sex and the Catholic Church. One aspect of
Church teaching which has always struck me as particularly out-
rageous is the high level of hypocrisy it inculcates in Irish life. As
a young man on one of my first visits to the Aran Islands in 1959,
I became friendly with an Inis More family, the mother of which
had become pregnant by a man who was not her husband. Long,

lonely months – while the husband was away from the island in a mental home, and with a lodger in the house – had produced a near-inevitable result. This was the island of 1959, where gossip, claustrophobia and a culture of surveillance were ubiquitous – and the woman's pregnancy led to a withdrawal of friendships, such that the woman gave up going to Mass on a Sunday. This was rare behaviour indeed for an Irish Catholic mother in those days.

On the morning of the child's birth, as the woman lay recovering in bed, the parish priest, a Father Varley, visited the house to stand over her and inform her that she was in mortal sin. What Varley did not realize, however, was that this culture of surveillance was absolute in its effects. An islander called at the presbytery to speak with the parish priest – and the result of the visit is best described in the island vernacular:

> ...called to the priest's house on business, but he got no answer, but bedad, all he got was the priest's arse going up and down. When he looked in the window, the priest was on the job with the nurse.

The incident occurred many years ago. All the participants in this sad drama are dead. Readers cannot be expected to know, without explanation, that the real point of that story is not the priest's hypocrisy, not the contrast between the way he judged the woman's sexual needs and the manner in which he satisfied his own. No: the real significance lies in the fact that, such was the awe with which the Church was regarded at this time, very little was ever said about the *in flagrante* moment. In over half a century of visiting the island, I never heard it discussed in a pub. It was instead a subject for mention around the fireside in low tones after the children were in bed.

The priest in due course got a rousing send-off from the

islanders when he left for another parish. He left Kilronan pier to the accompaniment of a fusillade of rockets from the encircling lifeboat, of which, like everything else on the island, he had been in charge. I happened to be on the boat, standing beside an American lady who remarked to the priest as the flags fluttered and the currachs rowed around us: 'You must be very proud, Father. They all love you so much; you must have done great work!' In a sense, the island was a microcosm of what Ireland was like in 1959. It demonstrated the attitude of society as a whole to the clergy – God's anointed as they would have been generally thought of – at this time, and in subsequent decades. This omertà theme is one to which we will return.

For the moment, however, let it be noted that the root circumstance in maintaining this strange, insulated Celtic bubble of Catholicity was education. The Church held the nation's schools in a vice-like grip. In 1961 – as if by way of marking the tenth anniversary of the Mother and Child scheme controversy which had so spectacularly underlined the Church's determination, and to ensure that Catholic doctrine would continue to control Irish attitudes to birth, life and death – Archbishop McQuaid issued a pastoral letter containing the following:

> Catholic pupils are not to frequent non-Catholic schools or schools that are open also to non-Catholics. Only the Ordinary of the place where the school is situated is competent to determine according to the instructions of the Apostolic See, in what circumstances it may be tolerated for Catholics to attend such schools and what safeguards are to be prescribed against the danger of perversion.

McQuaid's 'perversion' referred to the danger of coming into contact with Protestants. But while the policy he outlined

underlines the fact that the Church retained control of education, it also highlights the extraordinary irony implicit in this
situation. For, despite the sacrifices of the nuns, brothers and
priests who provided education in the Republic, the sector was
in poor shape. Certainly it could not be compared to the state
of education in Northern Ireland at the same time: here, with a
population around a third of that in the Republic, British government funding meant that there were in excess of *ten thousand*
more pupils in secondary education than there were in the South.

By the mid-1960s, it was clear that this situation was in dire
need of rectification. Now, the new generation inside Fianna
Fáil, which by then had replaced de Valera's palsied hands on the
levers of power, began the increased investment that revitalized
the Irish educational system. This investment, along with outside
influences like the arrival of television in 1961 and joining the
EEC in 1973, would ultimately bring about the diminution of
the clergy's role in education and in Irish life generally.

In contemporary Ireland, commentators are suggesting that
the fall in Church vocations is so extreme that there may be no
Irish ordinations at all in ten years' time. To understand the
extraordinary magnitude of this trend, it should be pointed
out that at the time of McQuaid's pastoral, there were 11,000
priests and nuns at work in Ireland and a total of 10,885 Irish-
born nuns, priests and lay workers at work in the mission
fields. And, as the fiftieth anniversary of 1916 was being com-
memorated, some one thousand lay missionaries left Ireland to
join the nuns and priests working abroad.

*

I write this in the approach to the centenary of the Easter Rising,
at a time when condoms are available in the lavatories of most

Dublin pubs. However, as late as 1973, the power of the clergy was such that Irish politicians feared to bring in legislation permitting contraception until the matter was addressed by the courts in the McGee v. Attorney General and Revenue Commissioners case. The Supreme Court ruled in December of that year that married couples had the right to make decisions in private about the size of their family. Mary McGee had challenged the right of the state to seize some spermicidal products that had been sent to her. The twenty-seven-year-old mother argued in court that further pregnancies would endanger her life. Although McGee won her case, the episode marked a beginning and not an end to the obstacles to contraception in Ireland. For years, such products could not be advertised or sold openly; and, as we have seen, Charles Haughey dealt with the question by tabling what he called an 'Irish solution to an Irish problem' in the matter of contraception: his Family Planning Bill of 1979 legalized the use of the pill – but only with a prescription, and accompanied by the fiction that the product was being used not for contraceptive purposes, but for regulation of the menstrual cycle only.

Around the time of the fiftieth anniversary of the Rising, I interviewed a number of Irish bishops on topics such as birth control. It was an exercise nobody else in journalism had undertaken at the time; and I could have paid for it with my career with the *Evening Press*. The Irish cardinal of the period, William Conway, wrote to me taking grave exception to my questionnaire, and told the six-monthly meeting of the hierarchy at Maynooth that year that they should be on their guard against a 'flagrantly anti-Catholic book' now being prepared by a journalist called Timothy Patrick Coogan. By chance, his letter arrived on the day that I interviewed the prime minister of Northern Ireland, Terence O'Neill. I found Conway's letter lying on the kitchen table when I got home late that night, and its effect was to seriously interfere with my sleep. But I wrote back to the cardinal telling him that I had issued a similar questionnaire to the horned Protestant prime minister of 'Ulster', but at least he had agreed to see me.

The interviews I did manage to secure with some members of the hierarchy are a valuable periscope into the thinking of those who shaped Irish opinion fifty years after the Rising. One was with Bishop Michael Browne of Galway, the very model of the crozier-swinging, commentating Irish bishop. He was known as 'Cross Michael', allegedly because he wore a particularly large pectoral cross, but there were other reasons also. Like many a cleric of his day, the co-relationship between sin and sex was a major preoccupation with him. I've known him to accost a girl in her early teens on the seafront at Galway and tell her that it was wrong of her to be wearing shorts. On the main swimming area on the front at Salthill, meanwhile, he caused a 'Men Only' sign to be erected, enabling him to both swim and sunbathe naked. When I asked him about birth control he replied: 'Women get interested in this stuff from the papers. Most of it is written in America and they think it's great. Of course, an awful lot of women are going out to work to pay for the telly and that sort of thing, and this makes some of them want small families.'

Browne made it clear that his opposition to the Mother and Child scheme had been based on Catholic teachings on birth control. He said that his stand was based on a patient's right to choose a doctor. The idea that a non-Catholic doctor might be placed in charge of Catholics was abhorrent to him. In maternity cases this might have led to an infringement of Catholic teaching. Such would have been the attitude of Catholic bishops in many parts of the world at the time. The difference in Ireland, however, was that this was the law of the land and continued to be so for many years.

But Browne wasn't satisfied with the law of the land. Much wants more, and – like many of his contemporaries – he believed that Catholic teaching came before the legislation of the state. Despite the exalted position of the Church in Ireland, he railed against what he saw as the 'disabilities' under which it laboured:

> The law of the Catholic Church in this country is that cleric may not sue cleric, and neither cleric nor layman may sue a bishop before the civil court. That rule is admitted by most lawyers to be lawful, and in accordance with public policy, as tending to prevent scandals. But it is not allowed to oust the jurisdiction of the court and no matter how flagrantly the rule be violated, the court will hear and decide any case brought before it.[14]

The bishop was consciously arguing for canon law to prevail in Ireland – just as some Muslim clerics seek to impose sharia law today. This attitude, as we will see, lay behind the Vatican's approach to clerical sex abuse in Ireland, which resulted in the historic clash behind Church and state half a century later.

Unconsciously, Browne – a large, imposing man whom many found overbearing – betrayed a factor in his own formation: that of privilege. Most Irish priests, and hence bishops, came from the better-off classes. Browne's overall judgement on the Mother and Child scheme was that it was a tragedy – though for his own distinctive reasons: 'A young man like [Noël] Browne, with an *ordinary* degree, becoming a minister!' (Noël Browne had come from a poor background and owed his education to a philanthropic Irish medical family, the Chances.)

Another bishop with whom I spoke, Cornelius Lucey of Cork and Ross, known for his outspoken commentaries on anything that caught his attention, had a more kindly slant on birth control but was still fundamentally opposed to it. He said:

> Do you think that people who have had too many children through irresponsibility are going to be more responsible in their use of contraceptives? The Church isn't opposed to control. It's the means which are used she is concerned with. Anyone who wants contraceptives in this country can get them if they want them. There will always be some people who want to avoid having children. But no one wants to give away a child when it arrives. The Whites say the Blacks have too many children, the rich say the families of the poor are too big, and so on.

The bishops were content with what a French diplomat – Paul Blanchard, who had spent time in Dublin – referred to as *le catholicisme du type irlandais*, which was basically the product of insularity, and which the bishops hoped and assumed would never alter. But even as I was posing these questions, the second Vatican Council was in full swing, and Lucey's answers on this topic revealed an attitude that was to cost the Church dearly. They were founded on a belief that no matter what happened outside Ireland, change or materialism would not affect the faith of the Irish people. Bishop Browne of Galway expressed his point of view as follows:

> Young people say these things, but they don't have a clear view of their country's history. The same sort of thing was said in the days of the Veto, the Fenian crisis and after the fall of Parnell. It was a commonly held belief that after independence Ireland would no longer be Catholic.

When I asked him what he made of the charge that there was a strong vein of superstition and unthinking acceptance in Irish religious practice as compared with, say, continental Catholics, he replied:

> You know the story of the Frenchman who was asked if he was a Catholic? *Are you a Catholic? But yes! Do you eat meat on Friday? Certainly. Do you go to Mass every Sunday? Non: je ne suis pas fanatique!* That was the kind of thing you get over there. The French and Italians have problems we simply don't have here. It comes to this. Which is more important: a Church with a thousand peasants attending Mass, or one professor? They sneer at us for attendance at Mass. But what are we to do? Give these things up?

Browne was certainly assiduous in following the prescriptions of the Irish hierarchy. When Dr Robert Corbett, Master of the Coombe Hospital in Dublin, was appointed in 1942 as professor of gynaecology at University College Galway (UCG), Browne objected on the grounds that Corbert had attended Trinity College Dublin. At the time, the Irish hierarchy still regarded it as a mortal sin for Catholics to attend Trinity without permission. Apart from being a distinguished obstetrician, Corbett was also a Catholic, but the controversy dismayed him and he left both his post at UCG and the country.

A few years later, in 1947, Bishop Browne played a part in another controversy which, although ludicrous on the face of it, nevertheless had a bearing both on why Northern Protestants looked askance at the South and on why so many Anglo-Irish Protestants of the 'Big House' type left the country after independence. The 'Blazers' affair, as it was known, originated in an instruction by Bishop Joseph Walsh of Tuam that Catholics should not associate with divorced persons. As it turned out, this direction was interpreted in extremely broad terms, most notably by Catholic landowners in Co. Galway, who forbade the Blazers Hunt – one of the most famous in the country – from hunting across their lands, on the grounds that the Assistant Master of Hounds was a divorced Protestant lady who had remarried. Browne was one of the most vociferous of the gaggle of western bishops who supported the ban on the Blazers. He dispute was punctuated by sonorous statements on divorce by their lordships, read from pulpit and printed in newspapers. The lady in question resigned as Assistant Master – and, to paraphrase Oscar Wilde, the untouchables ceased their pursuit of the unspeakable. The foxes of Galway were, presumably, greatly relieved at not having a divorcee directing their pursuit.

The attitude towards Vatican II of some members of the Irish hierarchy of the time is worthy of mention. Bishop Cornelius Lucey took the view that the Second Vatican Council was not particularly relevant to Ireland: after all, the Irish were happy enough with things as they were: living their lives, that is, under the thumb of the bishops. Lucey said:

> The Council is all right for a week or so, but it doesn't seem so interesting when you are watching it. A lot of problems they discuss are of no interest to us. The Jews, religious liberty, we already have it here. The only time there's any trouble, the Jehovah's Witnesses cause it. Our people don't want them.

By way of illustrating the bishop's take on the meaning of 'religious liberty', and its reference to Jehovah's Witnesses, it should be borne in mind that at the time there were occasional incidents in rural districts in which local people, often incited by the clergy, spoke harshly to Jehovah's Witnesses and turned them away peremptorily. At one stage, in fact, anti-Jehovah's Witness feeling reached potentially dangerous level of intensity. In 1956, at Clonlara, in Co. Clare, a group of Jehovah's Witnesses were attacked as they distributed leaflets and the episode fetched up in court. It transpired that a local curate, Father Patrick Ryan, had led some of his flock in an attack on two Jehovah's Witnesses. Apart from being punched and roughed up, the victims saw one of their Bibles being driven down the street with a hurling stick.

The case ended in remarkable fashion. Father Ryan and the other assailants were found guilty of assault, but were placed on probation. The two Jehovah's Witnesses, however, were bound to the peace: and District Justice Gordon Hurley ordered that they both produce personal sureties of IR£100 each, and secure independent sureties of the same amount. The District Justice's extraordinary verdict had less to do with any notion of law or justice than the fact that the bishop of the diocese, Joseph Rodgers of Killaloe, sat grimly in the court.

One would have imagined that the court's finding would have pleased the bishop – but not so. He wrote to John A. Costello, the Taoiseach of the day and himself a distinguished lawyer, complaining that:

> I find it hard to credit that the Attorney General, had he been fully aware of the pernicious and blasphemous literature distributed and sold in my diocese by these self-styled Jehovah's Witnesses, would have proceeded against one of my priests for upholding and defending the fundamental truths of our treasured Catholic faith. Your Attorney General prosecutes one of my priests for doing what I, and

all good Catholics here, regard as his bound-in duty and right. The matter cannot rest.

In his reply the Taoiseach wasted no time in discussing such concepts as freedom of expression or equality before the law, but said that he 'fully appreciated the just indication aroused among the clergy and the people by the activities of the Jehovah's Witnesses'.

The Clonlara episode did not exactly betoken the type of Republic which the framers of the 1916 Proclamation had had in mind. But the mindset of Rodgers, and indeed of Browne, was seen in operation shortly afterwards. The scene was the Wexford village of Fethard-on-Sea, and the year was 1957. If the Clare incident had attracted national attention, Fethard-on-Sea drew international coverage. And there was a cross-border dimension too, for Ian Paisley and his barrister friend Desmond Boal had a hand in proceedings, with Paisley quite validly exploiting what he saw as a typical example of anti-Protestant feeling in the Republic.

The case arose out of the Church's *Ne Temere* decree, which directed that in a mixed marriage the children must be brought up as Catholics. In the Fethard controversy, a Protestant mother, Sheila Cloney, had agreed to having her first two children baptized Catholics. When she decided to enrol them in the local Protestant school, however, trouble broke out. The local priest, William Stafford, called at her home to tell her that her children would have to enrol in a Catholic school. Cloney refused, and the situation escalated to a point where a boycott of local Protestant traders and farmers was organized by Stafford. Eventually Cloney left her husband Sean and went to Belfast, where she came into contact with Paisley.

The boycott caused a great deal of ill feeling, and devastated local Protestant-owned businesses. Bishop Browne was among the prominent people who supported the boycott: he preached a sermon in Wexford saying that if Protestants could use the weapon of discrimination against Catholics in the North, then southern Catholics were entitled to use the boycott weapon. The affair drew attention not simply in Ireland, however, but also worldwide: *Time* magazine, for example, coined the word 'Fethardism' to describe religious boycotting.

Taoiseach Éamon de Valera condemned the boycott, though he also urged Sheila Cloney to 'honour her marriage vows'. At length, Sean Cloney traced his wife to Orkney where they were reconciled: they returned home, the boycott ended – and the Cloney children were taught at home. Yet, had the local parish priest not intervened in the first place, the Fethard scandal could have been a situation where an Irish solution was found to an Irish problem. It was quite common (though not spoken of) for the *Ne Temere* decree to be got around in a variety of ways – including the children being raised, as they arrived, alternately as a Protestant, then a Catholic and so on.

Indeed, an Irish solution *was* eventually found to the Fethard-on-Sea boycott. Without any fanfare, a local priest went into a Protestant-owned shop and bought a packet of cigarettes, and from then on the boycott crumbled. It is said that one of the hidden forces involved in finding a solution to the affair was Archbishop McQuaid of Dublin: he had a good track record in mediating in disputes of a secular nature, for example helping to resolve trouble between Haughey and the Gardaí, and between de Valera and the teachers' unions. That said, it remains the case that he was generally regarded, with justice, as being strongly of the old school, anti-Protestant variety of bishop.

*

In their interviews with me in 1966, the Irish bishops did display a social conscience. They argued, for instance, that the wages of agricultural workers were insufficient to provide a decent livelihood, and that the government should subsidize them. Cornelius Lucey in particular went on to distinguish himself by his work in the developing world, particularly in Latin America. During the 1970s, he took what must have been a painful decision for him. As the Ordinary of the Diocese, Lucey disciplined his friend Father James Good for his opposition to the papal encyclical on birth control, *Humanae Vitae*. But two years later, when he retired with only two years left to live, he joined Good as a missionary in one of the harshest regions of the world, the Turkana desert in the north of Kenya.

In general terms, however, the bishops' interviews reflect the self-satisfied attitude of the Irish Church leadership of the time. There is no reason to label them as essentially unkind men – yet they were certainly either immune to, or unaware of, many of the problems that lay around them in Ireland. Their Church ran the institutions, the hospitals, schools and rest homes, without which misery, starvation and death would have been the lot of many. Yet there was a blindness in their approach, insofar as the problems of day-to-day living outside the high institutional walls was concerned, and a disregard of the consequences that flowed from inadequate social legislation, from poverty and from Catholic teachings on contraception and family planning.

Bishop Peter Birch of Ossory was the exception to the approach of the Church leadership of the period. Birch – like my father, a Kilkenny man – looked at the problems of Irish life, and did not like what he saw. He regretted the absence of a Communist party in Ireland which might have forced society to tackle the gaps in its social legislation; and he was prepared to speak out openly on taboo issues such as the sexual problems of people suffering from mental illness. The sort of initiatives he sponsored in his diocese indicated his awareness of the widespread social failings of the time. The world now knows that many of the Church-run institutions – the Magdalene laundries, for example – were hell holes: but this was not common knowledge at the time, and Birch's work in trying to remedy and alleviate the situation in such places was rare in the Ireland of the day. He was one of the few people in Ireland who tried to do something about a system that sealed its victims away from real life.

In Church-run orphanages, many children, reared as they were in dormitory, classroom and refectory, never saw an adult in a conventional domestic context. Birch ensured that kids were taken to homes where they could see how a cake was made, where an egg came from, where there were pictures on the wall. He utilized the voluntary organisations such as St Vincent de Paul to do something to combat malnutrition by teaching women how to cook. Local structures and powerful social mores militated against such efforts. I remember him telling me of a not untypical difficulty he encountered in trying to improve peoples' lives. It was a case involving a husband, who drank, and his wife, who was struggling to cope with a large family. Birch managed to get the husband off the drink and the woman into cookery class before he departed to attend the Vatican Council. When he returned months later, however, the woman was pregnant again and the man was back on the drink. Yet Birch did have a hand in some spectacular success stories. One of the personalities to emerge from his Kilkenny Social Services project was Sister Stanislaus, a member of the Sisters of Charity Congregation, who became one of the best-loved people in Ireland through the organization which she founded (now known as Focus Ireland) to help the homeless.

My episcopal interviews took place against the backdrop of the Second Vatican Council, which for a time appeared to contain the possibility of transforming the entire country. But it was not to be. Pope John XXIII was revered in Ireland: yet change, like peace, came dropping slow and yielded little more than churches that were different in shape and size to those formerly built; a good deal of theological debate between liberals and conservatives; and a spate of letters to the *Irish Times* about contraception. Dr John Charles McQuaid wrote his particular *finis* to the era by an announcement, on his return from Rome, that Vatican II was not going to cause changes to the lives of the faithful.[15]

Nor in a real sense did it. There was a superficial focus on ecumenism which did help to improve relations between Catholics and Protestants in the Republic. The rite of the Mass itself was modernized: now it was said in English rather than Latin, with the celebrant facing towards the congregation instead of facing away. But there was no movement on substantive issues such as that of women priests, married priests, contraception, divorce or abortion – and this attitude has remained consistent up to the present day. Old attitudes died hard and during McQuaid's reign at least, the ban on Catholics attending Trinity College Dublin under pain of mortal sin remained in place. McQuaid's influence ensured that this was carried to ludicrous lengths. The one area where Catholic and Protestant students shared university facilities was in the Veterinary College at Ballsbridge. But as the teaching of biology has a moral basis – at least in McQuaid's eyes – some attempts were made at keeping Protestant and Catholic teaching separate. Hence students at the college became acquainted with such unusual creatures as the Protestant horse and the Catholic horse, the Protestant cow and the Catholic cow. Legend has it that the piety of the Catholic pigs surpassed all.

The present weakness of the Irish Church comes in part from a modernizing world with which that Church has declined to keep up – and yet most of its wounds are self-inflicted and stem from a generally rigid cast of mind, one that is consistently resistant to change. Some of this, at any rate, has its roots in the deep past. One of the theories concerning the Irish version of Catholicism is that it can be traced to the foundation of Maynooth in 1795. Some of its earliest professors were French, revolution having caused them to be expelled from France. These men are blamed for infecting Maynooth's culture of teaching with Jansenism. Cornelius Jansen was the bishop of Ypres in the early seventeenth century. Jansen emphasized the doctrines of original sin, predestination and the necessity of divine grace, and some of his writings tended to generate a censorious, holier-than-thou attitude amongst his followers. To this might be added the dangerous certainty of the Jansenistic professors that they had a special insight into, and a special devotion to, the workings of God's mind.

Certain of the Irish Church's particular characteristics have been attributed to the doctrine known as Gallicanism. Gallicanism originated in seventeenth-century France, and it posited that the local state was entitled to as much authority as Rome itself over the local Church. It is certainly the case that the Irish Church had a very distinctive character from the seventeenth century through to the early part of the nineteenth century. It had a well-deserved patina of martyrdom, rooted in the image of the hunted priest, risking, and sometimes losing his life during the era of the penal laws for remaining with his parishioners. By the time Maynooth was inaugurated, therefore, the Irish Church was displaying a degree of divergence of opinion from Rome that the papacy could not and would not tolerate.

In the mid-nineteenth century, as the Famine was ending, Rome sent one of the Church's most effective administrators, Cardinal Paul Cullen, to Ireland with a mission to stamp out Gallicanism and Irish particularism, and to introduce instead a rigorous culture of ultramontanism and of obedience to Rome. The selflessness of the Irish clergy and nuns who did what they could to bring aid and comfort to their people during the Famine is widely known and appreciated. What is not so widely known, and certainly would not be widely appreciated, is the fact that at the height of the Famine, the Vatican ordered the Irish hierarchy to hold a collection to assist the pope, who at the time had been driven out of the Vatican by the French. This order was followed and as thousands of pounds flowed into Ireland, having been collected amongst Irish emigrants abroad, chiefly in America, very large sums also flowed out from the starving isle to help the pope.

Cullen was able to utilize to his own ends the extraordinary respect which the Irish held for their priests – the only sympathetic authority figures they encountered in their often wretched lives. The result was complete success for Cullen's mission – which was to carry through what the great Irish-American historian, Emmet Larkin, has termed a 'devotional revolution', in which traditional Irish religious customs were downplayed in favour of Roman ones.

It was not a straightforward task. In the wake of the Famine, Cullen was presiding over a prostrate people, suspicious of French or Italian republican influences; and he himself was a doughty and effective fighter in the battle with the Anglican establishment for control of Irish education. The latter wanted to introduce Bible reading to Irish classrooms so as to create an independence of thought amongst Catholics that would inevitably help to weaken the power of popery. Cullen, more than anyone else, saw to it that this aim was not achieved.

However, be it through Jansenism, Gallicanism, ultramontanism or simple insularity and lack of competition, the church of Cullen and his like ultimately wove a rope to hang itself – even if this would take a very long time to become manifest. Invoking the traditions of the past in its efforts to deal with threats to its authority from sources as diverse – as time went on – as the spread of education and television, the Church's spokespersons conjured a series of evils and temptations. They set forth the evils of immorality, which was always sexual immorality – contraception, divorce and so on – and, all the while, as a shocked public would later discover, many of these same thunderers were buggering little boys, keeping mistresses and, where money was concerned, keeping anything they could lay their hands on, even as they set themselves up as moral arbiters.

In the modern era, the fall from grace of one particular bishop has come to epitomize the general decline of the Irish Church. In 1976, Eamon Casey was bishop of Kerry when word came through that he had been chosen to succeed Michael Browne in the diocese of Galway. Casey's replacement of Browne seemed to indicate a profound psychological, stylistic and theological change in the Irish Church. Like Haughey, who became Taoiseach three years later, Casey was hailed as a modernizer. Both men were seen as the harbingers of a new era – as indeed they were, if not quite in the manner that people might have anticipated.

I attended Casey's consecration as a bishop in Kerry in 1969. During the ceremony, a Maynooth professor remarked to me: '[Casey]'s not a theologian, he's a tycoon'. This was a not unfair description. Dressed in business attire, Casey would have appeared the epitome of a smooth CEO with a zest for life. Yet he also had a feeling for the poor. While he was serving for a period as a young curate in England, he set up a housing trust that enabled indigent Irish emigrants to buy their own homes. His interests extended further still overseas: he helped support Trócaire, the Irish Catholic aid charity; and, after witnessing the assassination in 1980 of Archbishop Óscar Romero in the cathedral at San Salvador, he reacted angrily, lobbying the UN and the White House and, when President Reagan came to Ireland in 1984, joining in protests against the visit because of American foreign policy.

His larger-than-life personality appealed to the Irish. He wrote off BMWs with gay abandon and was the subject of a not unkindly joke: 'What's the difference between God and Eamon Casey?' Answer: 'God is everywhere, including Galway. Casey is everywhere *except* Galway.' Casey's father was a creamery manager and he was one of ten children. As the brightest and the best tended to do in those days, Casey entered Maynooth at the age of seventeen and was ordained in 1951 – appropriately enough, the year the Irish hierarchy assisted in the collapse of an Irish government.

In 1992, the news broke in the Irish media that Casey had had a long relationship with an American divorcée, Annie Murphy, and that the couple had a son together, born in 1974. Casey resigned his ministry and left the country: first for Britain and then Ecuador. Although all these facts are now well known, I only discovered when the Annie Murphy story broke that Casey had been the subject of a notable example of omertà within my own circle of friends: the details were known to many, but not broadcast or reported for some years. The *Irish Independent* published an interview with Annie Murphy (on

22 January 2012) in which she explained how she and Casey came to be involved in the first place. She said that when Casey picked her up at the airport when she first came to Ireland in 1973, 'a light went on, there was a spark, that was it... he was electric'. Annie had been sent to Ireland by her father, following a miscarriage and various other problems, and Casey was a distant cousin. He wasn't distant for long.

Annie shared digs at that time with a woman I've known since she was a teenager. When Annie returned from weekends with Casey, she told my friend about romping with her new lover, sometimes dressed as Eamon liked her – in a bikini. Annie scoffed at my friend's reception of her stories: 'You Irish girls are so prudish!' And yet, for all that the story was by no means a secret, it took its time to emerge into the public realm: beginning with a report in the *Irish Times* that an Irish bishop had had an affair and fathered a son – though still not naming the bishop concerned. My friend now told her husband: 'I'll bet that's Annie Murphy!' It was. My discreet friend had maintained silence for almost twenty years, lest she caused scandal.

Murphy published a book, *Forbidden Fruit* (1994), which detailed the course of her relationship with Casey; she appeared on RTÉ's *The Late, Late Show*, which still functioned at this time as a sort of national confessional. Though his outing as a father was, initially, a shock to the Irish system – a shock of seismic proportions – his earlier popularity reasserted itself: at least to the extent that vox pops and first-hand experience would seem to indicate that people would have been glad to see him back in Ireland working as a priest. Casey remained in his missionary banishment in Ecuador, before moving to a parish in southern England. In 2006, he was finally allowed to return to the west of Ireland, but was forbidden to say Mass in public.

My own sense is that Casey was too young when he became

a priest – and too human. Many years after his fall from grace, he confessed in an interview that he found celibacy difficult not merely for sexual reasons, but because he missed the companionship which celibacy denied him. This was one glaring dilemma ignored by Church orthodoxy – one, as we shall see, of many.

10

Stonewalled

Pope Francis is a decent man. He might yet succeed in doing something to revive the fortunes of the Catholic Church – if, that is, they don't murder him first.

Francis reckons that one in fifty priests is a paedophile: in an interview with the Italian newspaper *La Repubblica* in 2014, he stated: 'I find this intolerable'. As an Irishman, *I* find it even more intolerable to even make an attempt to speculate on the percentage of paedophiles amongst priests who are either Irish or of Irish descent. And yet such speculation seems unavoidable: paedophilia is unfortunately one of the areas in which the Irish demonstrably punch above their weight. There are, of course, apologists who, even in the face of a blizzard of evidence to the contrary, try to play down the incidence of paedophilia amongst the clergy. David Quinn, writing in May 2009 in the *Irish Independent*, attempted to show that the extent of clerical abuse is easily overestimated. Quinn quoted a survey conducted by John Jay College in the United States, which put the incidence at 4 per cent, or twice what the pope came up with several years later. Neither figure, however, helps us to understand just what contribution the Irish made to either statistic.

The point here is not a statistical one. The pope was and is trying to deal with reality, but Ireland has had to cope with a problem of a willed *unreality*, the toxic fig leaf of 'holy Ireland' which has remained at the centre of the Irish Catholic mindset for a very long time. The importance of maintaining this guise may be gauged from the following quotation from a statement issued by the archbishops and bishops of Ireland at their meeting, held at Maynooth, on 6 October 1925. The statement dates from a time when the echoes of the Civil War had not yet fully died away and just as the Irish state was attempting to carve out a place for itself in the family of nations:

> We have a word of entreaty, advice and instruction, to speak to our flocks on a very grave subject. There is danger of losing the name which the chivalrous honour of Irish boys and the Christian reserve of Irish maidens had won for Ireland. If our people part with the character that gave rise to that name, we lose with it much of our national strength, and still more of the high rank we have held in the Kingdom of Christ.
>
> Purity is strength, and purity and faith go together. Both virtues are in danger these times, but purity is more directly assailed than faith. The danger comes from pictures and papers and drink. It comes more from the keeping of improper company than from any other cause; and there is no worse fomenter of this great evil than the dancing hall.
>
> We know too well the fruit of these halls all over the country. It is nothing new, alas, to find Irish girls now and then brought to shame, and retiring to the refuge of institutions or the dens of great cities. But dancing halls, more especially, in the general uncontrolled of recent years, have deplorably aggravated the ruin of virtue due to ordinary human weakness. They have brought many a good, innocent girl into sin, shame and scandal, and set her unwary feet on the road that leads to perdition.

Given a few frivolous young people in a locality and a few careless parents, and the agents of the wicked one will come there to do the rest, once a dance is announced without proper control. They may lower or destroy the moral tone of the whole countryside.

Action has to be taken while the character of the people as a whole is still sound to stop the dangerous laxity that has been creeping into town and country.

Amusement is legitimate, though some of our people are over-given to play. What, however, we condemn is sin and the dangerous occasions of sin. Wherever these exist, amusement is not legitimate. It does not deserve the name of amusement among Christians. It is the sport of the evil spirit for those who have no true self-respect.

The occasions of sin and sin itself are the attendants of night dances in particular. There may be and are exceptions, but they are comparatively few.

To say nothing of the special danger of drink, imported dances of an evil kind, the surroundings of the dancing hall, withdrawal from the hall for intervals, and the dark ways home have been the destruction of virtue in every part of Ireland.

One way around the evil of dancing proposed by the bishops was to promote Irish dances because 'they cannot be danced for long hours... Irish dances do not make degenerates.'

The bishop's statement was but the tip of the iceberg, what the public heard and saw from press and pulpit. Far more deep-seated control was exercised by documents which the public never heard about. The Church's influence in the educational field can hardly be over-emphasized. Horrific episodes in Ireland's past, carried out in the name of the Protestant religion

– be it Cromwell's slaughters or the doctrine of *providentialism*, which justified the Protestant Establishment's opposition to feeding the starving Irish during the Famine – had hard-wired the priest into Irish consciousness as being the one sympathetic authority figure that could be relied on.

And Mother Church was ever vigilant to ensure that this image would be continuously reinforced in the classroom. For example, a diocesan decree of considerably more import than the much-discussed statement on dancing, revealed that in the state technical schools, where children received some rudiments of education as they were trained in various trades, even these rudiments were originally opposed by the Church. However, while the Catholic authorities reluctantly agreed to some subjects being taught, in addition to technical ones, they stipulated that:

> Care must be taken by every means that pupils in vocational schools are trained to the full in moral and educational training and are protected against dangers morally damaging to young people. Therefore, in these schools instruction should be given separately to boys and girls, indeed, insofar as possible in separate halls.[16]

Nearly all primary schools were of course under the control of the Catholic Church, through the offices of the local parish priest who could and did hire and fire teachers. In addition, as the century progressed, vigilant bishops discouraged entrepreneurial educationalists from setting up new schools by citing clerically run schools in proximity to the would-be interlopers' establishments. Behind the scenes, episcopal influence in the Department of Education ensured that other obstacles were raised. Somehow, even where independent schools managed to establish themselves successfully, departmental grants were either slow in coming or even withheld.

And on other flanks, the bishops strove to keep divorce, contraception and abortion at bay. In the long term, they have failed in the matter of contraception and divorce. And in the matter of abortion, they have failed on two fronts. Firstly, there was and is an abortion trail to Britain from Ireland, well-travelled by women denied this procedure at home. Secondly, they failed to stamp out abortion completely in Ireland itself. The most spectacular illustration of the dangers of the abortion trail to Britain came in the year that the bishops issued their broadside against dancing. It was hushed up and written out of contemporary Irish history, largely – let it be said – for kindly motives and not merely for fear of clerical displeasure. Red-bearded Darrell Figgis, one of the more visible figures in the ranks of Sinn Féin, was a talented novelist, and was one of those who organized the landing at Howth in July 1914 of the guns that made the Easter Rising possible; he was also the man Michael Collins put in charge of drafting a Constitution for the new Free State. But he was also a married man with a mistress, and his life was to enter a tragic spiral. First, in 1924, his wife committed suicide; then, a year later, his mistress Rita North, who was only twenty-one, became pregnant and went to London where she died during a botched abortion. Darrell Figgis gassed himself in a London hotel room a week later. Everyone knew about the tragedy but few spoke of it.

Meanwhile, the backstreet (and some front-street) abortions continued. I remember as a boy that one of the features of Dublin's Merrion Square, as one entered from Lower Mount Street, was what appeared to be aluminium pillars flanking the doorway of the office of the fashionable Dr Henry Coleman. Towards the end of the war years, Coleman's plate vanished from the fancy portico, and one heard the doctor's name discussed in hushed tones. I later discovered that he had run a flourishing abortion practice, charging Dublin's better-off women IR£60 a time, a very large amount of money in those days. Other well-known abortionists of the period charged approximately half that amount, but such fees were still utterly beyond the reach of working-class women who lived in a world where labouring men earned two or three pounds a week and live-in maids received twenty-five to thirty pounds a year along with their keep.

Ireland's most famous (or infamous) abortionist was Mary Anne (Mamie) Cadden – or 'Nurse' Cadden, as she was always known. Cadden was a former midwife, struck off for providing illegal abortions, and she was sentenced to death for the murder of Helen O'Reilly in 1956. The case aroused nationwide interest, because O'Reilly was the wife of a man whom the Germans had parachuted into Ireland during the Second World War to act as a spy. His father, a policeman who had arrested Roger Casement on the eve of the 1916 Rising, persuaded his son to give himself up – and the son survived the war safely in internment.

Helen O'Reilly died of an embolism in the course of an abortion procedure in Cadden's one-room basement flat in Hume Street, off St Stephen's Green. Cadden attempted to dispose of the corpse, but her strength gave out after she had carried the body up the flight of steep stone stairs leading to the street. She then abandoned the dead woman on the pavement, where the corpse was subsequently found by a milkman. Cadden was sentenced to death in 1956, but her sentence was commuted to penal servitude for life. She went mad in prison and died in a state asylum in 1959.

It is clear that the tragedies of Rita North and Helen O'Reilly derive from the denial of a woman's right to the control of her own body. Abortion is, as we know, a worldwide source of bitter debate, but the debate in Ireland has taken on a particular patina. It remains mired in the fetid, clerically derived, watchful surveillance culture of a society given to the denial of human nature and to the isolation and stigmatization of unmarried mothers and their children as though illegitimacy were as dangerous as ebola. After all, the zeal displayed in Ireland for the protection of the unborn child could hardly have been said to have been matched by a similar concern for the fate of the child who reaches full term.

In discussing abortion, one must always have due regard for the sensitivity of the issue. Yet it also has to be stated bluntly that Ireland has made a dog's dinner of its abortion laws, which remain basically rooted in a statute of 1861. There have been five separate referenda on the issue since independence, but uncertainty and legalism are still producing tragedy and worldwide opprobrium for the country. In 1983, apparently to forestall any attempt to legalize abortion via the courts (as happened over contraception), Church influence was brought to bear on the then Taoiseach Garret Fitzgerald. The result was a referendum which resulted in a provision being inserted into the Constitution safeguarding the right to life of the unborn.

In 1992, the country was again convulsed over abortion, this time in what was known as the 'X case'. This concerned a teenage girl who had been raped and made pregnant by a neighbour and who was brought by her family to Britain for an abortion. While the girl was in Britain, and with the rapist denying paternity, the family sought guidance from the Gardaí as to whether the foetus could be used for DNA sampling. Hearing of this, the Irish Attorney General, Harry Whelehan, moved swiftly to seek and obtain an injunction preventing the girl from procuring an abortion. The case was appealed to the Supreme Court where, by a majority of four to one, it was decided that the teenager would be permitted to procure an abortion if there was a risk to her life through suicide. Of course, it was these very pressures – both legal and media driven – on the girl that had apparently resulted in a risk of suicide in the first place.

Shortly after the judgement was delivered, however, fate delivered an Irish solution to an Irish problem: the girl miscarried. One can only speculate as to what extent the controversy and the intense publicity it generated may have precipitated the miscarriage. X's assailant, named in 2003 as Sean O'Brien, subsequently served three years for the rape, having had an original fourteen-year sentence reduced on appeal. (In 2002, he was convicted of sexual assault and false imprisonment of another fifteen-year-old girl, and received a three-and-a-half-year sentence.) The X case resulted in three questions being put in a further referendum, which took place in November of 1992: first, a proposal that abortion would continue to be banned even if the mother was suicidal; second, a stipulation that the prohibition would not inhibit a pregnant woman's right to travel; and third, a guarantee that no barrier would be placed on the dissemination of information about abortion in other countries. The first proposal was defeated, the other two were carried.

Yet confusion over Irish law continued, when in 2005, three women known only as A, B and C, who had had abortions in Britain, brought a case to the European Court of Human Rights (ECHR), arguing that the lack of clarity in Irish law violated provisions of the ECHR. Two of the women were Irish, one Lithuanian. The court found that the Irish women's rights were not violated through being forced to travel. However, the ECHR found that Ireland *had* violated the Convention by not establishing a transparent system under which a woman could discover whether or not she was entitled to an abortion.

This last question arose forcefully and tragically in 2012 when an Indian woman, Savita Halappanavar, was denied an abortion in Galway. She was admitted to University Hospital Galway suffering from a miscarriage on 21 October 2012. She was then seventeen weeks pregnant. She asked repeatedly for an abortion, but was refused on the grounds that the foetus still had a faint heartbeat. Reportedly, Halappanavar was informed by a sympathetic member of the staff that an abortion was not possible as this was a Catholic country and a consultant had said that a foetal heartbeat was present. The remains of the foetus were finally removed on 24 October, by which stage Halappanavar was seriously ill. She died of sepsis and multiple organ failure on 28 October. Her death led to huge Irish and international protests and legal proceedings initiated by her husband are before the courts at the time of writing. The death of the thirty-one-year-old Indian citizen was both a tragedy in itself and a very black mark against Ireland internation-ally. As a result of the Halappanavar case, the Dáil passed the Protection of Life during Pregnancy Act in July 2013. This bill, which was designed to placate public protests over Savita's death, allowed for abortion where a woman's life was at risk, including a risk from suicide.

In July 2014, however, a woman known as Miss Y, who was threatening suicide, was denied an abortion under the Act. As a result she went on hunger strike – at which point another Irish solution to an Irish problem was found, with the baby delivered by Caesarean section at twenty-five weeks. In December 2014, a brain-dead woman was kept alive against her family's wishes so that the foetus in her womb could be delivered safely. After the woman had officially been declared clinically dead for three weeks, the High Court ruled that life-support procedures could be ended as there was no prospect of the foetus either surviving or developing normally even if it survived in the mother's womb for the further two months of pregnancy required.

Against such a context, one can certainly understand why a leading gynaecologist – Dr Peter Boylan, a former master of the National Maternity Hospital – said after the Halappanavar case that the lack of clarity in the Irish abortion law situation meant that medical practitioners 'had a sword of Damocles hanging over their heads'. One wonders how many unsuspecting Irish women may find one hanging over their heads also, should complications arise during their pregnancies – to say nothing of the psychological problems faced by women who become pregnant either through incest or rape.

*

Attitudes to abortion have, historically, been filtered through a specifically Irish Catholic attitude to sex and sexuality. I have glanced at its consequences, by turns tragic, scandalous and bizarre. But I now must turn to another dreadful and persistent stain on Irish life. I refer to the issue of paedophilia, the story of which has been seeping out slowly in recent years, and whose consequences Irish society has barely begun to address.

In the course of the 1980s, it began to emerge that some clergy were (and consistently had been) making widespread use of paedophilia as an outlet for their sexuality. A series of inquiries was held, including the Murphy Inquiry, which reported in 2009. The results that emerged were consistently shocking, and seismic in their consequences for the relationship between Church and state, and between Church and Irish Catholics in general. For now, Irish citizens learned in detail of horrific sexual crimes committed by priests and religious against children in Catholic dioceses all over Ireland. The four archdioceses – Dublin in the east, Armagh in the north, Tuam in the west, Cashel in the south – all had their share of abused and abusers. It appeared that some districts had particularly deep pools of iniquity within their borders: Cloyne in Co. Cork, the subject of a dedicated report which I shall examine below; and Ferns in Co. Wexford. The overall effect was, and is, that the scourge of paedophilia ravaged the Irish belief system. A faith that was part of Ireland's DNA was wounded critically.

The diocese of Ferns was the terrain of the notorious paedophile Father Seán Fortune, whose crimes were well known and commented on throughout the diocese. Fortune's behaviour was detailed in a report carried out for the Irish state by Judge Frank Murphy. Two of Fortune's victims described how Fortune had pushed them into the cubicles of public lavatories and raped them. In the case of 'Colin', the priest left him telling him he was a good boy. Colin ran home, removed his bloodied underclothing and never told anyone.

'Daniel' was first raped by Fortune when he was thirteen. The priest then gained such psychological ascendency over him that when, in manhood, his business collapsed he actually went to Fortune for financial assistance. In return he was required to perform sexual favours for Fortune three times a week. When, in 1999, Daniel eventually complained to Fortune's bishop, Brendan Comiskey, about his experiences, Comiskey showed himself to be aware of Fortune's behaviour: 'Fortune is an abomination,' he told Daniel. But this came somewhat late in the day. Fortune at the time was facing sixty charges of sexual abuse. Rather than await a court hearing, the priest committed suicide three weeks after Daniel's complaint.

At least Fortune's victim Daniel survived to talk about his experiences. The Ferns Inquiry also heard about others who did not. The mother of 'Brendan' told the inquiry about weekends during which Fortune took Brendan and others away on outings, one of which was a week-long course on religion in Maynooth. On returning from one such outing Brendan could not walk properly and told his mother he had haemorrhoids. The mother of 'Keith' pathetically told the inquiry how she and her husband had heard the rumours about Fortune – but like many other parents, they reacted by thinking how terribly wrong it was for people to be saying such things about priests. Both Brendan and Keith committed suicide.

The blind-eye policy towards Wexford might have continued nationally and the Ferns Inquiry never been initiated had it not been for a BBC documentary made by one remarkable young man. In the film *Suing the Pope*, Colm O'Gorman details his experiences and those of others at the hands of Fortune and his ilk. O'Gorman, who received €300,000 in compensation for his childhood experiences, founded One in Four, a group devoted to helping the victims of clerical abuse; later, he took over the running of the Irish branch of Amnesty International.

Fortune was not even the most notorious of Ireland's paedophile priests. That hateful accolade belongs surely to Father Brendan Smyth, who devastated the lives of many children and their families over several generations. Smyth joined the Norbertine order in Northern Ireland in 1945, and went on to molest children there, in the Republic, the United States, Italy and Wales. His activities were well known to his clerical superiors who disgracefully evaded the consequences of his actions by moving him frequently from parish to parish. It subsequently came to light that at least one of Smyth's colleagues, a Father Bruno Mulvihill, had repeatedly complained about his activities to senior Church figures – but without success. Indeed, Smyth's superiors at Kilnacrott Abbey in Co. Cavan shared the blame with various bishops for not having taken action to investigate these most serious allegations. By 1975, however, the destruction in Smyth's wake had reached a point where Church authorities were forced to hold an inquiry into his behaviour.

They did so by employing a liberal dose of the omertà principle that would eventually destroy the career of one of the Church's high fliers, Cardinal Sean Brady. Brady, then a priest and teacher at St Patrick's College in Cavan, was the notary taking the statements of children who had been abused by Smyth. The children were forced to swear vows of silence about the proceedings of the inquiry; Brady subsequently handed their signed statements over to the Ordinary of the Diocese. Neither Brady nor the bishop took any further action, and – scandalously – Smyth was allowed to continue with his offences for another twenty years. A warrant for his arrest was finally issued in Belfast in 1991, after he had abused four children from the Falls Road. Smyth went on the run in the Republic, living mainly at Kilnacrott Abbey.

The RUC was at length made aware of this situation, and contacted the Dublin authorities, seeking Smyth's extradition. But for a reason never satisfactorily explained, the request remained undealt-with in the office of the Irish Attorney General, Harry Whelehan. Readers will recall that this was the office that acted with such speed in the 'X case', when it became known that a young woman was planning to travel to England for an abortion. Eventually, Chris Moore, a journalist with Ulster Television, produced a film highlighting the failure of both Brady and the Norbertines to do something about the paedophile in their midst, reporting on the RUC extradition request, and highlighting the inexplicable delay on the part of the Attorney General. Channel Four added another programme which highlighted these mysterious legal delays. The controversy surrounding the Smyth affair would lead to the fall of the Fianna Fáil–Labour coalition government in November 1994. Smyth himself was eventually extradited, tried and sentenced to twelve years in prison; he died in jail in 1997. He was so hated throughout the country that he was buried in darkness, by the light of car headlights, in Kilnacrott Abbey and his grave protected with a shield of concrete to protect it from attack.

It was not only the nature of the crimes – the betrayal of trust, the preying on vulnerable youth, with all its damaging consequences for later life – that shocked and horrified Ireland. The arrogant and miserly attitude of the Church's response to the crimes of its minions was also deeply shocking. In Ireland, as elsewhere in the developed world, there are certain notifiable diseases, which, should they befall, must be notified to the authorities so that infection can be contained. But having not only failed to protect its flocks from the depredations of paedophiles, the Church compounded its crime by consistently moving the abusers onto other parishes or communities, where they could again spread their contagion with impunity. Then, when this malpractice was at length laid bare, the Church, guided – or, more accurately, misguided – by Rome, fought tooth and nail to pay as little compensation as it could to its victims.

By March 2010, the disaffection in Ireland had reached such proportions that the pope of the day, Benedict XVI, wrote a pastoral letter to the Irish faithful, apologizing for the abuse. The pontiff also appointed a very high-level group composed of cardinals and nuns from Canada, the US and Britain to investigate both the abuse issue and the training of priests in Ireland.

The pope's initiatives were greeted with limited enthusiasm. Of more import to Irish Catholics was the fact that, despite the torrent of evidence of abuse both during and before that time, in the period between 1975 and 2011 only six priests were convicted of their crimes.

Public engagement with the papal moves was also very considerably eroded by the terms of a deplorable compensation deal struck in 2002 between eighteen religious congregations and Michael Woods, a politician representing the outgoing Fianna Fáil government, who served as minister for education. This agreement lumbered the Irish taxpayer with far greater costs than those accruing to the Church, by agreeing to indemnify the religious orders against legal liabilities. This provision appears to have cost the state – to date – some eight to ten times the Church's bill, which was said to amount to €128 million. Indeed, it later emerged that this included a number of properties which had already been handed over to the state.

By 2012, when Richard Boyd Barrett, the Independent TD for Dún Laoghaire, made public the details of the deal, it was revealed that costs had escalated to more than one billion euro, with lawyers alone extracting some €160 million in fees. The total bill was made up of compensation claims, the cost of running a redress board composed of judges and other experts, and sundry legal costs. On top of all this, victims who availed themselves of the redress scheme were enjoined to secrecy and forced to agree to forego their rights to seek additional compensation from the courts.

Secrecy of another sort was perhaps the most unusual feature of this landmark agreement in the history of the relationship between Irish Church and state. Woods signed off on the deal on the eve of the 2002 general election; and this was given as the reason why the agreement was not brought to cabinet before it became a fait accompli. Subsequent to its signing, the Minister for Justice, Michael McDowell, who at the time of the agreement's conclusion was the Attorney General, said he disagreed with the claim that his office had been 'involved to an appropriate level at all times' and 'was involved in all relevant stages where the legal advice was required'. After McDowell's public contradiction, Woods claimed that McDowell, '*was* actively involved' at every *relevant* stage in the preparation of the indemnity deal agreed with the religious orders to compensate victims of abuse in residential institutions. Woods then changed tack, and defended the exclusion of McDowell and his officials from the meetings as follows: 'The legal people simply couldn't have attended – it was a no-go area for them – they had fallen out with the religious.' He claimed that his strong Catholic faith made him the most suitable person to attend the talks. Woods' exclusion of state expertise from the talks, however, did not apparently impress the country's financial watchdog. John Purcell, the Controller and Auditor General, told the Dáil's Public Accounts Committee that 'greater diligence' would have added 'extra rigour' to the state's negotiating strategy. The fundamentally unsatisfactory nature of the deal Woods struck with the Church certainly could not be denied: in June 2009, its terms were revisited, and, on this occasion, the eighteen religious congregations involved in the abuse scandals promised further funds and agreed to an audit of their finances to determine their ability to pay.

Mean-spirited and ungenerous as was the Irish Church's initial financial response to the crimes of its pastors towards their flocks, there are indications that it was probably a great deal more generous than would have been the case had certain powerful Vatican figures had their way in deciding how crimes of clerical sex abuse should be handled. We have this insight because the sex and paedophilia scandals provided the unlikely context for a partial lifting of the veil of secrecy that normally lies over Dublin–Vatican relationships. This came about as follows. By 1997, the Irish Church generally was taking heat over the clerical sex abuse issue – and no one more so than the archbishop of Dublin, Cardinal Desmond Connell. Connell had been an unlikely choice as leader of the see of Dublin, the largest, richest and most socially complex diocese in Ireland. Connell was a member of the conservative Holy Ghost Congregation, and a former teacher of metaphysics at University College Dublin. His only actual pastoral experience, so far as anyone knew, came as a result of being chaplain to a convent of the enclosed order of Carmelite nuns. But he was also known to be a friend of the influential Cardinal Joseph Ratzinger, prefect of the Congregation of the Doctrine of the Faith – and later, of course, Pope Benedict XVI.

Whatever the reasons for his elevation, Connell in the late 1990s was not a happy man. He and his fellow bishops had formulated a policy document for dealing with the abuse issue, which involved mandatory reporting of the guilty to the civil authorities. But, in a manner reminiscent of Bishop Browne's attitude in the Ireland of the 1930s, the powerful Cardinal Darío Castrillón Hoyos – prefect of the College for the Clergy and one of the Vatican's leading policy-makers – slapped down the Irish bishops. Their 'framework document', he told them, was only a discussion document, and it did not conform to the 'canonical norms now in force'. Connell and his colleagues were infuriated by Hoyos' unhelpful response: after all, these 'canonical norms', which consisted largely of omertà and a passing of the parcel, had resulted in both the laity and the media baying at the Irish bishops' doors.

But the word of the Vatican remained law: and now Rome instructed the Papal Nuncio to Ireland, Archbishop Luciano

Storero, to officially inform the Irish bishops that the policy which they had drawn up was indeed only a 'discussion document'. The letter – which, as with much of the Church's activity at this time, became public via media investigation – was revealed on RTÉ's *Would You Believe* television series in January 2011. It went on to say that the Vatican had serious moral and canon reservations about the Irish bishops' policy. When the letter became public knowledge the Vatican then tried to argue that the Nuncio's letter was not a rejection but merely an invitation to review the document carefully!

While loyally maintaining omertà, Connell and his episcopal colleagues eventually managed to obtain a meeting with Hoyos. The meeting was held in 1997 in Sligo, in conditions of great secrecy; the media would not get wind of it for over ten years. At the meeting, the normally peace-loving and soft-voiced Connell led the charge in seeking guidance in how to deal with a problem that was almost completely outside the realms of the experience of most of those present. Irish indignation, however, was no match for Vatican guile. Connell is said to have almost 'come over the table' at the Vatican cardinal when the latter informed the meeting that the duty of the Irish bishops towards their priests was to act 'as fathers, not policemen'.

Hoyos had also criticized the American hierarchy for their zero-tolerance approach to paedophilia. Indeed, in 2001 he actually wrote to a French bishop congratulating him for not notifying the authorities about a priest, who was eventually jailed for eighteen years for raping a boy and abusing ten other minors. He sent this letter, in his official capacity as head of the Congregation for the Clergy, after first showing it to Pope John Paul II.

The authority for dealing with clerical sex abuse was subsequently handed over to the Vatican Congregation which once ran the Inquisition, the Congregation for the Doctrine of the

Faith. This was a move favoured by Ratzinger, who had been arguing for some time that this should be the case. The Hoyos episode sheds some light on the pressures which subsequently caused Ratzinger to make history by becoming the first pope to retire. Indeed, it also sheds some light on as to why his successor, Francis, should so forthrightly condemn members of the College of Cardinals.

The *Would You Believe* disclosures cast the elderly Connell in a new, and more favourable light. Previously, this prelate's reputation had been one of the first to be shredded as a result of the findings of the Murphy report. Judge Yvonne Murphy's team criticized Connell for his tactical use of that moral sleight of hand known as 'mental reservation' in order to avoid telling the bald and unvarnished truth to the Murphy Commission.[*] Mental reservation permits one to indulge under certain circumstances in *suppressio veri*: a suppression of the truth which does not actually or actively involve falsehood. Connell told the Murphy Commission that the archdiocese was on a 'learning curve' on the abuse issue from 1998, the year of his appointment. Connell, however, had clearly learned quickly where money was concerned: for he had been insuring the archdiocese

---

* An article in the *Irish Times* of 26 November 2009 regarding the Dublin archdiocese report provided examples of the effects of 'mental reservation' as described by abuse victims Marie Collins and Andrew Madden. According to the article, 'Cardinal Connell emphasized he did not lie to the media about the use of diocesan funds for the compensation of clerical child sexual abuse victims. He explained to Mr Madden he had told journalists "that diocesan funds ARE [report's emphasis] not used for such a purpose; that he had not said that diocesan funds WERE not used for such a purpose". By using the present tense he had not excluded the possibility that diocesan funds had been used for such purpose in the past. According to Mr Madden, Cardinal Connell considered that there was an enormous difference between the two.'

against liability payments to abuse victims. Payments were made to victims from a secret 'stewardship trust' that he controlled and the existence of which was unknown to parishioners until 2003. Connell had previously categorically denied that victims were paid off, saying that if any money had changed hands it would have come from the priest's private means. This statement involved him in widespread criticism when it was discovered that he had in fact sanctioned a loan to a Father Ivan Payne to pay off an abuse victim.

Connell's stonewalling approach led him to refuse assistance to a victim of one of the archdiocese's worst abusers, Father Paul McGuinness. It was shown that, in 1996, he told neither the victim, Marie Collins, nor the police what he knew about McGuinness, although he later apologized for this and also relaxed his policy on not handing over documents concerning other abuse cases to the Murphy Inquiry. The inquiry also found that Connell had been economical with the truth on a number of abuse cases; and that he had been slow to release required documents, although it did praise his growing willingness to co-operate as he came to terms with the scale and impact of the abuse issue. This was the first time in Irish history that a senior cleric had been forced to give an account of his stewardship in such circumstances. All bishops submit their resignations to the pope on reaching their seventy-fifth birthday. Connell's was accepted after his seventy-eighth. He was replaced in 2004 by Archbishop Diarmuid Martin.

The significance in general of the Murphy Report is that it surveyed some of the most damning cases of cover-up of the entire era in Irish history – extending over the reign not merely of Connell but of three of his predecessors: Archbishops McQuaid, Dermot Ryan and Kevin McNamara. As McQuaid had been appointed in 1940 (and did not resign until 1972), it became undeniably clear that the attitudes of Castrillón Hoyos and others like him in the Vatican had prevailed in Dublin for a period of more than sixty years – and in all likelihood much longer. The Murphy Report spelled out in detail just why this occurred. This was Vatican policy at work, not merely a handful of elderly celibates seeking to sweep scandal under the carpet. The report outlined the manner in which forces influencing the character and the codes of Irish society were formed. Bishops, on their ordinations, were obliged to take an oath of loyalty to the Holy See. They were heavily guided towards obeying the law of the Holy See – that is, canon law – rather than the law of Ireland, or any other country for that matter.

The report also made it clear that while Connell was struggling to come to terms with the abuse issue – sometimes in ways which ultimately led to his being severely criticized by the inquiry – he was at the same time being strongly urged by the archdiocese's canon lawyers to in effect bend his loyalty to the Holy See over the laws of Ireland. No wonder, then, that there was a dismaying sameness *worldwide* to the Catholic Church's response to the abuse issue: after all, the Church in different parts of the world was responding to the same voices and demands from Rome.

The Murphy Report, meanwhile, also sheds damning light on the state of the Church's insight into paedophilia itself. It quoted the results of a secret Vatican inquiry into paedophilia which accurately diagnosed the nature of the affliction and concluded that those subject to its urgings found them 'uncontrollable'. Awareness that this is the case, of course, makes the Church's 'pass the parcel' policy even more inexcusable: knowingly sending men who could not control themselves amongst vulnerable children would be monstrous in any stratum of society – but for an institution that claims to uphold moral standards to do so surely creates a new low in hypocrisy. This is particularly the case when the fundamental reason for that policy appears, in typical Vatican-speak, in a letter from Storero to the Irish hierarchy. Speaking of the bishops' document, he warned the Irish that 'nothing contained in it would give rise to difficulties, should appeals be lodged to the Holy See'. In other words, Rome was not to be lumbered either with bills or compensation claims either from the laity or the clergy.

Murphy marked a watershed period, and one of the first churchmen to realize this was Connell's successor as archbishop, Diarmuid Martin, who was bolstered by the fact that before being appointed to clean up Dublin, he had been one of the Vatican's most experienced and senior diplomats. On his appointment, Martin called his priests together for a private meeting at which he showed them an advance copy of the Murphy Report – and told them that on reading it, he was so sickened that he felt like climbing into a bottle of whiskey. He warned his hearers that there was to be no more covering up of these crimes. Apology and contrition was what the situation called for, and an abuse-free future the expected norm. So far as an outsider can tell, Martin has seen to it that, in the archdiocese of Dublin, his wishes have been followed. In 2011, however, he had reason to speak publicly – outside the confines of a private gathering of priests – on continued Vatican footdragging on the child abuse issue.

The cause of Martin's righteous anger was yet another horrendous report – on this occasion into abuse in the diocese of Cloyne. And this time, it was evident that times truly had changed, for the Taoiseach of the day also had occasion to speak out in overt criticism of the Vatican. Martin's criticism was of attempts from within the Church to obstruct the Cloyne investigation; and of the failure of 'cabals' within the Church to square up to the enormity of the crimes being investigated. It must have been one of the few occasions in history – if not the only one – that the word 'cabal' was used to denounce the Church from within, by an authoritative and respected Church figure:

> There may be a cabal in Cloyne. They may have friends in other parts of the Irish Church. They may have friends in Irish society. There may be friends in the Vatican. The numbers that are involved in this are few. The damage these people cause is horrendous. It's for all of us to see where they are, but in the long term I have to take responsibility that in Dublin there are not cabals who reject our child protection laws. Everybody knows there are people who have challenged what I do, there are people who challenge what the diocese does, and people challenge what the national norms are. They exist. The way we get out of cabals is by those of us who are convinced of what we are doing, being strong together.

Martin's comments were made on RTÉ radio in the wake of Taoiseach Enda Kenny's speech, on 20 July, which condemned the Vatican for its undermining of the Irish bishops' mandatory reporting policy. Kenny's speech was electrifying:

> The revelations of the Cloyne Report have brought the government, Irish Catholics and the Vatican to an unprecedented juncture. It's fair to say that after the Ryan and Murphy Reports Ireland is, perhaps, unshockable when it comes to the abuse of children. But Cloyne has proved to be of a different order. Because for the first time in Ireland, a report into child sexual abuse exposes an attempt by the Holy See to frustrate an Inquiry in a sovereign, democratic

republic... as little as three years ago, not three decades ago. And in doing so, the Cloyne Report excavates the dysfunction, disconnection, elitism... the narcissism that dominate the culture of the Vatican to this day. The rape and torture of children were downplayed or 'managed' to uphold, instead, the primacy of the institution, its power, standing and 'reputation'. Far from listening to evidence of humiliation and betrayal with St Benedict's 'ear of the heart'... the Vatican's reaction was to parse and analyse it with the gimlet eye of a canon lawyer. This calculated, withering position being the polar opposite of the radicalism, humility and compassion upon which the Roman Church was founded.

Martin said that he had been impressed by the emotion in the Taoiseach's speech, which showed that Kenny clearly felt deeply about the issue. Though he questioned the essence of Kenny's remarks – that the Vatican had sought to undermine the workings of the Cloyne Report – he said he too was both disappointed and angry at what the report had revealed.

However, the Vatican – or at least its spokesperson, Federico Lombardi – claimed in response to Kenny's words that there had been nothing in the advice issued from Rome to encourage bishops to break or ignore Irish law. Lombardi's comment, however, was another classic example of Vatican double-speak. True, a canon lawyer could argue that the official Vatican statement to the Irish hierarchy did not contain an *incitement* to break the law. But the reality was that the bishops had, in effect, been verbally *encouraged* to do so by Cardinal Hoyos, when he told them at the meeting in Sligo that they should not act towards their priests as policemen. The time for toleration of double-talk, however, was fast running out.

By means of Wikileaks publications, the Irish public had learned that in February 2010 the American embassy in Rome had reported to Washington that the Murphy Commission had written to the pope asking to be given any information contained in Vatican files. The requests, however, had not even been acknowledged. Far from being outraged by 'the rape and torture of children', indeed, the Vatican had taken umbrage at the Murphy Commission's temerity in even making its approach. The Vatican insisted that the Murphy request should have been made through the Irish government via diplomatic channels, on the grounds that the Holy See was a sovereign state. The US diplomatic cable informed Washington that: 'Many in the Vatican were offended by requests for information by the Murphy Commission which they saw as an affront to Vatican sovereignty.'

The US diplomat further noted that the Vatican, while concerned to prevent any crimes from taking place in the future, was angered by the Irish government's failure to 'step in to direct the Murphy Commission to follow standard procedures with Vatican City'. So, crocodile tears having been duly shed, the reality of the Vatican concern lay with *process* rather than with victims. Unfortunately, the Irish Taoiseach of the time, Brian Cowen, had caved into Vatican pressure. After several fruitless requests by the Murphy Commission for information, a rocket had been received from Cardinal Bertoni at the Irish embassy in Rome demanding that diplomatic channels be used. Cowen's response had been in line with the ineptitude with which he was facing the state's financial crisis. In the Dáil he defended the Vatican's failure to respond to Murphy, saying that the Vatican had acted 'in good faith'. It was not unreasonable, he said, to argue that the Holy See and the Nuncio believed the matter was more properly addressed through diplomatic channels. Enda Kenny, however, said that the Vatican had been discourteous. This view was shared by a majority of the public. The Murphy Commission, after all, was an official government body established by Cowen, and was, as the Vatican well knew, a response to the unparalleled state of anger and distress in Ireland caused by the abuse. Using delaying tactics while hiding behind diplomatic niceties impressed no one.

Now, however, the 'cabal' wing of the College of Cardinals was unmoved by the unrest in one of its hitherto most docile and lucrative provinces. This pendulous, pretentious and enpurpled gaggle of prelates saw fit to express its displeasure publicly. Following Taoiseach Enda Kenny's speech, the Papal Nuncio to Ireland, Giuseppe Leanza, was very publicly recalled to Rome for 'consultations' on the Cloyne Report. The recall of an ambassador by any temporal power is one of the highest expressions of diplomatic displeasure which can be conveyed between governments. For the Vatican to do so from a country with Ireland's history of involvement with Rome was quite extraordinary. Traditionally the Papal Nuncio was the doyen of the diplomatic corps accredited to Ireland. But this belt of the Vatican crozier did not noticeably affect the course of an increasingly steely-eyed Irish government policy towards Rome.

Following the recall of the Nuncio in July 2011, the Irish government announced in November that the Irish embassy to the Vatican was to be closed. This mission had always been regarded as a key Irish listening post, and the Villa Spada itself was generally seen as being one of the most – if not *the* most – valuable of Ireland's overseas properties. The announcement of its closure, made by the Tánaiste Eamon Gilmore, attempted to distance the closure from sex abuse scandals by saying that the

Department of Foreign Affairs gave 'particular attention to the economic return from bilateral missions'. Gilmore said that the closure was part of the government's effort to pay for its obligations under the austerity programme then in force in order to meet the costs of a bailout by Europe and the International Monetary Fund. Similar closures were envisaged for Iran and for an Irish government office in Timor Leste.

However, having donned the fig leaves of Iran and Timor Leste, Gilmore then made it quite clear what the government attitude was toward the Vatican:

> I remain of the view that the 1997 letter from the Nuncio provided a pretext for some to avoid full co-operation with the Irish civil authorities... The sexual abuse of children is such a heinous and reprehensible crime that issues about the precise status of documents should not be allowed to obscure the obligation of people in positions of responsibility to deal promptly with such abuse and report it.

Rome did now move promptly. On 26 November 2011, a little over three weeks after the recall of the Nuncio, Rome named a whizz-kid New Yorker, Charles John Brown, to succeed Leanza. He was given a day to think about it, before he accepted the appointment. Brown spoke blandly about the need not to exaggerate the importance of what he termed 'this delicate moment' in Dublin–Rome relationships. A former aide to and favourite of Pope Benedict, Brown told the *Irish Times*:

> The Nuncio is a representative of the Holy See on the ground there. It is not that, in any sense, he is in control of the Church in Ireland. It is the bishops of Ireland who are in control of the Church in Ireland.

It is probably fair to deduce from this the terms of the briefing which Brown received in the Vatican before taking up his new post. Speaking of reforms within the Irish Church, he said:

> As for reforms to the Irish Church, I am agnostic about this. I need to study all that material and then talk to the Irish bishops... The Church was left behind the curve on all of that, the Church has to modernize and to find new ways of presenting her message to people in this new context of the materialism and consumerism of a society that is now more similar to other European countries than it was in the 1980s.

My mother had a saying – and I recalled it on reading this statement. She used to say: 'That remains to be seen – as the cat said when it came out from behind the piano.' Decoded, the Nuncio's message might be interpreted as saying that Ireland is no longer a backward country that could be relied upon to do as it was told; and the Vatican brand would have to be repackaged and sold to a population that was lamentably given over to consumerism and materialism. There may be some veneer of truth in this statement, but the unholy reality of Ireland's second colonial ruler, Mother Church, was not one about which one could be 'agnostic'. Children were raped and tortured by the Church in Ireland – and this same Church did everything it could to evade responsibility for these crimes.

One cannot, after all, be bland about the buggery of children. In the next chapter, I will look more closely at the regime of institutional and clerical abuse which has stained the history of modern Ireland.

11

Institutional Abuse

THE ALL-PERVASIVE INFLUENCE OF THE CHURCH IN IRISH education had a Janus-faced aspect. One side of the picture shows priests and nuns running first-class, elite schools which turned out young ladies and gentlemen to either take their place in Irish society or go abroad well equipped to deal with life in other countries. The other side of the educational picture, however, reveals scenes of the indefensible being perpetrated on the defenceless.

Clerical abuse, sex scandals and the Church's underhand methods of attempting to deal with these problems resulted in damage to society that was unparalleled in post-1916 Ireland. Among the victims, of course, were those certain individual members of the religious and clergy who were subjected to false allegations as to their behaviour. The best-known case is perhaps that of Father Kevin Reynolds who, in an RTÉ programme aired in 2011, was falsely accused of raping and impregnating an African woman. The programme was broadcast despite the fact that Father Reynolds had offered to take a paternity test to prove his innocence; he subsequently received damages.

An even more disturbing example, perhaps, was that of a nun who actually went to prison because of false allegations. Nora Wall – formerly Sister Dominic of the Sisters of Mercy Order

– was actually given a life sentence of which she served four days before being released. Her case was subsequently determined to be a miscarriage of justice based on the evidence of two young women with psychiatric problems. As the *Irish Times* noted at the time, Wall's case was probably influenced by the climate engendered by RTÉ's *States of Fear* programme, which dealt with institutional abuse by nuns and clergy. It is certainly the case that countless thousands of decent nuns and priests, who were serving out their roles as best they could, wrongly suffered guilt by association with the abusers. Great social opprobrium was engendered by paedophile priests, as well as by normal heterosexual clerics who strayed beyond the bounds of celibacy to father children, while still preaching abstinence and condemning abortion, contraception and divorce.

The worldwide Church had sufficient knowledge of the nature of paedophilia to act in ways other than cruelly transferring the transgressors to fresh parishes and victims new. But lessons learned abroad were very slowly applied in Ireland; and then generally, initially at least, only under duress – as a result of the fallout from media coverage and the work of campaigning abuse victims. There were certainly a number of sources of information into the behaviour of certain members of the clergy and religious orders. Myriad inquiries were instituted into activities in various dioceses and institutions – industrial schools, reformatories, orphanages and Magdalene laundries – run by the Church. A further and deeply disturbing source, meanwhile, became manifest in January 2014: a local historian, Catherine Corless, made discoveries in the Tuam area of Co. Galway which seemed to indicate that up to eight hundred inmates of a nearby Bon Secours convent, a mother and baby home, may have been buried in mass graves adjoining the former site of the home. Some of these infant corpses may have been buried in what was the site of a large septic tank. Another rumour – being investigated at the time of writing – is that vaccine trials may have been conducted at the institution.

A formal inquiry was established in July 2014 under Judge Yvonne Murphy, one of the heroines of the child abuse saga. At the time of writing, this Tuam Inquiry is still in progress: Judge Murphy's courageous and professional pursuit of her inquiries in the teeth of Vatican disapproval and obfuscation, however, was groundbreaking, and engenders hope that the new inquiry will be equally clear and unequivocal in its findings. Murphy's work, after all, helped to serve notice on the hitherto male-dominated corridors of power that the new and formidable force in Irish life signalled by the presence in politics of such women as Mary Robinson and her successor Mary McAleese could and would have an influence on Irish political and religious discourse. In the midst of scandal and betrayal, this is one development in Irish life which does offer hope for the future.

Certainly one feels the need for such hope after studying the work of another inquiry, the Ryan Commission, which investigated the history of abuse in boys' reformatories, children's homes, hospitals and orphanages in Ireland. Under the chairmanship of Judge Sean Ryan, it began its work in 2000 and reported in May 2009. Ryan shone a light on some very dark places in Ireland: these reformatories were a Victorian idea which continued long into the twentieth century, providing in the process a festering source of cruelty and abuse. The schools were places of harshness where sexual abuse, savage beatings, neglect of children's health and emotional needs were commonplace and where the diet was of a particularly low standard – this even when the congregations running them had large farms at their disposal. The Department of Education was kept informed of the regimes in both reformatories and industrial schools through the visits of departmental inspectors, and yet the government hesitated to intervene for reasons both political and economic.

The former were based on straightforward fear of the Church's influence. The second were rather more complicated, and were based on the fact that the various congregations saved the state money by investing heavily in the building and running of these institutions. Although the Church certainly still had the wherewithal to ensure that children were properly fed in these places, the state, by turning a blind eye to how the institutions were run, was saved the expense which intervention might have incurred. And blind the eye certainly was. I myself have come across reports in the Public Records Office in Dublin from inspectors who tried to do their job by informing their superiors of what was going on in such notorious reformatories as St Conleth's at Daingean in Co. Offaly. Their reports were ignored.

The reformatories ostensibly aimed at providing a means of betterment for boys labelled 'delinquent', whose principal educational influence otherwise was likely to have been restricted to whatever they might have been expected to learn in prison. Take the Oblate Fathers, who intended that the first reformatory, situated at Glencree in Co. Wicklow and opened in 1859, was to be modelled on the progressive Mettray system* which had taken root on the Continent and in Britain. This system involved having the youths live in separate houses in small communities which were regarded as families. Religion was central to the lives of these 'families' both for the improvements

---

* Named after the Mettray penal colony in the village of Mettray in the French département of Indre-et-Loire, which opened in 1840.

it was hoped to bring to the boys themselves and in order to keep proselytizing Protestantism at bay. It was intended that discipline be strict but not cruel.

The family-style setting idea, however, did not flourish in Ireland. There was a general public awareness – or perhaps shameful private awareness would be a better way of putting it – that something was fundamentally wrong with these institutions. Yet this issue was simply, in the true Irish way, never discussed. Omertà played its part; so did emigration, which helped to dispel any problems out of sight and mind. Some of the doctors who attended these institutions and signed death certificates for children who died of malnutrition, systematic abuse and – sometimes – savage violence must have been fully aware of what was going on. Yet, willingly or unwillingly, they allowed themselves to be part of the problem, rather than the solution.

From the outset, the experiment suffered from the absence of the ideal small houses in which the Mettray inmates lived. Glencree was an old army barracks which, along with adjoining lands, was given to the reformatory project by the local landowner, Lord Powerscourt. The disciplinary aspect of the Mettray system certainly remained – but the familial one did not; instead, a rule of great harshness evolved here just as it did in other institutions. Daingean was another former barracks site, and punitive military discipline here became the norm. Indeed, Daingean became a place and a byword for reformatory horror. The following is an account by one Don Baker, who in 1963 was committed to Daingean by the courts:

> Shortly after that he called me down from the dormitory at night and he flogged me. They'd beat us on the stairs below the dormitories and the sound of the strap hitting you would echo all over the place. I was stripped naked and

had to lie spread-eagled on the stairs. One brother stood on my hands to keep me there and another held my legs. Then the brother, who had made my life such a hell in the church, flogged me with a leather. I always felt that this was his way to get me – if he couldn't get me sexually, then he could do it by beating me.

There may well have been a sexual aspect to that particular brother's assaults on Baker, but beating was a way of life at Daingean as it was in every other reformatory. The minister for education in May 1999 was Micheál Martin, and he read into the Dáil record an account by a visiting committee to Daingean three years after Baker had left. They described how the manager of Daingean, Father William McGonagle, had described to them 'openly and without embarrassment' how corporal punishment was administered in Daingean:

Ordinarily the boys were called out of the dormitories after they had retired, and that they were punished here on one of the stairway landings. The boys wore night shirts as sleeping attire when they were called for punishment. Punishment was applied to the buttocks with a leather.

When asked why he allowed boys to be stripped naked for punishment, Father McGonagle replied in a matter-of-fact manner that he 'considered punishment to be more humiliating when it was administered in that way'.

Further psychological pressure was applied by having those who were awaiting a beating stand on the stairs immediately above those who were being leathered so that they could see what was going to befall them when their turn came. Needless to say, such treatment made boys want to run away from reformatories. The punishment for this on recapture, however, was further savage treatment. The Rosminians who ran St Joseph's industrial school at Ferryhouse, Clonmel, for example, administered justice in ways that were ubiquitous:

> The three lads were marched in wearing nothing but wet swimming togs. This was so it would hurt more and so the bruising on their backsides wouldn't be as marked. Each of them was spread over a table, with brothers holding then down. Then another brother beat them with a thick leather strap. The head priest told us this is what we would get if we even thought of running away. The beatings went on for about an hour, the boys were screaming and roaring. One of them fought back, and they beat him all the more.

This, it should be pointed out, was the scene in an industrial school and not a reformatory: these were additional institutions in which the inmates had been placed not because of crime, but allegedly to save them from bad conditions at home. But the same conditions and regimes tended to appear.

As for the Magdalene laundries, these were originally founded to shelter 'fallen women' such as prostitutes or women who had become pregnant out of marriage. They flourished in an atmosphere of penance and guilt. Discipline was harsh, diet poor and the inmates were relentlessly exploited by being forced to work for nothing in the laundries run by the nuns. The girls received little or no education. The first Irish asylum was founded in 1765 in Dublin and the asylums finally closed their doors in 1996. Three years before, there had been a major outcry over the discovery of the remains of approximately 155 females in a graveyard of the former High Park Convent in Drumcondra, which had been sold for building purposes. Owing to the lax recording practices tolerated by the authorities where clerical institutions were concerned, some sixty of these bodies were never identified and were ultimately cremated. But these pathetic victims did not die entirely in vain. A hard-fought campaign mounted by survivors of the laundries and their families secured compensation for the abuse suffered by the victims of the Magdalene system – 600 were still alive in March 2014 – which finally resulted in the Irish state acknowledging the harm and hurt caused to the women.

A report was compiled by Senator Martin McAleese who, as a result of the campaign, had been tasked with investigating conditions in the laundry. The McAleese Report was criticized by survivors for glossing over their experiences, yet it contained sufficient information to cause the Taoiseach, Enda Kenny, to issue a formal apology. Speaking in the Dáil in February 2013, he said: 'I, as Taoiseach, on behalf of the state, the government and our citizens, deeply regret and apologize unreservedly to all those women for the hurt that was done to them. This is a national shame for which I'm deeply sorry and offer my full apologies.' Kenny said it was a 'brutal and inhuman regime which Irish governments turned a blind eye to'. A €50 million compensation fund was set up by the state: but not only did the orders involved not contribute, the Vatican joined in the sorry affair by wrongly informing the Irish minister for justice that the nuns were prepared to pay compensation.* By the

---

* The Vatican made a public announcement (reported in the *Irish Times* of 2 April 2014) confirming that four congregations of nuns were willing to pay compensation. However, some of the congregations concerned subsequently said they would not pay. The minister for justice, Alan Shatter, then wrote to the Vatican seeking clarification. A month later (see *Irish Times* 7 May 2014) Archbishop Silvano Tomasi

time of the Taoiseach's apology, the four orders involved – the Sisters of Mercy, the Sisters of Our Lady of Charity of Refuge, the Good Shepherd Sisters and the Sisters of Charity – were known to have made hundreds of millions of euro in profit from the sale of properties during the Celtic Tiger boom.

*

Nothing in the Irish Church or in the Irish educational system could be regarded as being more essentially Irish than the Irish Christian Brothers. Since 1802, this order – founded by a wealthy Catholic businessman, Edmund Ignatius Rice – provided free education for the Irish Catholic poor. Founded at a time when the penal laws were still a potent force in Irish life, and in the wake of the removal of the Irish parliament by the Act of Union of 1800, the order was permeated by a strongly nationalistic spirit, and as the century wore on, Irish Christian Brothers schools became bastions of the Irish language and of Gaelic games.

At the time, as we have seen, the object of the British-controlled national school system was to de-nationalize children – one of its textbooks directed a child to be 'thankful that I am a happy English child upon whom fortune has smiled'. The Brothers' philosophy, then, inevitably ran counter to the Establishment view. For some, both before and sometimes after independence, the Brothers' schools were seedbeds of revolution. Several leaders of the 1916 rebellion and the

made a public statement that the nuns had paid over €400 million in compensation, but that the state had 'mishandled the money' and then come back looking for more cash. The nuns were not willing to provide this, he said. The spin put on all this was that the Vatican had somehow become confused between claims – and the sums of money involved – arising out of differing forms of abuse.

subsequent independence movement received their education from the Christian Brothers, and as late as the IRA campaigns of the 1950s Special Branch detectives picking up an IRA volunteer on the border could say with certainty: 'He was one of Brother X's pupils.' There were many Brother Xs.

Elsewhere, I have likened the education provided by the Brothers to that of war surgeons in the field, compared to the work of consultant specialists in advanced peacetime operating theatres. They got the Irish poor onto their educational feet and sent them into the battle of life with at least a chance of survival, and even, as Irish history shows, of advancement. The Brothers, therefore, were considered to be above reproach – and this continued to be the attitude of official Ireland until the dawning of the era of scandal and betrayal. There had, naturally, been rumours that apart from an excessive devotion to corporal punishment, other bad things took place within the Christian Brothers' domain. But the state chose not to investigate and to focus instead on such iconic images of the Brothers as the famous Artane boys' band, which entertained the crowds at Croke Park on All-Ireland day. With their skilful playing, in their blue- and red-piped uniforms, the members of the band seemed to epitomize all that was best about the Brothers' endeavours – disadvantaged lads from an industrial school visibly demonstrating the Brothers' gift to them of life-enhancing skills. It was a tableau that perfectly depicted the links between the Church and the manly Irish culture that places Gaelic football and hurling at the highest pinnacle of Irish devotion to sport.

In a bilingual RTÉ television programme *Trom agus Eadrom* ('Heavy and Light') in 1976, Brother Joseph O'Connor – who had become a national figure through his development of the band – was the subject of a particularly laudatory tribute. The overwhelming consensus amongst those who either took part in the programme or viewed it was that good Brother O'Connor had received no more than his due. Ten years later, as the era of scandal and betrayal brought more and more unwelcome truths into the light, a different picture of the now dead Brother O'Connor formed in the glare of inquiries and television programmes. One man told of how, following some classroom misdemeanour, O'Connor made him take off his clothes and then:

> Right there in front of the whole class, he sat down on the bench, on the desk with his foot on the bench where the boys would sit and write, and his other foot on the ground. He opened his cassock and put me across it and put his left hand under my private parts. He was squeezing me and beating the living hell out of my bare backside. He was foaming at the mouth, jumping and bopping. He was having a sexual orgasm in front of the whole class of boys. And I wasn't the only boy he done. He did things to me that I wouldn't even tell my wife about, they were so shameful. Some of the things he did I can't talk about now. It's too painful.

This is only one of the many anecdotes which survivors of the Artane regime told of O'Connor's behaviour. One victim described how Brother O'Connor induced him to bend over by dropping sweets on the floor – and then pulling down his trousers and beating him all over his body with a leather cosh until he became unconscious. The boy had been placed in care because he had been born outside of wedlock. His mother chose to visit him shortly after the beating but was sent away: she was told that she could not see her son because he had contracted TB.

Other victims of Artane have told how they were beaten

and raped repeatedly by different Brothers. One boy described how in a beating for running away his wrist was broken and some of his teeth were knocked out. He had to sit in agony while his head was shaved by another boy. Any other boy found talking to him was beaten. A litany of frightful tales could be told: such as that of a man who said that his sex education consisted of being forced to watch two younger boys masturbating a Christian Brother. Then he was forced to beat them before being 'fondled' by the same Brother. The man said that this happened for five consecutive nights with ten different boys.

The outcomes of such episodes for the inmates of Artane and the other institutions run by the Brothers include suicide, inability to communicate with their children, barriers between them and their wives, and feelings of anger and shame that remained with them to the grave. The outcome for the Brothers themselves is perhaps best described in the terse unemotional prose of a report of September 2013 by the National Board for Safeguarding Children in the Catholic Church in Ireland, which reviewed the Brothers' Irish province. Out of a total of 870 allegations of sexual abuse made against 325 Brothers, only 12 convictions had been secured. But as a result of the complaints and bad publicity, the Brothers had closed all of the industrial schools and had moved out of direct education provision, transferring responsibility for their entire educational network to mainstream schools. But the fatal dagger to the heart of the illusory prototype of the Brothers' achievement was delivered by a paragraph which said: 'The Christian Brothers' membership in Ireland now stands at some 267 with an average age of 74 years. There are no new Brothers in formation and the province's historical base in Ireland has reduced substantially.'

It was a sad end to a chapter begun by Edmund Ignatius

Rice over two hundred years ago. If ever there was a case of the good being interred with the dead, and of the evil living thereafter, it is the story of the Irish Christian Brothers.

*

At the time of writing another wide-ranging investigation is analyzing what took place in Church- and state-run institutions in Northern Ireland between 1922 and 1995. The Historical Institutional Abuse Inquiry has been described as the largest investigation into institutional child abuse in the United Kingdom's history. It is chaired by a retired judge, Sir Anthony Hart, and it is also expected to deal with allegations that the British state was implicated in abuse at the notorious Kincora Boys' Home in Belfast, where boys were routinely raped by loyalist paramilitaries and members of the British security forces. One of those in charge of the home was the late William McGrath, once a political associate of Paisley and a political extremist who established the far-right 'Tara' organization – and a voracious paedophile. McGrath's notoriety eventually led to his being charged with various acts of rape and buggery. He received a sentence of four years' imprisonment in 1981, of which he served two. McGrath died in 1991, taking many of his secrets to the grave. But the brief glimpse of his career, which the publicity surrounding his trial elicited, did help to shine a light on the deeds of darkness which are sometimes made possible by the mishandling of institutions set up for the protection of vulnerable boys and girls.

The Historical Institutional Abuse Inquiry is also hearing reports of matters common to other institutions south of the border. The Sisters of Nazareth are among the Church orders being investigated: and whatever findings eventually emerge concerning these allegations, the Nazareth nuns have already performed better than some of their fellow religious south of the border in as much as they have readily admitted to at least part of their wrongdoing. In this case, their actions centre on the wrongs inflicted on vulnerable women, and on the taking of children for forcible adoption.

Sister Brenda McCall, representing the Sisters of Nazareth, has acknowledged, for example, the suffering caused to the children sent to Australia as part of a scheme by the Australian government to bring white children of 'good stock' into the country. McCall told the inquiry that the Sisters of Nazareth were involved in sending 111 children to Australia in the scheme over a period of years until the late 1950s. She noted:

Looking back, there was a grave injustice done to these children in sending them out. And not just to the children but to their families as well. I think no matter the most eloquent apology or the most beautiful monument or no matter how much money they receive, it will never make up for what we took from them. I know some made good lives for themselves. But having been out to Australia and spoken to some migrant children, they still have this, 'what if, what if I had stayed in Ireland?', even though they had made good lives for themselves out there. We have to acknowledge – that is, the British government, the Australian government, the churches, the congregations and institutes. We all have to put our hands up and acknowledge that maybe it was not the right thing to do, even though it was done in the best interests of the children at the time.

The belief that the Church was acting 'in the best interests of the children' helped to cover up one of the worst aspects of the history of such institutions: the way in which Church–state collusion worked in practice. The state ensured that the institutions were kept supplied with new inmates, and in effect paid for them. They were funded through capitation grants and their managers, in collusion with local clergy, saw to it that numbers were kept up, by arranging to have children committed to the institutions on the grounds of anything from family incapacity to mental health. A Department of Education memorandum accurately describes how the courts and the clergy together ensured that a flow of capitation grants continued to pour into these institutions:

> The fact [is] that the managers have an organized system for 'touting' for children. They have social workers who act as a sort of agent and get children committed to the schools. We have no means of preventing this practice but I suggest that we consult the department of local government with a view to getting the assistance of the local county managers to ensure that children are not committed without sufficient reason and to obtain periodical reports on the parents' means when children are committed on the grounds of poverty.[17]

Little or no improvement resulted, and, by turning a blind eye, the state achieved the cheapest possible method of dealing with some of the weakest and most vulnerable in Irish society.

★

The medical profession does not come well out of this history. The tradition of omertà and the fact of Church and state being hand in glove in so many ways, spawned evils other than the medical condoning of such barbaric practices as symphysiot-omy. Some doctors willingly joined in the abuse of residents of institutions. The following letter from the file of an abuse victim was published in the *Sunday Independent* on 22 December 2002.

> Dear Mr X
> You must remember that record-keeping was not a prior-ity generally in psychiatry when you were a patient. While certification of insanity seems formal and stigmatising I can assure you that it was simply 'a transfer process' by which persons in custody were moved to Dundrum. What I am saying basically is that although you were certified insane, insanity or madness was not necessarily validated by that opinion. Doctors used the certification process simply as a transfer document: that is the way it was. It is no longer so, but that will not relieve you, I am sure. Equally the decertification process, which again referred to insanity, was no more than a transfer process back into the prison system. There is nothing in your file to suggest insanity or psychosis, that's all I can reassure you of.
>
> Dr *****.

Such a mindset helps to explain how one facet of institutional care – sustained malnutrition – was allowed to continue. The diet in these institutions was, by and large, appalling. I have spoken to survivors of these homes who told me they frequently ate grass.[18] And from interviewing survivors I found a 'normal' day's menu often consisted of the following: breakfast – bread and dripping; lunch – two potatoes and cabbage water; tea – two slices of bread. The various investigations have established that children frequently surreptitiously ate pigs' feed, and stole raw potatoes from the fields to be eaten at night.

Department of Education reports contain cases such as that of Lenaboy outside Galway city, in which the dismal conditions described by an inspector were ascribed to a septuagenarian nun who had spent her earlier life running a Magdalene laundry. The nun herself was described as 'a miserly, ruthless old woman, who has as her objectives the reduction of the debt on the institution. She has been hardened by age and a lifetime spent in a Magdalene home.' It would certainly seem that a certain attitude of mind was required to run such homes, and that mindset was by no means confined to Catholics. Protestant institutions of a similar type – for example, Dublin's Bethany home run by evangelical Protestants to house 'fallen women' – also produced claims similar to those made about the Magdalene homes. The Bethany home also had a high incidence of mortality; and children here too were sent to locations outside the jurisdiction. Shamefully, the Irish government at the time of writing has refused to compensate the Bethany victims along the lines of the Magdalene sufferers, even though the latter campaigners have joined forces with the Bethany survivors in support of their claims.

Ireland must hang her head in shame at this infamous perversion of the 1916 Proclamation's aspiration to cherish all the children of the nation equally. In these institutions, it seems rather that children were all victimized equally.

12

The Corruption of a Nation

I N THIS BOOK, I HAVE EXAMINED THE SORT OF MORAL sickness which has infected the Catholic Church in Ireland, frequently to devastating effect. Lives have been destroyed, or blighted at best; and the institution of the Church itself eaten from the inside, as termites eat the foundations of a house. But there are other sorts of moral sickness, and these too have eaten away at Ireland. I refer, of course, to the sickness that comes from the sort of financial corruption that seems ubiquitous and endemic in Irish politics and business. Such corruption has been exposed again and again in the history of modern Ireland, without ever, it seems, being rooted out. In addition, the very systems set in place to identify and punish such corruption have also been found wanting. The result is a loss of public confidence in Ireland's political structures, in the rule of law and in governance in general.

In March 2012, Judge Alan Mahon noted that corruption in Ireland:

[C]ontinued because nobody was prepared to do enough to stop it. This is perhaps inevitable when corruption ceases to become an isolated event and becomes so entrenched that it is transformed into an acknowledged way of doing business. Specifically, because corruption affected every level of Irish political life, those with the power to stop it were frequently implicated in it.

Judge Mahon knew what he was talking about. He presided over an investigation into planning matters and corruption in public life: and his tribunal turned out to be one of the longest and most expensive public inquiries ever held in Ireland, running for some fifteen years and costing up to €300 million. The Tribunal of Inquiry Into Certain Planning Matters and Payments began in November 1997 under Judge Feargus Flood. He was succeeded as Chairman in 2003 by Judge Mahon, assisted by two other judges, who reported in 2012. Mahon's inquiry, moreover, was but one of many. State tribunals in recent years have investigated matters ranging from the infection of citizens with 'dirty' blood, causing hepatitis, to unpleasant activities in Ireland's economically crucial beef industry. None of these investigations lasted as long or cost as much as Mahon; indeed, some were short, swift and economical. Each, however, played its part in exposing corruption and mismanagement in Irish public life and business, and shaking public confidence.

Other scandals, meanwhile, remain unsatisfactorily or poorly investigated – and among these, it seems to me, one scandal looms large. Of all the rotten things that have occurred in Ireland from the 1970s onwards, indeed, I would suggest that the worst was perhaps the Stardust nightclub fire of February 1981. The Stardust was located in the Artane area of north Dublin, part of Charles Haughey's constituency. The owner of the Stardust, Patrick Butterly, was a prominent member of Fianna Fáil and a major contributor to party funds. Patrick Butterly also shared Haughey's interest in horses. The fire which tore through the nightclub claimed the lives

of forty-eight young people and severely burned and trau-
matized hundreds more. Among the many condolences that
poured into Haughey's office were messages of sympathy from
Margaret Thatcher and Queen Elizabeth II. The fire resulted
in Haughey's cancelling a scheduled Fianna Fáil ard fheis and
postponing a planned general election.

The story of the Stardust fire, already dreadful, becomes
immeasurably worse when one considers that there had already
been another disastrous fire in Ireland, from which clearly no
lessons had been learned. That tragedy took place in 1943,
when wartime censorship, shortage of newsprint and the then
limited news coverage provided by Ireland's state broadcasting
system played their part in restricting coverage and discussion of
the event. The fire took place at a Co. Cavan orphanage which
was part of an industrial school complex run by the Poor Clare
nuns, an enclosed order whose members never set foot outside
their convents, and who led lives defined in their rulebook as
'consecrated and virginal chastity, bridal love... embraced in
poverty and lived in obedience directed towards Christ'.[19]

Whether or not such rules had, as local folklore suggests, a
bearing on what befell in 1943 must be a matter of speculation.
But what we do know is that the two fires – at the Stardust and
in Cavan – shared extraordinary characteristics. In both cases,
a lack of fire safety regulations was a factor. In both cases,
some of the best legal brains in the country and two of the
country's best-loved artists were involved. In the case of Cavan,
the senior counsel representing the state electricity board, Tom
O'Higgins, later became a presidential candidate and ultimately
Chief Justice. The official report on that fire was compiled for
the government of the day by Brian O'Nuallain, who became a
famous writer under the pseudonym Flann O'Brien.

In the Artane fire, the lawyer who conducted the Inquiry into the Stardust fire, Ronan Keane, also became Chief Justice in later life. The artist involved, Christy Moore, was and is one of Ireland's best-loved singers: his song 'They Never Came Home' became an anthem for the families of the Stardust victims in their campaign to establish the truth about the disaster. It also, however, resulted in Moore being hauled into Dublin's High Court on the grounds of contempt of court: in the wake of the fire Patrick Butterly claimed that the song suggested that the only cause of the deaths was the chaining of some fire exits. The song was deleted from the singer's album; and Moore had to pay some IR£60,000 in legal costs. At the time of writing, however, the song has been reissued on another Moore album without any further objection. The Butterlys themselves received compensation through the courts, following a finding by the Keane Inquiry that the fire could have been caused by arson. As we will see, however, new evidence produced long after the inquiry proved that the fire was *not* caused by arson.

'We are all Fianna Fáilers,' Butterly told the writer Tony Canavan in 1999. Butterly was then eighty years of age: he died not long after the completion of the privately circulated memoir that Canavan helped him compose. Butterly continued: 'What you had these people for was to help get things. I don't mean by giving them money. But if you wanted to know something about your business or you wanted someone who could do something, you didn't get the answers by writing into the papers. You asked these people.' [20]

Both the Cavan and Stardust fires now seem to have been caused by an electrical fault, but in both cases the exact causes have not been established. The orphanage fire is said to have started in a laundry in the basement, but remained undiscovered until 2 a.m. when a girl who had woken up in her dormitory informed one of the nuns. In the street outside the convent, people saw smoke and tried to get into the locked convent. At length, they were admitted by one of the children.

The nuns by this time had herded all the other children into one dormitory. They could have been led out of the building – but instead the nuns persuaded the locals who had gained entrance to attempt to put out the fire. By then, however, the fire had taken such a hold that this proved impossible; indeed, some of the would-be rescuers were lucky to escape with their lives from the laundry area. Eventually a man arrived with a ladder and a local hero with the appropriate name of Louis Blessing managed to reach one of the dormitory windows and bring five of the trapped children to safety. The remaining thirty-five children perished.

It was said afterwards that the reason the nuns directed firefighters to the laundry and prevented them entering the dormitory area in the early stages of the blaze was that they did not wish the children to be seen in their night attire. The inquiry, however, absolved the nuns from all blame and instead criticized the unorganized local fire service, which consisted mainly of a horse and cart with what was alleged to have been a faulty hose pipe and no pumping apparatus. A fire engine finally arrived from Dundalk, forty-five miles away, along what at the time were very narrow twisting roads – but it was too late to deal with the blaze. No one apparently thought to have recourse to the fire services in the town of Enniskillen – across the border in Co. Fermanagh, but considerably closer than Dundalk.

The final stage of the drama was the issuing by the department of local government of a forty-seven-page fire-safety recommendation document: *Fire Protection Standards for Public Buildings and Institutions*. The recommendations were intended to cover buildings for which 'a department of state has any responsibility or for which it has power to make rules and regulations in respect of the inmates'. It later appeared that two of the principal figures connected with the Cavan inquiry did not agree with its findings. O'Higgins and O'Nuallain collaborated in composing the following verse:

> In Cavan there was a Great Fire,
> Judge McCarthy was sent to Inquire,
> It would be a shame,
> If the nuns were to blame
> So it had to be caused by a wire.

Prior to the Stardust fire, meanwhile, there had been several reports of breaches of fire safety regulations at the premises. Just over three weeks before the fire on 19 January 1981 a fire officer with Dublin Corporation, Martin Donohue, had visited the building and found problems. Because of stacked boxes, he had difficulty in passing along corridors – this on a night when some 2000 people were present, while the licence only allowed for a maximum of 1400 people. Donohue had earlier cited a number of occasions on which he found exit doors locked and caused them to be reopened. As a result of his complaints, Dublin Corporation wrote to Patrick Butterly summarizing Donohue's objections to the way Stardust was being run. The letter said:

The Inspector for Places of Publican Resort (electrical) visited the premises on 15 January 1981 at 9 p.m. and noted the following:

1. Exit passageway at side of stage obstructed with cases, boxes etc.
2. Overcrowding – the number of persons present in the Cabaret Room was greatly in excess of the permitted number of 1400 for which exiting is provided. This

constitutes a very serious infringement of the bye-law...
which requires that special care should be taken to ensure
that the means of escape provided for all persons on the
premises are at all times maintained unobstructed and
immediately available. Unless I receive your immediate
assurances that the exit ways will in future remain unobstructed and immediately available at times when the
public are on the premises it will be necessary to instigate
proceedings against you for contravention of the above
bye law. And also to raise the matter during the hearing
for application of renewal of your annual licence.

In his reply, Butterly said that he immediately complied with
regulations when breaches were brought to his attention. He
claimed that the excess attendance was caused by people using
forged entrance tickets. The fire occurred three weeks later.
The subsequent inquiry found that Butterly habitually ordered
that exit doors be kept locked at least until midnight, apparently to prevent people getting in without tickets.

The inquiry had been the subject of controversy from the
moment it was established. The highly respected lawyer Mary
Robinson, later president of Ireland, criticized the fact that the
inquiry had no power to investigate what were alleged to be
failures to implement several recommendations made in reports
on fire prevention made over the years. In particular, Robinson
underscored the fact that building regulations introduced in
1976 had not been conformed to. And Robinson apart, there
were criticisms of the fact that the only technical advisor on
fire matters to the minister for the environment, a Captain
John Connolly, had not been included in the tribunals panel.
Such a fire expert would have been automatically included in
an inquiry in other countries.

On the night of the Stardust fire, an atmosphere of panic prevailed. There were difficulties in finding either fire extinguishers, unbarred windows or unlocked doors. Sections of blazing material fell from the ceiling on the heads of the screaming youngsters. Firemen could not gain access. Smoke and darkness further impeded them: it was as though the Cavan orphanage fire had never occurred and the reams of resulting safety recommendations had never been written. Later in 1981, I happened to be in the area and I inspected the scene of the disaster. I have visited most of the prisons in Ireland and the diamond-shaped pattern of the bars on the Stardust windows put me in more in mind of the windows of the prison at Long Kesh, rather than of a dance hall frequented by young people. I sat there for a long time by myself in a state of fury – and fury was not my reaction alone. There was much public disquiet and anguish on the part of the relatives of the fire victims.

Not long after the fire, Haughey oversaw the establishment of an inquiry into the blaze under the chairmanship of Judge Ronan Keane. As might be expected, Keane was scathing about the chaining of doors and fire exits. He said that Butterly, whose evidence he treated with 'great reserve', had shown a 'reckless disregard' for safety. Keane issued a list of precautionary recommendations which were incorporated into public buildings of all sorts throughout the country thereafter. From the victims' relatives' point of view, however, the findings were a disappointment insofar as issues of both accountability and compensation were concerned. The inquiry found that the cause of the blaze was probably arson: not alone did this absolve Butterly of legal responsibility for the fire, it also enabled him to receive IR£580,000 compensation from Dublin Corporation. The arson finding also caused resentment amongst the victims' relatives at the thought that their loved ones – or anyone in the building that night – might be stigmatized as having engaged in criminal activity.

The relatives fought a continuous battle both to establish the truth of what happened at the Stardust and to obtain compensation. They have so far been unsuccessful in their last objective, but their protests did secure a major alteration in Keane's findings. In 2006, following ongoing protest and pressure, the government ordered a revisiting of Keane's findings. Paul Coffey, SC, was instructed to conduct a fresh inquiry – and he found that: 'The cause of the fire is unknown and may never be known. There is no evidence of an accidental origin and equally no evidence that the fire was started deliberately.' This of course was at variance with Keane's finding which enabled Butterly to successfully claim compensation. On 3 February 2009, the Dáil voted that no one in the Stardust on the night of the blaze could be held responsible for it. As a result the original public record was corrected and the finding that it was due to arson was removed. This still did not bring compensation any nearer for the victims' families. All the state provided for them were their legal costs.

Public opinion, however, had been powerfully affected by the findings of an edition of RTÉ's flagship current affairs programme, *Prime Time*, broadcast on 14 February 2006. This produced a map of the building not considered by the Keane Inquiry. The map shown to the inquiry had indicated that there was a storeroom over a basement. In fact there was no basement: the storeroom was instead located in the roof space above the first floor. It is said to have contained barrels of highly flammable cooking oil and self-combustible materials such as cleaning polishes and floor waxes, the existence of which the Keane Inquiry was not aware. Alongside the storeroom, moreover, was a room containing electrical appliances from which, the programme said, people had seen smoke emerging and had heard sounds of sparking in the weeks preceding the fire. In addition, witnesses interviewed on *Prime Time* claimed that they saw flames coming from the roof of the building eight minutes before flames appeared in the ballroom below. It appears reasonable, therefore, to speculate that the fire could have started in an area above the ballroom, rather than in it.

There the matter lay until 11 February 2014, when a Garda inquiry was opened into evidence given before the Keane tribunal. It is understood that a researcher, Geraldine Foy, who worked with the victims' committee for several years, produced the material which was being investigated by the police. A fire expert, Robin Knox, also worked with the victims' committee. At the time of writing the findings of this latest Garda inquiry were being sent to the Director of Public Prosecutions.

But also at the time of writing, the families of the victims of the fire have not received any compensation. Patrick Butterly never faced any charges; and he never made any apology for what happened on Valentine's Day 1981. But in his unpublished memoir, Butterly complained about getting nothing out of the fire, and grumbled that all his compensation went on legal fees.

The only definite conclusion of the Stardust affair is that the rain glistens on the little marble headstones marking the graves of the Stardust victims in St Fintan's cemetery nestling on the Hill of Howth overlooking Dublin Bay.

*

Irish public opinion generally regards the tribunal era as having commenced with the Beef Tribunal of 1991. This tribunal helped to foster a general impression that politics and the beef trade were inextricably linked, for good or ill – and it did so in a manner damaging to both the taxpayer and the international reputation of Irish meat. The tribunal cost IR£34 million in legal fees alone; additional costs arose during its course, and these were rightly or wrongly also associated in the public's mind with the tribunal's activities.

The Beef Tribunal played a part in the fall of not one but two governments. First Desmond O'Malley led his Progressive Democrats followers out of their coalition with Fianna Fáil after Albert Reynolds referred to him as being 'dishonest' while giving evidence to the tribunal in 1992. Two years later, in July 1994, after the inquiry had ended, Reynolds – without consulting his Labour coalition partners – went public to say that its findings vindicated him. This, together with the suspicions and tensions generated by the Brendan Smyth affair, led to the Labour Party leader – and Tánaiste – Dick Spring withdrawing his support. The government fell in December 1994, to be replaced by a 'rainbow coalition' of Fine Gael, the Labour Party and Democratic Left.

The tribunal cast the Irish meat industry in an extremely unfavourable light. As has happened so often in Ireland, the report was initiated not by state action but by a television programme. This was screened on 13 May 1991 as part of ITV's *World in Action* series. Between the programme itself and a series of allegations made in the Dáil by opposition deputies, a picture of fraud and skulduggery was painted: the result was that a man who figured largely in the allegations, Charles Haughey, ordered the establishment of a tribunal of investigation under the chairmanship, initially, of Justice Liam Hamilton.

At the heart of the inquiry was a government decision in 1987 to extend the state insurance scheme on beef destined for Iraq to a level in excess, in fact, of the amount actually exported. This decision was taken against advice by officials, and it amounted to a fraud on taxpayers. It mainly benefited the AIBP Group controlled by Larry Goodman and, to a small extent, Hibernia Meats, controlled by Oliver Murphy. Writing about the tribunal era, Matt Dempsey in the *Farmers Journal* delicately described the situation of the time of the export guarantees as 'opaque'. As he said, 'The connection between agri-industry and politics was real and at times seemed to be all-pervasive.' Throughout the tribunal's hearing, the relationship between Haughey and Goodman was stressed and the influence of Goodman on the Department of Agriculture was also held up to scrutiny. Estimates at the time placed the share of national GDP accounted for by the Goodman business empire at approximately 12 per cent.

However, the tribunal found that both the Goodman and Hibernia companies were filling their contracts with beef which was either purchased from the EU's beef mountain (that is, accumulated by the EU intervention policy) or was not produced in the Republic at all. Therefore, despite the fact that sales to Iraq were being subsidized, the subsidies were not actually helping to increase the prices paid to Irish farmers. The tribunal found that fraudulent practices were rife throughout the industry, in Goodman's factories and in others owned by Fianna Fáil supporters. However, the tribunal found no evidence that Goodman either knew of, or condoned, these practices.

Hamilton's report consisted of 900 pages, which were not easy for a layperson to follow. Moreover, while there was much handwringing and suspicion, the result in political terms was both unexpected and extraordinary. The government changed. In 1992, in the course of the tribunal, Desmond O'Malley, the Tánaiste and leader of the Progressive Democrats, the junior partner in the coalition government, had criticized Reynolds over the granting of the export credit scheme during the latter's spell at the Department of Industry and Commerce. When Reynolds' turn in the witness box arrived, he retaliated by calling O'Malley dishonest. The PDs now moved a motion of no confidence and the government fell. Fianna Fáil was decimated in the subsequent election and it seemed that a new government was about to be formed between Labour and Fine Gael. However this did not materialize owing to a demand by the Labour leader, Dick Spring, to make the post of Taoiseach a rotating one, in which he and the Fine Gael leader, John Bruton, would alternate.

The result was that Fianna Fáil was returned to power – with a ballot box in one hand and a beefburger in the other. Albert Reynolds became Taoiseach at the head of a coalition with the Labour Party whose leader, Dick Spring, became Tánaiste. (It was at this point, as I have noted, that Reynolds turned his attention to the nascent peace process in Northern Ireland.) Two years later, in 1994, the subsequent issuing of the Hamilton Report lit the fuse that caused this partnership too to blow up. Reynolds greeted the publication of the report with a statement claiming that it vindicated him completely – before Spring and Labour had had time to consider the 900-page document. The ill will generated by this precipitate announcement appears to have been a factor in causing Spring to withdraw his support for Fianna Fáil in a row over the handling of the case of the notorious paedophile priest, Brendan Smyth. And so this government collapsed too, and Fianna Fáil was ejected from power. The Beef Tribunal did not result in anyone going to jail. Larry Goodman's costs were paid for by the state. Liam Hamilton was subsequently appointed Chief Justice – and at least some of the sort of abuses mentioned in his report continued within the beef industry.

Years later, in 2014, there was further tension surrounding the beef industry. In November of that year, the Irish Farmers' Association picketed supermarkets and major meat plants, protesting at the low level of prices being received from Irish factories compared with those on offer in Britain. A farmer's wife summed up the farmers' grievances with the meat processors succinctly: 'They are on the rich list. We are on the poor list.' Talks initiated by the minister for agriculture, Simon Coveney, defused the row; and new agreements on pricing animals according to age and weight were concluded. Whether these will initiate a new era of harmony has yet to be demonstrated. But what could be said with certainty is that at the time of writing, the Irish meat industry remained as it had been: not for the faint-hearted.

*

By the time of the 2014 row, Charles Haughey was long gone, dying in a state of disgrace over revelations at yet two more tribunals, the McCracken and Moriarty Inquiries. History will probably record that Haughey's downfall was caused by one woman and contributed to by a second. The first was his mistress, Terry Keane, whom we have mentioned previously. The second was Margaret Heffernan, the heir to the Dunnes Stores Irish retail chain. This tough businesswoman wrested control of the family business from her brother Ben in 1992, after the latter had appeared on a balcony of a room on the seventeenth floor of the Grand Cypress Hotel in Orlando, Florida, threatening to jump. After he was talked down, police discovered that with him in the hotel bedroom were a prostitute and some of the cocaine which had led him to the balcony in the first place. Dunne escaped the wrath of the Florida police at a subsequent court case: he was fined but was not sent to prison on drug charges.

However, he did not escape the wrath of Margaret Heffernan so easily. She and her brother Frank Dunne went to war with their sibling and effectively took control of the family business. In the course of the litigation, Heffernan discovered that Ben Dunne had been making payments to various people, including Haughey, who was now living in retirement. When Heffernan confronted Haughey about documents uncovered by the accountancy firm Price Waterhouse as part of her legal battle with Ben Dunne, however, Haughey completely denied that there had been any payments.

Heffernan, however, was not so easily put off – and her inquiries began lifting the lid on the corruption that was steadily eroding not merely the links between big business and politics, but the very nature of Irish democracy itself. Part of the Price Waterhouse documentation found its way into the hands of an investigative journalist, Sam Smyth, who revealed that Ben Dunne had certainly not been partisan in his bestowal of cash on politicians. A leading Fine Gael politician, Michael Lowry, had also benefited. Lowry, at the time minister for transport, energy and communications, owned a company called Streamline Enterprises which received £208,000 from Dunne. This was ostensibly for supplying refrigeration equipment – but in fact it had gone towards building an extension to Lowry's home. This revelation caused Lowry to resign from the cabinet and as a member of Fine Gael. Meanwhile the Heffernan legal juggernaut rolled on, and Judge Gerard Buchanan was asked to determine whether or not there was a case for a sworn public inquiry tasked with discovering whom Ben Dunne had been paying and for what. In February 1997 Buchanan's report established that there was indeed a case.

This led to the establishment of an inquiry under Judge Brian McCracken to investigate just what Dunnes Stores had been doing with its money. The McCracken Tribunal was to prove the first stage of a triple rocket of inquiries that would ultimately blast the reputation of Haughey and a number of other politicians into smithereens. The other two inquiries were the Moriarty Tribunal, into payments to politicians generally; and the Flood/Mahon Tribunal into corruption in planning matters and the building industry, which we have already encountered

The McCracken Tribunal revealed that Haughey had received some IR£1.3 million from Ben Dunne – although McCracken suggested that the reason for Dunne's generosity was merely to secure Haughey's friendship. But in 2005, the Moriarty Tribunal found that Haughey had done considerably more than bestow friendship on Dunne: he had, for example, arranged meetings between Dunne and the then chairman of the Revenue Commissioners, Séamus Paircéir, which resulted in a tax assessment on the Dunne family trust being reduced from €39 million to €16 million. This saving of €23 million, however, was not the end of the story. The bill was wiped out completely before an appeals body, with Paircéir – who had by that stage retired from the Revenue Commissioners – acting as a tax advisor for Ben Dunne.

The Moriarty Tribunal also found that Haughey received more than IR£8 million from various people, including Ben Dunne. He took some fifty thousand pounds from a Saudi businessman to help him gain Irish citizenship, and had a million pound-plus overdraft settled with Allied Irish Banks (AIB) for almost a half million less. AIB tended, after all, to look more kindly on the overdrafts of a Taoiseach than those of an ordinary citizen; another former Taoiseach, Garret Fitzgerald, had an IR£200,000 overdraft written off in 1997 after he lost heavily when the share price of Guinness Peat Aviation collapsed. In Fitzgerald's case, however, the Moriarty Tribunal found that, unlike Haughey, Fitzgerald had disposed of assets in an effort to reduce his indebtedness.

Before the tribunals began, it was still possible to meet people in Ireland who would say things like: 'I know Haughey's a crook, but he's a good crook. He'll make money for himself, but he'll make money for the country too. That's why I voted for him.' The tribunal era, however, largely put an end to that point of view. In 1998, an opinion poll found he was rated the most hated man in Ireland. Not surprisingly the Moriarty Tribunal found his behaviour was 'unethical'; and more damagingly for the fabric of Irish public life, Moriarty also accused him of 'devaluing democracy'. One incident in particular destroyed Haughey's credibility with people who had still maintained a sneaking regard for him. He had organized a collection for Brian Lenihan – former Tánaiste and foreign minister and one of his closest personal and political friends for several decades – when the latter was found to need a liver transplant operation. He underwent the procedure in May 1989, but the tribunal found that of the IR£270,000 collected in funds, Haughey had appropriated a 'sizeable proportion' for his own use. Money collected for the Fianna Fáil party also seems to have found its way into Haughey's personal accounts – or at least into his lifestyle.

While Moriarty was trying to unravel the sources of these expenditures, Haughey claimed that he was not aware of the details of his personal finances. All these matters, he said, were handled by his accountant, the banker Des Traynor, who controlled the Guinness and Mahon bank in Dublin. Traynor was also chairman of one of the largest Irish companies, Cement Roadstone Holdings (CRH) and throughout the late 1980s and early 1990s, he also ran the Ansbacher scam from the offices of CRH. The Ansbacher scam, which ran from 1971 until the early 1990s, meant in effect that wealthy Irish people could hold money offshore and beyond the reach of domestic taxation, mainly in the Cayman Islands. But at the same time, they could have access to their funds in Ireland, again without paying any tax. Haughey was a major beneficiary of this scheme, for which no one was ever prosecuted, although it was reckoned to be one of the largest tax evasion schemes of the era. The Revenue Commissioners reckoned that, while they were able to secure €113 million in taxes and penalties, a successful prosecution could not be mounted against any of the people involved in these illegal activities for two main reasons. Firstly, a successful prosecution would have required original documentation and this was not forthcoming from the Cayman Islands. Secondly, there was a ten-year statute of limitation on such cases.

It was revealed in 2013 that some 289 instances of illegal tax evasion had been discovered in the Ansbacher undergrowth, including some relating to individuals who were either elderly or in bad health. Age and infirmity were, seemingly, among the reasons why no prosecutions were brought against certain of those implicated in the scam. As for Haughey himself: his evasions had contributed significantly to the length, and cost, of the Moriarty Inquiry, but although the Moriarty and McCracken mills ground slowly, they eventually discovered the facts – and, in later reports, made a number of discreditable findings about other prominent people in Irish society and public life which are discussed below.

Eventually the era of scandal would result in a number of prominent people going to jail. But Haughey himself would not be among their number. He was unexpectedly rescued

– inadvertently – by one of his arch-enemies, the co-founder of
the Progressive Democrats, Mary Harney. She gave an interview to the *Irish Independent*, just as the state was considering
bringing charges against Haughey arising from McCracken:
in this interview, she told the newspaper that she believed he
'should be convicted: that [the argument that he was too old to
go to jail] does not wash with me'. The judge who should have
tried the case found that it would be impossible for Haughey
to get a fair trial, and he walked scot-free on that occasion.
He also emerged free of a claim for €2 million brought against
him by the Revenue Commissioners arising out of Dunne's
gifts – this time by successfully appealing the claim to the
Appeals Commissioner, Ronan Kelly. However, he later paid
€6.5 million to the Revenue Commissioners in back taxes and
penalties. To meet his legal fees, which must have been astro-
nomical, Haughey sold his Abbeville estate for €45 million, but
this transaction was on a sale-and-lease-back basis; he continued to live in Abbeville until his death in 2006.

The effect of such endlessly lurid findings on the public
mind can well be imagined, and there was a good deal more to
come from Moriarty. Indeed, even as Moriarty was doing its
work, further equally disgraceful revelations were being made
before the Flood/Mahon Tribunal investigation into corruption
in planning and in the building industry.

*

The Celtic Tiger nickname first appeared – or so the lore has it
– in 1994, bestowed on the Irish economy by one Ken Gardiner
of Morgan Stanley. The moniker was testament to Ireland's
ostensible kinship with the Asian so-called 'tiger' economies:
and on the surface, indeed, Gardiner's comparison appeared

well founded. Between 1995 and 2000, the Irish economy grew by 9 per cent annually. Most of this consisted of actual economic growth – but as time went on, the nature of this growth became increasingly problematic. The trouble with the Celtic Klondike thus created was that the growth became increasingly property-centred and was paid for with cheap credit supplied from European and especially German banks. 'Development' and 're-zoning' were the buzz words of the day. It was a scenario tailor-made for the growth of corruption.

It was against this background that the Flood/Mahon Tribunal began sitting in November 1997. Its findings were referred to the Criminal Assets Bureau, the Director of Public Prosecutions, the Revenue Commissioners and the Standards in Public Office Commission. But, as we shall see, the activities of the tribunal itself were to be the cause of much bewildered, and increasingly annoyed, shaking of heads.

The entire tribunal juggernaut was set in motion by a small advertisement offering IR£10,000 pounds for information leading to convictions for corruption in the Irish planning world. The advertisement was placed on the back page of the *Irish Times* in July 1995 by a barrister, Colm MacEochaidh, and Michael Smith, a former chairman of An Taisce, the body charged with overseeing Irish planning and environmental matters. Initially, the placing of the advertisement appeared to be a most public-spirited and beneficial action. The series of events which it set in train, however, would cause many Irish citizens to wonder just how beneficial the tribunal process actually was to the state.

At the time of the advertisement's appearance, one James Gogarty, a former Garda and an engineer, was in dispute with his employers on the matter of his pension rights. The company was JSME, a large structural engineering firm owned by Joseph Murphy. Around the time Gogarty fell out with his former employers, and as a result of his dispute, Gogarty turned whistleblower. He alleged that a Fianna Fáil Minister, Ray Burke, received payments to ease the passage of a planning proposal made by Murphy in conjunction with two brothers, Tom and Michael Bailey, to develop a 700-acre site in north Dublin. All charges against both Joseph Murphy Snr and his son, Joseph Murphy Jnr, were dropped. However, Gogarty's decision to turn whistleblower ultimately resulted in the Baileys having to make the biggest tax settlement – some €25 million – in the history of the state. Gogarty's spirited evidence was instrumental in the establishment of the Flood/ Mahon Tribunal, and his appearance as a witness made him something of a national figure during the tribunal's hearings. It later transpired, however, that some of Gogarty's allegations did not stand up and this resulted in some major reversals of the tribunal's findings, including that of corruption against Burke; he and other witnesses may now claim their legal costs, which will most likely run into the tens of millions of euro.

The legacy of the tribunal, then, remains to be established – but it can be said with some confidence that his appearance before it put a definitive end to the career of the then Taoiseach, Bertie Ahern. Ahern had already been criticized by the Moriarty Tribunal as a result of his unorthodox financial habits: as Fianna Fáil's treasurer and designated signatory of cheques, he had developed a system of signing blank cheques and leaving them for his then boss, Charles Haughey, to complete as he chose. Now Mahon judged that Ahern had received money for which he could not or would not account. One source was alleged to have been the property developer Owen O'Callaghan: both Ahern and O'Callaghan denied this, with Ahern claiming that cash flowed from 'dig-outs' organized by friends to help him over the costs of his legal separation from his wife in the 1990s.

At the time Ahern was minister for finance, yet he said that he did not have a cheque book or a bank account of his own. This circumstance would appear to have rendered nugatory an allegation put to him by the tribunal that volumes of sterling currency were being lodged to his name. Later, however, his constituency secretary, Gráinne Carruth, admitted to the tribunal that she, as part of her duties, regularly paid sterling into an account in his name, and returned the receipts to Ahern. Carruth's annual salary in 1994 was €3,432; the particular lodgement which caught the eye of the tribunal was for £15,000 sterling, paid into the accounts of Ahern and his daughters – and, inevitably, the Carruth episode had a disastrous effect on Ahern's popularity, undermining his image as a typical jovial and goodhearted Dubliner. Had the loyal Carruth continued to defend her boss, she could have been both fined and jailed. Ahern soiled his image yet further, meanwhile, by claiming that the cash had come from betting on horses.

As a result of fallout from the tribunal, Ahern, former minister Pádraig Flynn and a number of Dublin city councillors resigned from Fianna Fáil. Burke was sentenced to six months in prison for tax evasion (of which he served four and a half months); and the Fianna Fáil TD Liam Lawlor was jailed not once but three times in the course of the tribunal – firstly for failing to turn up, and then, when he did appear, for repeatedly obstructing the tribunal's workings. The result of such relentlessly greedy, smoke-filled backroom wheeling and dealing was of course collateral damage – and a lot of it. One consequence – made manifest during the years of the financial crash and the austerity it brought on the long-suffering Irish public – was the building of now empty and unsaleable 'ghost' estates all over the country. These hurriedly thrown-together eyesores could well have taken their architectural inspiration from Pete Seeger's song: 'Little boxes on the hillside, little boxes made of ticky-tacky... and they all look just the same'. Even when building rampages of this kind did not result in unsaleable eyesores and widespread bankruptcies, such lunatic property speculation had additional evil side effects: building took place on water tables; the laying of concrete and tarmacadam interfered with the normal run-off of rainfall, leading to flooding and pollution. The upkeep of infrastructure, such as the repair of Ireland's antiquated water and sewerage systems, was ignored; lakes, rivers and beaches became polluted by agricultural and human waste.

★

I want to conclude this survey of the disgraces perpetrated on the citizens of Ireland with a brief mention of one of the worst examples of the heartbreak caused by a fell combination of official neglect and corruption. I refer to the case of Brigid McCole, who was poisoned by the Irish state. This horrible story lies at the heart of the story of the Lindsay Tribunal, which was set up in 1999 to investigate the infection of haemophiliacs with HIV and hepatitis C as a result of contaminated blood products supplied by the Blood Transfusion Service Board (BTSB).

An earlier tribunal, chaired by Judge Thomas Finlay and established in 1996, had been critical of what was done to citizens of the state in this regard; however, a number of issues were left unresolved – including that of compensation. Campaigners, notably the Positive Action group, were active in seeking further redress. Their activities were more than justified by the findings of a new tribunal chaired by Judge Alison

Lindsay, which met for the first time in 1999. The Lindsay Tribunal found that a 'minimal' figure of 250 Irish haemophiliacs had been infected with HIV or hepatitis C while receiving treatment from the BTSB before 1985. Illnesses which patients died from as a result included kidney failure and cirrhosis of the liver.

The tribunal was critical of the National Haemophilia Treatment Centre (NHTC) for its slow response to the risk of HIV infection. Lindsay found that patients were routinely started on, or home-treated, with possibly dangerous blood products after a risk of infection had been discovered. Though safer heat-treated products had become available, unheated blood products were probably not recalled. There was an 'unacceptable' delay in notifying victims of the results. The tribunal was informed of instances of tests being taken for HIV in 1985 but some patients not being told of the results until 1987. The tribunal heard that the National Haemophilia Treatment Centre NHTC received results from Britain in March and April of 1985 but that Professor Ian Temperley, the NHTC director, took a sabbatical from May to October without instituting a system for informing patients of the results. Temperley's counsel, Brian McGovern, SC, told the tribunal that Temperley had been hospitalized because of 'unbearable pressures at work'. His sabbatical had been arranged before it was known when HIV tests would become available. Locums did inform some patients, but the tribunal commented that it was 'most unfortunate' that the professor was absent at the time. The tribunal was also critical of the failure to ensure that blood products were heat-treated so as to reduce the risk of infection.

The issue of HIV and contaminated blood has caused controversy in many countries including France. In the case of Ireland, it should be borne in mind that, while most of the blood used by the BTSB was sourced locally, some of it came from American suppliers. This included blood taken from prisoners and drug addicts. The statistical consequence of this may be partially assessed by the fact that, by the time the first tribunal reported, the death toll amongst some 1700 people who had received blood or blood products found to be contaminated with hepatitis C was over 10 per cent: that is, 188 deaths.

What all this meant in *human* terms is best exemplified by the case of Brigid McCole. She was the wife of a hill farmer in Co. Donegal, and she died in 1996 at the age of fifty-four from hepatitis C, having received contaminated blood in 1977. She was not diagnosed with the condition until 1994. Her legal case began, after many delays, the following year, at which point she was refused consent to use an alias in court. This decision assisted the state, as it rendered other victims more likely to make use of the government's preferred compensation scheme, rather than take a case in open court. McCole, in having the temerity to pursue her case through the courts, was now exposed to the full anger and vengefulness of the state.

The McCole case was subject to delay after delay until 8 October 1996 – and McCole herself died on 2 October, six days before the case was due to open. Since 1995, the state had known (because the Attorney General had given the government his advice on the matter) that it was liable in the McCole case: it also knew, however, that Brigid McCole herself was dying – and as a result it persisted with a stonewalling, delay-ridden defence, teamed with explicit threats that McCole would be pursued for enormous costs if she lost the case. Twelve days before her death, the BTSB wrote to McCole's solicitors:

If your client proceeds with her claim for aggravated and exemplary/punitive damages against our client and fails, then our client will rely on this letter in an application to the court against your client for all costs relating to the claim for such damages and for an order setting off any costs to which your client might otherwise be entitled.

For years, McCole's husband and their twelve children had witnessed her slow progress towards death. Four years after her death, her husband Bernard (Brianie) drowned himself in a lake a mile from their home. Friends and neighbours agreed that he had never recovered from Brigid's ordeal and death.

Brigid McCole received little justice from the Irish state (her estate was paid the sum of IR£175,000 in compensation): but her sufferings probably cost the minister responsible, Michael Noonan, the leadership of his country. He took a hard line on Brigid McCole's case: 'callous' would be a mild descriptive term. Amongst the steps he took was a threat of legal proceedings issued to Brigid's ageing mother when she wondered aloud how her daughter came to contract hepatitis C. He subsequently made repeated public apologies for his behaviour but was forced to relinquish his brief leadership of Fine Gael following his party's disastrous electoral showing in the general election of 2002. Noonan is now finance minister and oversees Ireland's world of austerity.

13

The Golden Circle

ONE DAY A MAN WHOM I DID NOT KNOW, ALTHOUGH HE lived in my locality and walked the same streets I do – got into his car, a taxi, and drove to a nearby graveyard. He was driving a taxi because his business had failed. In the graveyard, the man tied a rope around the branch of a tree, fed the other end into his car, tied it around his neck and drove off – with results better imagined than described.

In a very real sense, that man's blood is on the hands of the people who, in betraying the vision of 1916, have mismanaged Ireland so badly. These people, it seems to me, are responsible for the escalation of suicide rates in the Republic by about 40 per cent. In addition, they have created emigration, unemployment, homelessness and widespread heartache, attacked the weak and the poor, and in general rent the fabric of Irish society as the centenary of the Easter Rising approaches.

One of the striking features of the financial crash which occurred in Ireland in 2008 was that most of the words written and spoken about it were couched in economic and financial jargon, impenetrable to the layperson. The people of Ireland had to sit distractedly before television sets as the crash progressed, and listen to people gravely questioning whether the difficulties were caused by a liquidity crisis or a credit crisis

– when what they actually wanted to hear, of course, was the answer to two different questions: were their jobs safe? And were their savings protected? Very often the answer was no.

One point insistently made – put to the people by the Irish, international and financial authorities – was that the citizens themselves were somehow to blame for their country's economic calamity. The crash was not solely related to the Lehmann Brothers bankruptcy of 2008 or the world's banking situation: instead, there was a notion put about that the Irish public was responsible for its own misfortune. The people had partied their way to the crash. But there is only a veneer of truth in this analysis. In fact, the disaster could be charted with near-actuarial accuracy by the extent of the departure by Ireland's leaders from the idealism of the 1916 leadership. Such people might wear Armani, their contemporary cash registers might be computers, but their souls and their vision were still what Yeats had described in his poem 'September 1913':

> What need you, being come to sense,
> But fumble in a greasy till
> And add the halfpence to the pence
> And prayer to shivering prayer, until
> You have dried the marrow from the bone;
> For men were born to pray and save;
> Romantic Ireland's dead and gone,
> It's with O'Leary in the grave.

After all, by now it will be evident to readers that the seemingly never-ending conveyor belt of scandals in contemporary Ireland indicates a serious weakening of the country's moral codes. There was a gross failure of leadership amongst the political and clerical elites, a Gadarene rush over the financial clifftop which stampeded the Irish to their economic doom. This stampede was accompanied by a chorus of Gordon Gekko's dictum that 'greed is good', sung by cabinet ministers, bank directors and corrupt accountants and stockbrokers alike. In the media world, the newspapers were wafer-thin on analysis, but bloated with property supplements. As for dissenting voices, they were few: there was only deathly silence on the part of the Department of Finance, the Central Bank and the regulatory authorities.

The Irish government had presided over the growth of the crisis with a laissez-faire attitude of non-interference with the market: it might have borrowed its ideological garb from the Whig approach to dealing with the potato shortage which led to the Irish Famine. In the early stage of the Irish crisis, the reaction of Brian Cowen's Fianna Fáil government was the familiar one: women and children first, and they set about an attempt to deprive the over-seventies of their medical cards that entitled them to medicines and free GP care. Predictably, this partially successful move ignited an explosion which deservedly helped to swell the reaction to the austerity which came later and which, deservedly, blew the Fianna Fáil government out of office.

The situation for which every member of that Fianna Fáil cabinet bears a collective responsibility came to a head in extraordinary fashion – at a meeting in Government Buildings on the night of 29 September 2008, at which the Irish banks revealed that not only did the emperors of Irish finance have no clothes, but that the Irish people would have to buy them a whole new wardrobe. The immediate result was that the government had to introduce an austerity budget the following month which raised taxes and slashed state benefits. As was done during the Famine – when the Encumbered Estate Act enabled the British government to purchase distressed estates at knock-down prices – an agency was set up to acquire distressed businesses, buildings and development projects: the National Asset Management Agency (NAMA). NAMA imposed what was euphemistically termed a 'haircut' on the value of these properties: over the following years, the vulture capitalists of the world would gorge on the rich pickings of the decaying Irish economic battlefield.

However, after two punishing years of rising unemployment and general misery, the Irish banks still were not trusted sufficiently by the international financial community to be able to raise finance. And so, after a period of denials and general obfuscation, the Taoiseach Brian Cowen had to go on television in November 2010 to announce that the Irish government had been obliged to appeal to Europe to save the situation: the European Commission, European Central Bank and International Monetary Fund (IMF), generally known as the Troika, were coming.

Austerity was on the way. After completing their work, the members of the Troika, led by Ajai Chopra of the IMF, concluded their Irish sojourn by heading for the best Indian restaurant in Ireland, Rasam in south Dublin. Unfortunately the menu they created for Ireland was not as palatable as Rasam's cuisine. It was heavily reliant on bread and water, and in effect imposed further stringencies on the cuts and hardships that followed the banks' bailout in 2008. Well might *Vanity Fair* publish a piece headlined 'When Irish Eyes are Crying'.

★

The activities of the main Irish banks in the course of the economic boom had caught the attention of journalists across the world. Formerly dour, conservative and staid institutions had gradually grown hard-edged and brash over time – and competitive too, jostling each with another to throw soft loans at their customers and to invest without due discipline. AIB, Ireland's largest bank, had already had to be bailed out in the not-too-distant past: in March 1985, the Irish government provided funding to safeguard the bank's existence following the collapse of the Insurance Corporation of Ireland, in which AIB had invested heavily. It's an ill wind, however, that blows no one any good: the morning after that 1985 bailout, the bank's CEO Gerry Scanlan bought 50,000 shares in AIB – which netted him a tidy profit as the share price rose sharply to reflect the government's comforting intervention. As I have already noted, Garret Fitzgerald would subsequently find AIB so sympathetic to his difficulties that they forgave his overdraft. In the meantime, no public investigation was conducted into how AIB's investment in the Insurance Corporation of Ireland went so badly wrong: Scanlan went on to become chief executive of the Dublin Stock Exchange.

Were lessons learned? Hardly. Writing in the journal *Administration* in autumn 1997, two economists, Patrick Honohan and Jane Kelly, attempted to place the Insurance Corporation of Ireland incident, which they described as Ireland's largest financial crash, in the context of world banking crises. Their judgement was that, against the international background:

> Ireland's experience seems *relatively benign*, confidence in the banking and wider financial system has remained unimpaired, few depositors or policy holders have lost money (and none from the Insurance Corporation of Ireland affair) and the burden on the taxpayer from these incidents has been relatively low by international standards.

At the time of writing, Honohan is governor of the Central Bank of Ireland.

In the years following the ICI crash, meanwhile, AIB continued on its merry way, pleased to take advantage of the consistently benign Irish banking environment. From the 1980s onward, for example, the bank led the way in scooping up deposits throughout the country after a Deposit Interest Retention Tax (DIRT) was introduced. These accounts were essentially bogus: their holders were required to be non-resident, and by no means all of them were. A farmer in Kerry, for example, could walk into a local AIB bank where the manager had been an old school friend, look him in the eye and unblushingly open an account with an address in another country. The custom gave rise to the story of the Kerry farmer who in one of these transactions gave his address as 'Main Street, New York'. The advantage to AIB and the other banks of the DIRT scheme was that a higher interest was charged on the bogus offshore accounts, thus boosting both bank profits and bankers' bonuses. When the scam was at length uncovered by the *Sunday Independent* in 1998, both the Central Bank and the Revenue Commissioners denied that they had ever been aware of its scale.

Scanlan told the DIRT Inquiry in 1999 that bogus non-resident accounts were not confined to AIB but were an industry-wide problem. He said that in 1991 AIB concluded an agreement with Revenue that there would be no retrospective action concerning 'reclassified' accounts which had previously been 'wrongly' described as non-resident. He subsequently apologized to the official concerned after the official challenged his assertion that a deal with Revenue, involving the official, had been hammered out at a football match.

The DIRT scandal was one example of a slipshod attitude to financial and ethical prudence which has characterized AIB for many years. This attitude is best summed up, perhaps, by the financial scandal involving Allfirst Bank of Baltimore, Maryland, which was a wholly owned subsidiary of AIB. In 2002, it was revealed that over the course of several years an Allfirst currency trader, John Rusnak, had run up losses of some $690 million. Rusnak had been buying and selling currencies, mainly dollars, in exchange for Japanese yen in the belief that the yen would weaken against the dollar. It did not, though Rusnak somehow managed to cover the losses. AIB's internal controls allowed this to go unnoticed for possibly seven years. In the end, however, the losses were discovered: six executives of the American AIB subsidiary were fired and Rusnak himself served roughly six years of a seven-and-a-half-year sentence, some of it in home confinement. US state prosecutors held him liable for the lost hundreds of millions and stipulated that, throughout his earning life he must pay compensation in proportion to his income. Back in Dublin, however, where Scanlan had moved to the Dublin Stock Exchange, AIB chief executives kept their jobs. Whatever they knew, or did not know, about Rusnak's activities will never be discovered: but in various media interviews at the time, bank officials who either worked with Rusnak or heard of his activities while they were working in other banks indicated that they were generally aware of what he was doing. Yet – and rather like Nick Leeson's operations which brought down the venerable Barings Bank in London in 1995 – everybody's business was seemingly no one's business.

And there were many more scandals to come. In 2004, for example, another contribution was made to AIB's malodorous history, with the bank fined €65 million for overcharging on foreign transactions, something which had apparently been going on for over ten years. In 2009, Tom Mulcahy, the former CEO of AIB, resigned as Aer Lingus chairman. His letter of resignation was delivered to the minister for transport on a Saturday and accepted by the minister at lunchtime. Mulcahy was one of two former and (at the time) three current AIB executives who had 'tax issues'. These executives were not merely some of the bank's top people, but – as happened throughout the banking industry – had gone on to work in other branches of finance. The 'tax issues' arose out of the operations of an investment company called Faldor, set up in the British Virgin Islands to hold funds on behalf of the AIB executives and some of their friends.

Arising out of the Faldor operation, Scanlan paid Revenue €206,000 in undeclared tax, corporation tax and penalties. He subsequently issued a statement saying that he and his wife had not invested in Faldor. They had invested in an AIB investment product which had then invested in Faldor without their knowledge. He said 'immediately subsequent to being contacted by AIB in October 2003, we contacted the Revenue to make an unprompted voluntary disclosure so that any liability arising could be determined and settled'. He would have sued the bank had it not been for his previous happy relationship with AIB. Three other former senior executives, or their estates, were subject to lesser sums for undeclared tax and penalties. They were Roy Douglas, Diarmuid Moore and Patrick Dowling (deceased). Ironically Tom Mulcahy, who lost his job at Aer Lingus, may not have had cause to resign. He did so because AIB had issued a statement saying two of its un-named former executives had tax issues following the bombshell announcement that five of its former executives were involved with Faldor. He was led to believe that he was one of the 'tax issues two' and decided to resign following an intervention by the minister responsible, Mary Harney, who, believing the AIB statement, ruled that no one with tax issues could head a state company. Months later, however, after an extensive examination of Mulcahy's records, Revenue pronounced him tax compliant.

The Financial Regulator, Liam O'Reilly, said that the Irish Financial Services Regulatory Authority would be working with financial institutions to ensure that they operated in a 'culture of integrity' – to which this writer at least would respond that bringing about such a culture within the Irish banking system would be a task equal to the labours of Hercules.

Meanwhile, following in AIB's footsteps, but going further, another hugely disruptive force was at work in Irish banking circles. In 1986, one Seán Fitzpatrick became chairman of the relatively small Anglo Irish Bank. Under Fitzpatrick, the bank began a period of rapid expansion: and when he at length stepped down as chairman in 2005, the bank's annual profits were reaching in excess of €500 million a year. The only problem was that Fitzpatrick achieved such figures by concentrating heavily on the property market. His successes emboldened AIB and Bank of Ireland – the country's second-largest bank – to follow suit, gambling and dealing unwisely to such an extent that the financial sector of Europe's most western country became imbued with the spirit of the Wild West.

The only problem with this was nobody ever seemed to be told to get out of Dodge; instead, everybody seemed to want to get in – via the property market. Dodge is but a metaphor, but there was nothing metaphorical about the money, the savings, the investments ploughed into a rapidly overheating property market in the boom years. And one piece of property in particular became an apt symbol of these Wild West days. The Galway Tent, an actual tent erected as a fundraising space at the annual Galway Races, became Fianna Fáil's most high-profile, notorious and noxious venture. It carried the Western motif and high-roller gambling to the limit: tables cost between €2500 and €3500; food and wine of the best flowed as developers, bankers, businessmen of all sorts rubbed shoulders with Fianna Fáil ministers and even the Taoiseach of the day. Although both Ahern and Cowen vigorously deny it, a public perception persists that the tent gave the favoured access to deal-brokers and the powerful in politics. Outside the tent, over a number of days, racegoers literally gambled away millions: some property whizzkids thought nothing of paying out further hundreds of euro to hire a helicopter to take them from Galway city to the racecourse. All this while outside in the real world, Irish life flowed on untouched and unknowing. Did all the Irish party? No, they did not.

One would have thought that someone might have alerted the leaders of banks and the members of their boards to the dangers of what was going on. Did they know? If they did not know, why not? As this is being written, a banking inquiry is attempting to get at the answers to these questions, but it has limited powers. At this point, and into the future, all that can be said with certainty is that no one in government, and very few in the worlds of economics and the media shouted stop. It must be stressed that a handful of economists *did* speak up for the virtues of prudence. They included Paul Curran, George Lee, Pat Leahy and notably the commentator David McWilliams who vainly but repeatedly sounded tocsins of alarm in the media for a period. Morgan Kelly, an economics professor at University College Dublin, carried out in 2007 a survey of property bubbles in other parts of the world, notably Japan, and concluded that Ireland was heading for a crash of at least 60 per cent in property prices.

But neither Kelly's drastic warnings nor the commentators' prophecies penetrated the walls of government, the Galway Tent or the Department of Finance. Between 1995 and 2000,

Irish GDP had grown annually at rates of 7.8 and 11.5 per cent. A slowdown occurred between 2001 and 2007, but growth still remained strong – between 4.4 and 6.5 per cent. During that period Irish GDP rose until it became the second highest in Western Europe. As a result of such a context, voices such as those of Kelly were derided as interfering with progress. Bertie Ahern, the Taoiseach through the course of the boom, rejected Kelly's findings in the most vigorous way possible. In 2007, speaking in terms which came back to haunt him and for which he subsequently apologized, he commented that: 'Sitting on the sidelines, cribbing and moaning, is a lost opportunity. I don't know how people who engage in that don't commit suicide because frankly the only thing that motivates me is being able to actively change something.'

In 2008, however, the global financial crisis exploded – and the walls came tumbling down. In March of that year, a sudden and cataclysmic fall in share prices on the New York Stock Exchange was mirrored on the Irish Stock Exchange: in what became known in Ireland as the St Patrick's Day Massacre, the Anglo Irish share price collapsed. In New York in September, the Americans allowed Lehmann Brothers to fail. Amazingly, there were still people who attempted to boost the property industry, or at least that portion of it devoted to building castles in the air. On 17 September 2008, the prominent property developer and solicitor Noel Smyth wrote an article in the *Irish Times* in which he said: 'None of our banks in Ireland are in the remotest area of trouble or of any concern.' The article did not mention that he was a large customer of the two Irish financial institutions about to be hardest hit by what lay around the corner: Anglo Irish Bank and Irish Nationwide building society.

In his article, Smyth had suggested that the government should step in and guarantee all deposits in the banks. This was in fact a sensible suggestion, but two weeks later, on 29 September, it was catastrophically conjoined with a government guarantee not merely of deposits but of *debts*. It took a little while for people to realize that the latter were included; initially many people, myself included, thought that the government had acted wisely and well in stopping the rot in public confidence over their bank deposits. By now, banks all over Europe would have failed had they not been propped up by means of state intervention: in the United Kingdom, Bradford & Bingley; in Germany, Hypo Real Estate (which had a Dublin arm, Depfa); in Iceland, Glitnir and others; and in Belgium, Fortis. The Irish government was well aware that Anglo Irish Bank was heading for that list – and so was Anglo Irish Bank itself.

The bank guarantee, however, was subsequently revealed as the worst decision in Irish financial history. Professor Bill Black, an American white-collar crime expert, would later tell the state inquiry into the banking crisis – ongoing as I write – that the bank guarantee was the 'most destructive own goal in history'. It was, he said, an 'insane decision'. Black, who is an associate professor of law and economics at the University of Missouri, Kansas City, commented that in his experience: 'The Irish bank guarantee was the worst response in history; to my knowledge nobody ever did that, nobody responded as stupidly as the Irish government by giving an unlimited guarantee they turned a banking crisis into a fiscal crisis.' With further American candour, he blamed the guarantee on 'lying bankers and incapable regulators'.

And Black's thoughts certainly stand up to scrutiny. As part of the guarantee programme the government underwrote Anglo's vast debts, now approaching €34 billion. Private debts were now socialized – shifted on the state's balance sheet – and thus made the responsibility of the citizens who had had no part in running them up in the first place. The finance minister at the time of the bailout, Brian Lenihan Jnr – at this point suffering from what would prove to be terminal pancreatic cancer – had proposed nationalizing Anglo and Irish Nationwide and 'burning' the bondholders (cutting them, and their debts, loose), but – according to evidence given to the banking inquiry by Patrick Honahan, the governor of the Central Bank – this was not favoured by Taoiseach Brian Cowen. In his statement to the banking inquiry in 2015, Cowen said of his exchanges with Lenihan on the night of the bank guarantee: 'there was no question of our conversation being in any way adversarial or confrontational with each other. Both of us were deliberating with each other and striving to find the best course of action for the country at this point.'

This decision becomes more understandable – if not quite forgivable – when it was discovered that the government had come under intolerable pressure from both the European Central Bank (ECB), and the US in the person of Timothy Geithner, the Secretary of the US Treasury. His worry was *contagion*: if the Irish started burning bondholders, the billions of dollars of American bonds held across Europe would also be in jeopardy. The Irish taxpayer, then, was obliged to find the €34 billion necessary to keep Geithner and the ECB happy. But there was no happiness for the Irish taxpayer.

A key aspect of the banking saga, and one which was a cause of very considerable public rage, was the extent to which it shone a light on the attitudes of banking executives. This light shone most mercilessly on Anglo in particular, but most observers felt instinctively that similar attitudes could be met with amongst other bank executives. The revelation of hubris amongst Anglo executives in particular, however, came through later, in the form of transcripts of tapes of internal phone calls recorded by Anglo itself, released in 2013. The tapes were made as Bertie Ahern's time in government was coming to an end in 2007: that is, a year before the bank guarantee, and they reveal that Anglo top executives were well aware of the perilous state of their bank.

The executives concerned were David Drumm, who had succeeded Fitzpatrick as the bank's Chief Executive, and John Bowe, Anglo's Head of Treasury. Against the backdrop of a worsening international financial situation, Drumm discusses with Bowe whether they should 'just shut down the fucking loans. Just don't do any.' He suggests that the staff should be reassigned to other duties such as tidying files and planning future bond issues. Drumm's most surprising suggestion is that the staff should 'brush up on their fucking German'. The pair – and this, remember, is a year before the banking guarantee – then go on to discuss how they could get the board's approval for shutting down on lending.

In a tape made just before the bank guarantee, Bowe is heard telling another Anglo executive how the bank is planning to inveigle the state into becoming involved in lending money to Anglo. The government has been asked for €7 billion, in the belief that once the hook went in and such massive lending commenced, the state would be unable to shut off the flow. The other executive, Peter Fitzgerald, at this point director of retail banking, is surprised and asks Bowe how they had come up with the figure of seven billion. The tape records Bowe laughing as he replies: 'Just as Drummer [David Drumm] would say, "picked it out of my arse".' Bowe then goes on to lay out the bank's strategy. He says:

If they [Central Bank] saw the enormity of it up front, they might decide they have a choice. You know what I mean?

They might say the cost to the taxpayer is too high, if it doesn't look too big at the outset, if it looks big, big enough to be important, but not too big that it kind of spoils everything, then, then I think you have a chance. So I think it can creep up.

Fitzgerald, obviously pondering the import of this, replies: 'Yeah. They've got skin in the game and that is the key.'

The tapes had an entirely predictable effect, with what became known as the 'German tape', made immediately after the bank guarantee, inflaming public opinion. Drumm is recorded singing 'Deutschland, Deutschland, über alles', and laughing as he directs his executives to 'get the fucking money in'. The tape caused a degree of shock and offence in Germany itself, with many Irish people taking it on themselves to ring the German embassy and apologize. The Taoiseach, Enda Kenny, ordered an inquiry into 'the axis of collusion', and a parliamentary inquiry was eventually set up.

Understandably, the one thing above all that Irish citizens wanted out of the disaster of the banking crash was *answers*: and with a view to giving them these, the government held a referendum in October 2011. The object of the referendum was to amend the Constitution so as to allow parliament special powers of investigation. The public, however, refused to concede these powers and the referendum failed. One reason for the failure was most certainly a general disenchantment with politicians and a reluctance to concede any more powers to them, especially in the light of the disaster which had befallen the country. But an influential 'No' argument was put forward in a letter to the newspapers signed by eight former Attorneys General (including Patrick Connolly, Peter Sutherland, Dermot Gleeson, Harry Whelehan and Paul Gallagher). The letter noted:

The proposal in relation to Oireachtas inquiries seriously weakens the rights of individual citizens, firstly to defend their good names and secondly to have disputes between themselves and the Oireachtas concerning their constitutional rights (especially their rights to fair procedures) decided by an independent judiciary.

The letter also criticized the government's move to cut judicial pay along with that of other citizens because of the financial crisis. It said: 'The proposal to allow proportionate reductions in judicial remuneration (which we support in principal) provides insufficient protection for the independence of the judiciary.'

The referendum failed, then – and in the meantime, the effect of Ireland's new and extraordinary indebtedness began to unfold. Essentially, it meant that in effect the Irish Republic lost its sovereignty. This is not overstating the case. In the aftermath of the bank guarantee, the Republic depended on emergency funding from the ECB, but on 19 November 2010, Jean-Claude Trichet* of the ECB wrote to Lenihan telling him that unless Ireland accepted a bailout programme (meaning a diet of economic austerity), emergency funding would be cut off. Lenihan and Ireland had no choice but to accept – and it was at this time that the Troika hit town.

---

* The 'haughty' Trichet, as the *Irish Examiner* described him, refused to come before the banking inquiry in 2015, only agreeing to take questions from members of the Public Accounts Committee, at the end of a lecture he gave in Dublin. Trichet rejected claims that he had 'blackmailed' Lenihan, thus: 'We had helped Ireland more than any other country. We were the institution that was helping Ireland much more than any other central bank did for any country [worldwide]... Brian knew we were helping Ireland more than any other country. We were together on the same side trying to get out of a situation that unfortunately was the most dramatic you could imagine.'

There was little sympathy for Ireland as the crisis unfolded – notably from the Germans, the very people who had lent the money that fuelled the property boom in the first place. Given the sort of skulduggery that characterized business in the Irish banking industry, perhaps this German attitude is understandable. Yet those with long memories remembered how after the war, the victorious Allied powers wrote off half of Germany's debt. And there is no need to stress the fact that this debt was incurred for rather less forgivable reasons than the Irish one. France and Germany, however, really knifed Ireland in October 2010, in the course of a G20 meeting in Deauville. Here they announced that, henceforth, bonds from the peripheral countries would not be honoured. The acronym PIGS used to describe these countries – Portugal, Ireland, Greece and Spain – says something about the attitude in a two-speed, German-led Europe regarding the smaller nations. So much for the original vision of the founding fathers of the European Union, Monnet and Schuman, who saw the new Europe, emerging from the debris of the Second World War, as a place of enlightenment and prosperity for all. Today's EU has turned into a debt-collecting agency for the Germans.

A further, tangible example of short-term commercial hard-headedness came in the form of the interest rate which Europe charged Ireland for the money it was forced to borrow as a result of the bailout. The Europeans got the money at 2 per cent and charged the Republic 9 per cent for the privilege of borrowing it, although this rate was subsequently reduced. Putting the matter in a nutshell, the IMF EU bailout meant that Ireland received €85 billion in financial support – to which Ireland contributed €17.5 billion, by means of raiding everything in her already depleted larder, including the state's pension funds. The European IMF loan was repaid by the implementation of fierce austerity measures, including cuts in private and public sector workers' pay, pensions and living standards. Many people who, on reaching the age of seventy, normally received free medical treatment, lost this entitlement. Additional taxes were introduced, including a Universal Social Charge, essentially a levy which hit poor and rich alike; a property tax; and a water tax. A sizeable section of the Irish electorate took to the streets to protest against this last measure.

Economic activity was hard hit, jobs and homes were lost and, as we have already seen, Irish suicide rates soared. Older people have been particularly badly affected, by a combination of all the foregoing cuts, including reductions to their pensions, and the fact that the savings they had placed in bank shares on the advice of stockbrokers were wiped out overnight. And yet there was a surprising degree of docility in Ireland in the face of cuts, austerity and revelations of financial impropriety. What was the source of such passivity? Psychiatrists with knowledge of Irish history trace it to the condition of 'learned helplessness' at which I have previously glanced, acquired during the Famine and as a consequence of the stultifying effects of the authoritarian nature of the two colonialisms. The really surprising aspect of this docility was the humble manner in which the Irish public accepted one of the main provisions of the European/IMF loan: namely that every three months emissaries from Europe and the IMF showed up in Dublin to monitor Ireland's progress towards fulfilling the bailout conditions and allocating praise or blame for progress or lack of it, as the visitors saw fit. The men in suits with the briefcases told the people of Ireland how, or if, they should spend their pocket money.

Every so often, meanwhile, some European bureaucrat would drop into Dublin to pat them on the head and make encouraging noises about what good Europeans they were. Among these cheerleaders is Christine Lagarde, the French politician who is now the managing director of the IMF. With a finely attuned sense of the Irish people's sensibilities she showed up in Dublin as this book was being written to commend the Irish for the manner in which they were dealing with austerity – carrying an Hermès handbag costing over €7000.[21] It was all a very long way from that ringing declaration of independence with which the 1916 Proclamation began.

Today, the indications for the Irish banking industry are not encouraging. The softly softly political approach to the banks continues, even after their own irresponsibility had placed them in the hands of the government and ravaged the national finances and caused extraordinary social damage. Today, ordinary tax-payers who had contributed the money which bailed out the banks are still being harassed by phone calls from the banks demanding payments for mortgage arrears. Suicide patrols were still manning the riverbanks and some harbours, on the lookout for people who appear likely to kill themselves – while the banks pass onto their mortgage customers the reductions in the interest rates which the banks themselves enjoy.

But speaking (perhaps appropriately) on 1 April 2015, the Taoiseach merely said of the banks' behaviour that he would ask them to show their customers 'a degree of understanding' and pass on lower ECB rates. As the Irish economy shows signs of improvement and property prices increase slightly, however, the banks are finding it more profitable than heretofore to seize peo-ple's homes. Something of a market for them stirs into life again. More hard-faced dealing; more house price increases – and for the Irish economy, another boom-bust cycle down the road.

The lessons of this (not yet concluded) phase of financial storm and collapse seem glaringly obvious. The financial sector in Ireland is in dire need of ethical political oversight and of correct governance: the sort of oversight and governance that plans prudently for the medium and long term, that pays due regard to the social dividend that ought to flow from financial sector, that attends to more than short-term financial gain and personal enrichment. An overarching lesson to be learned is that the relationship between bankers and politicians in Ireland is much too close – unhealthily close, disastrously close, as has become all too apparent in recent years.

Have such lessons been learned? Have they been taken on board and acted upon? The answers to these questions are surely and categorically *No*. Speaking in Paris on 9 April 2015, Patrick Honohan declared that change was necessary: 'The Irish legislative framework deserves to be strengthened to take account of egregious recklessness in risk-taking by those who were in charge of failed financial firms.'

The banking industry in Ireland, however, remains poorly regulated, and its activities continue to be overseen by politicians wedded to a notion of the virtues of light-touch oversight. The smallness and intimacy of Irish society lends itself to such a culture, of course – but nevertheless, it is certainly not beyond the wit of our politicians and administrators to establish a system of governance that is fit for purpose. The consequences of *not* doing so are all too evident. Indeed, the people of Ireland will be paying for past failures in this sector – literally paying, indeed – for generations to come.

In such a context, symbolism is important – and so it is worth noting that the government has sanctioned the completion of what was formerly intended to be an extravagant new headquarters for Anglo Irish Bank beside the River Liffey in Dublin's Docklands. The building will now provide a new headquarters for Ireland's Central Bank – which already, of course, possesses a very large existing headquarters on Dame

Street. My own inclination would be to leave the Central Bank where it is, and to use the new Docklands building as a university-run centre for the study of white-collar crime.

There is a lack of knowledge available to the citizen about decision-taking and how government and higher financial business is conducted. In theory, the legislation is there to provide the Irish citizen with knowledge, facts and figures. There is a Public Accounts Committee (PAC), a Freedom of Information Act, the parliamentary question mechanism. But none of these function as well as they ought. The PAC, for example, is essentially muzzled: its legal remit is to examine only public spending which falls within the view of the Comptroller and Auditor General. Bodies which receive their money from other sources in addition to that of the taxpayer – such as the Health Service Executive – can legitimately claim that they have no duty to answer to the PAC. And it is known that the Committee's own legal advisor has warned its members about the dangers of straying outside its remit. Thus, quite legally, a serious restriction exists in the principle of the public's right to know. The Dáil passed that legislation and it should revisit it and remove that prohibition.

Another restriction lies in the fact that the politicians and the public service collude together to circumvent the provisions of the Freedom of Information Act. It is not that the paper trail is tampered with as such – but rather that pains are taken to avoid a paper trail in the first place. Much business is carried out verbally and off the record. As for the parliamentary question: it can be sidestepped readily enough. It is often remembered that the late Judge Liam Hamilton, perhaps the best man in Ireland to judge, noted that the expense and bureaucracy of the Beef Tribunal over which he presided could actually have been avoided had parliamentary questions been answered properly in the first place. After what Ireland has passed through in recent years, one would have thought that the lessons of Hamilton's observation would have universally been accepted and acted upon – yet in fact there is a tendency in the *opposite* direction. At the time of writing, a (temporary) restriction to parliamentary privilege occurred that was unequalled in the history of the state. The episode was so unusual that it attracted the attention of the distinguished British media commentator, Roy Greenslade. As Greenslade reported in the *Guardian* in May 2015:

> An injunction granted by the High Court restricted the Irish media, both electronic and print, from reporting comments in the Dáil by independent Deputy Catherine Murphy on the dealings of the owner of the biggest electronic and print media company in the country, Denis O'Brien, with the Irish Bank Resolution Corporation [IBRC, the state vehicle created to handle the affairs of the former Anglo Irish Bank].

Murphy revealed that O'Brien had secured an interest rate of 1.25 per cent from the IBRC – when, according to Murphy, the IBRC could reasonably have charged an interest rate of 7.5 per cent. In fact the legal position was unclear; the injunction had been obtained by O'Brien against RTÉ. In letters written on the eve of the June bank holiday, O'Brien's lawyers claimed a report of the Murphy Dáil speech would breach the injunction. As breach of an injunction is a contempt of court, the unstated but obvious threat was that reporting the Dáil proceedings could lead to criminal proceedings against anyone who reported the Murphy Dáil speech. However, not only had the injunction order not been finalized, it had not been copied to any other media organization so, apart from RTÉ, the media was in the dark as to the actual terms of the injunction. After the bank holiday weekend RTÉ returned to the High Court for clarification as to whether the injunction prevented it from reporting utterances made in the Dáil, which utterances are expressly afforded constitutional privilege. The *Irish Times* (also threatened by O'Brien) joined that application.

On 2 June 2015, the judge who had granted the injunction indicated that he had never intended to restrain TDs from making comments in the Dáil, nor to prevent the reporting of them, and he lifted the injunction in respect of the information made public by Ms Murphy. He also directed the release of a redacted copy of his judgment outlining the reasons for the granting of the injunction. However, an application RTÉ to discharge the remainder of the injunction restraining publication of certain information relating to the banking relationship between O'Brien and IBRC was refused by the High Court the following week.

O'Brien followed up his injunction initiative by launching proceedings against members of the Dáil's Committee on Procedures and Privileges for failing to protect him from Murphy's allegations and those of the Sinn Féin finance spokesperson, Pearse Doherty. He has not been without supporters in his efforts. The influential Fine Gael strategist, Frank Flannery, told the *Sunday Times* on 8 August 2015 that absolute privilege in the Dáil 'tramples on the rights of citizens'.

One of the most striking images of the entire controversy was that of Catherine Murphy holding up to the cameras the copy of an official response she had received to her queries under the terms of the Freedom of Information Act. It consisted of line after line of redacted type: and Deputy Murphy said that it had taken her nineteen parliamentary questions to get to the bottom of the matter. O'Brien was of course fully entitled to secure the best deal he could from IBRC and to seek to have his privacy protected: and yet the whole jolting experience could have been avoided if the Irish system allowed simple questions to be answered in a straightforward fashion when issues affecting public finances arise.

Another such issue has arisen at the time of writing – one which affects in this case not the Dáil, but the Northern power-sharing administration at Stormont. As I remarked earlier, the wreckage of the Irish economy created rich pickings for vulture capitalists who swarmed into Ireland to acquire businesses which had been taken over by the state's National Asset Management Agency (NAMA). One such, the American private equity company Cerberus, acquired almost the entire Northern Ireland portfolio of these assets for some €1.5 billion. Some estimates have valued the properties as originally worth €5 billion – but the sale price was not the issue that seized the public's attention. Speaking under legal privilege in the Dáil, independent Deputy Mick Wallace revealed that, arising from the sale, several million euros had been deposited in an Isle of Man bank account – for distribution amongst some of the parties involved, apparently as fixers' fees.

Wallace further alleged that the money was destined for a senior Northern Ireland politician or party. The First Minister, Peter Robinson, leader of the DUP, Northern Ireland's biggest political party, denied that either he or his son Gareth (who runs a PR company that had undertaken some work for one of the parties involved) had done anything wrong. His only motivation or involvement in the affair had been, he said, to attract employment to the North. A prominent Northern Ireland lawyer, Ian Coulter (who had controlled the Isle of Man account into which the money had been transferred), also denied any wrongdoing. The matter is now being investigated by the authorities. In addition to the foregoing, the Public Accounts Committee was told by the NAMA Chairman, Frank Daly, that a prominent Northern Ireland businessman, Frank Cushnahan (who had resigned from NAMA for personal reasons in 2013), was due to receive payment in relation to the acquisition of the northern properties from another American company, PIMCO. NAMA subsequently ceased negotiation with PIMCO when it became aware that a third of a €15 million acquisition fee was to go to Cushnahan. What the Public Accounts Committee can do about the matter is not clear: but when Shane Ross, a prominent member of the Committee, was asked for his opinion after the story broke, he replied: 'It stinks.' He said that, after learning of the PIMCO fee proposal, NAMA should have scrapped the whole sale process and started again.

For too long, it seems to me, the principal law governing the business and professional arena in Ireland has been the Old Pals Act. What is clear is that the Public Accounts Committee has not the powers it needs to police the Irish political and economic landscape. What is required is resolute government action on the proposal which the Fine Gael–Labour coalition made when it first took office after the crash: namely, that a referendum be held to alter the Constitution so that the Dáil be empowered to set up committees armed with the powers to compel witnesses to appear before them, to make judgements on the evidence heard and if necessary to report matters to the Attorney General, the Director of Public Prosecutions or whoever.

Similarly, the charades surrounding the operation of the Freedom of Information Act and the vital democratic institution of the parliamentary question must be ended. The intrusion of the former Attorneys General into debate on amending the Constitution was most unfortunate. Giving parliamentary committees extra powers obviously carries risks – but if Irish society deems parliamentarians sufficiently responsible to be given the power to appoint Attorneys General, then society is entitled to assume too that their representatives are responsible enough to be entrusted with the task of finding out what has been done in the name of the people. The word accountability should come first in the dictionaries of those who serve the public in any capacity.

However, while the foregoing are unquestionably serious matters requiring attention, it is possible to end on a positive note, but it has to be a tempered one. A people with the resilience and the courage that saw them through the Famine has after all come through the worst of the bank-induced crisis. The people elected a government in which right and left combined to take the dreadful but, overall, necessary decisions needed to get through. The Taoiseach, Enda Kenny, established a sort of economic war cabinet evocative of Lloyd George's ultimately successful kitchen cabinet which steered the United Kingdom through the First World War. Generally speaking, the people accepted this leadership, and at the time of writing the tears are drying as unemployment and emigration ease, though they have yet to cease entirely. There are signs of economic green shoots.

Spiritually, the Church lags behind in terms of restoring lost respect; and it is not to be expected that old levels of authority will ever, or should ever, be restored. However, the principles of service to others and of voluntarism remain a large factor in Irish society, and one would not like to think of them as being irredeemably compromised. There is one important national body, which exists on a combination of local community effort, voluntarism, idealism and a decent sense of nationhood – and it continues to grow in strength. This, of course, is the Gaelic Athletic Association (GAA), the most important sporting and cultural organization north or south of the border. In the face of intense competition from other sports – such as soccer and rugby – the GAA's games attract ever growing crowds and membership from families, young and old, men and women. Stadia are mushrooming and players are vying to be included, without pay, on both Gaelic football teams, and those of the ferociously skilful game of hurling.

While Church and state are working out their new roles in the centenary period of the 1916 Rising, the GAA does provide a working model of what the 1916 Proclamation described as the pursuit of the 'happiness and prosperity of the whole nation... cherishing all the children of the nation equally'.

Notes

1 Quoted in Diarmaid Ferriter, *Judging Dev*, Royal Irish Academy, Dublin, 2007.

2 Quoted in Tim Pat Coogan, *Eamon de Valera: The Man who was Ireland*, Hutchinson, London, 1993.

3 Terence Dooley, *The Decline of the Big House in Ireland*, Wolfhound Press, Dublin, 2000.

4 Seán Moylan during the Treaty debate, 21 December 1921. Dáil Éireann Official Report: Debate on the Treaty between Great Britain and Ireland, n.d. p.146.

5 Quoted in Tim Pat Coogan, *Ireland in the Twentieth Century*, Palgrave, New York, 2006.

6 Taken from table of statistics on jailings in Tim Pat Coogan, *The IRA*, Harper Collins, London, 1971, and in several subsequent editions.

7 Tim Pat Coogan, *Ireland Since The Rising*, Pall Mall, London, 1966.

8 Paisley repeated this justification for his bigotry several times, notable in a day-long interview with Deborah Ross in the *Independent*, 22 May 1998.

9 In a speech at a Vanguard rally in Belfast's Ormeau Park, 18 March 1972.

10 Frank Kitson, *Low Intensity Operations: Subversion, Insurgency and Peacekeeping*, Faber and Faber, London, 1971, reprinted 1991.

11 Later collated in Anthony Bainbridge, Robin Morgan and James Adams, *Ambush: The War Between the S.A.S. and the I.R.A.*, Pan, London, 1988.

12 Joseph McGuire, quoted in Tim Pat Coogan, *On The Blanket: The Inside Story of the IRA Prisoners' 'Dirty' Protest*, Palgrave Macmillan, London, 1980.

13 Tim Pat Coogan, *On The Blanket: The Inside Story of the IRA Prisoners' 'Dirty' Protest*, Palgrave Macmillan, London, 1980.

14 Michael Browne, *Legal Disabilities of the Church in Ireland*, Maynooth, 20 July 1930.

15 Dr John Charles McQuaid, sermon, 'No change will worry the tranquillity of your Christian lives', 9 December 1965.

16 Diocesan decree 274, quoted in Seamus O'Buachalla, *Educational Policy in Twentieth-Century Ireland*, Wolfhound Press, Dublin, 1988.

17 SpEd G001/e Daingean Reformatory, Department of Education, NAI.

18 Tim Pat Coogan, *Ireland Since the Rising*, Hutchinson, London, 2003.

19 See www.poorclares.ie

20 Patrick Butterly, Memoir, quoted in the *Sunday Business Post* 12/02/2006.

21 *Irish Independent*, 20 January 2015.

Acknowledgements

In addition to the selection from my works listed below, I benefitted from the researches of a number of outstanding Irish journalists who have produced books on the contemporary crisis. These are listed below. I have made considerable use of the coverage of contemporary events by the major Irish newspapers, and also a number of online publications. Official publications, including the reports of the various tribunals, were also helpful. I am also indebted to such ground-breaking TV programmes as RTÉ's *States of Fear*.

A special word of thanks is due to my friend Commandant Pat McKevitt, for presenting me with a copy of the Pearse letter published in Chapter One. As readers will see for themselves, this important document makes it clear that – given the divisions in nationalist ranks and the IRB's lack of armament – the IRB leaders knew they were going out to defeat and almost certain death in pursuit of their ideal.

I would also like to thank Denis McClean, who cast a kindly and knowledgeable eye over the work in progress. A special word of thanks must go to Neil Hegarty, a prince amongst editors. Richard Milbank, publishing director of Head of Zeus, was also co-operative and wise in his suggestions at various stages of the book's progress. The opinions expressed in the book are of course my own.

Bibliography

Coogan, T.P., *Ireland since the Rising*. Pall Mall, London, 1966

_____ *The Irish – A Personal View*, Phaidon Press, London, 1975

_____ *The IRA: A History*, HarperCollins, London, 2000

_____ *On the Blanket: The H-Block Story*, Ward River Press, Dublin, 1980

_____ *Ireland and the Arts*, Namara Press, London, 1983

_____ *Disillusioned Decades: Ireland 1966–87*, Gill & MacMillan, Dublin, 1987

_____ *Michael Collins: A Biography*, Hutchinson, London, 1990

_____ *De Valera: Long Fellow, Long Shadow*, Hutchinson, London, 1993

_____ *The Troubles: Ireland's Ordeal 1966–1995 and the Search for Peace*, Hutchinson, London, 1995

_____ *The Irish Civil War* (with George Morrison), Macmillan, London 1998

_____ *1916: The Easter Rising*, Weidenfeld & Nicolson, London, 2004

_____ *Ireland in the Twentieth Century*, Palgrave, New York, 2004

For insights into contemporary crises and events I am indebted to the following works:

Collins, S., *The Haughey File*, O'Brien Press, Dublin, 1992

Collins, S, *The Power Game: Ireland under Fianna Fáil*, 2nd edition, O'Brien Press, 2001

Cooney, J., *John Charles McQuaid, Ruler of Catholic Ireland*, 2nd edition, O'Brien Press, Dublin, 2003

Curran, R. and Lyons, T., *Fingers: The Man Who Brought Down Irish Nationwide and Cost Us €5.4bn*, Gill & Macmillan, Dublin, 2013

Dooley, T., *The Decline of the Big House in Ireland*, Wolfhound Press, Dublin, 2001

Dunne, D. & Kerrigan, G., *Round up the Usual Suspects: The Cosgrave Coalition and Nicky Kelly*, Magill, Dublin, 1984

Fetherstonhaugh, N. & McCullagh, T., *They Never Came Home: The Stardust Story*, Merlin, Dublin, 2006

Keogh, D., *Jews in Twentieth-Century Ireland: Refugees, Anti-Semitism and the Holocaust*, Cork University Press, Cork, 1998

Kerrigan, G. & Spiers, D., *Goodbye to all That; A Souvenir of the Haughey Era*, Blackwater Press, Dublin, 1992

Leahy, P., *The Price of Power: Inside Ireland's Crisis Coalition*, Penguin, Dublin, 2009

McGarry, P., ed., *Christianity: Articles from the Irish Times series*, Veritas, Dublin, 2001

McWilliams, D., *Follow the Money*, Gill & Macmillan, Dublin, 2010

McWilliams, D., *The Good Room: Why we ended up in a debtors' prison – and how we can break free*, Penguin, Dublin, 2012

O'Toole, F., *Meanwhile Back at the Ranch: The Politics of Irish Beef*, Random House, London 1994

Ross, S., *The Bankers*, Penguin, Dublin, 2009

Ross, S., *Wasters*, Penguin, Dublin, 2010
Ross, S. & Webb, N., *Untouchables*, Penguin, Dublin 2012

Newspapers

Irish Examiner
Irish Independent
Sunday Business Post
Sunday Independent
The Irish Times
The Sunday Times
Vanity Fair

Picture Credits

1. 1916 Proclamation (Corbis)
2. Thomas Clarke (Hulton Archive/Getty Images)
3. Seán Mac Diamarda (Sean Sexton/Getty Images)
4. Pádraig Pearse (Hulton Archive/Getty Images)
5. James Connolly (Topham Picturepoint)
6. Thomas MacDonagh (Wikimedia Commons)
7. Eamonn Ceannt (Topfoto)
8. Joseph Plunkett (Bureau of Military History Collection, Dublin, Ireland)
9. Dublin after the Easter Rising (Universal History/Getty Images)
10. Éamon de Valera under arrest (University College Dublin Archives)
11. The first Dáil Éireann (General Photographic Agency/Getty Images)
12. Black and Tans (Corbis)
13. Signing of the Anglo-Irish Treaty (Time Life Pictures/Getty Images)
14. Michael Collins (Popperfoto/Getty Images)
15. Irish Free State cabinet (Walshe/Getty Images)
16. Éamon de Valera and Archbishop Edward Byrne (Keystone/Getty Images)
17. Alex Spain (Wikimedia Commons)
18. Dublin mothers (Hulton Archive/Getty Images)

19. Churchgoers after Mass (The LIFE Picture Collection/ Getty Images)
20. Dr Noël Browne (Topfoto)
21. Archbishop John McQuaid and Pope Pius XII (Topfoto)
22. Seán Lemass and Jack Lynch (Jim Gray/Keystone/Hulton Archive/Getty Images)
23. Ian Paisley (John Downing/Express/Hulton Archive/Getty Images)
24. Belfast riots, 1969 (Keystone/Getty Images)
25. 'Bloody Sunday', 1972 (Getty Images)
26. Charles Haughey and Neil Blaney (Irish Times)
27. Austin Currie and John Hume (Bentley Archive/Popperfoto/ Getty Images)
28. Bobby Sands (STF/AFP/Getty Images)
29. Bobby Sands' funeral (Press Association)
30. Stardust nightclub (PA Photos/Topfoto)
31. Father Alec Reid (Rex Shutterstock)
32. John Major and Albert Reynolds (Peter Macdiarmid/Getty Images)
33. Mary Robinson (AFP Photo/Max Nash/Getty Images)
34. Bertie Ahern (Oliver Hoslet/Corbis)
35. Éamon Casey (PA Photos/Topfoto)
36. Father Seán Fortune (Irish Times)
37. Same-sex marriage referendum (Paul Faith/AFP/Getty Images)
38. Brian Cowen and Brian Lenihan (Bloomberg/Getty Images)
39. Enda Kenny (Bloomberg/Getty Images)

Index